# JAN KOCUR

*A story of*
SLOVAK PRIDE, AMERICAN PATRIOTISM,
& THE GOLDEN AGE OF THE SLOVAK LEAGUE OF AMERICA

by Richard D. Kocur, Jr.

Modra Publishing

ISBN: 978-0-979-0300-0-0
LCCN: 2009940671

Modra Publishing, San Diego
www.modra-publishing.com
info@modra-publishing.com

# Dedication

*To the unsung hero of the story, Margaret Zbojkova Kocur.*

# Acknowledgements

*I started this project never really expecting it would be any more than an interesting piece of family history. The more I learned, however, the more I believed the story of Ján Kocúr was worth telling. I could never have realized that goal without the help, guidance, and dedication of many people. Each individual I've come in contact with has provided valuable assistance, whether they realize it or not, in seeing this book to where it is today. I am very grateful.*

*I would like to thank everyone in my family for their support and interest in this project over the last four years, especially my parents Jane and Dick Kocur. Also thanks to Andrew Hudak and Joseph Hornack from the Slovak Institute in Cleveland, Ohio for their dedication to preserving the memory of Slovak pioneers like Ján Kocúr and for their aid in uncovering so many of the documents used to piece together this story. Thanks to Jana Madar for her help in translating the many documents, letters, and articles from Slovak to English and opening a whole new perspective on a long ago time.*

*I would also like to thank to Carol Kocur, Barbara Stephens, Jen Kissel, and Margarete Minar for their aid in reviewing, commenting, editing, proofing, and polishing this work. I am grateful for the help of those individuals who read through the work in progress and agreed to contribute their expert perspective for the finished product; Joseph Senko, Daniel Tanzone, Andrew Hudak, Andrew Masich, Stefan Kucik, M. Mark Stolarik, and Sister M. John Vianney, S.S. C. M.*

*Finally, a heartfelt thank you to Donna Griffin Albert for her considerable and talented work on the art, design, and layout of this book.*

# Table of Contents

**Chapter**

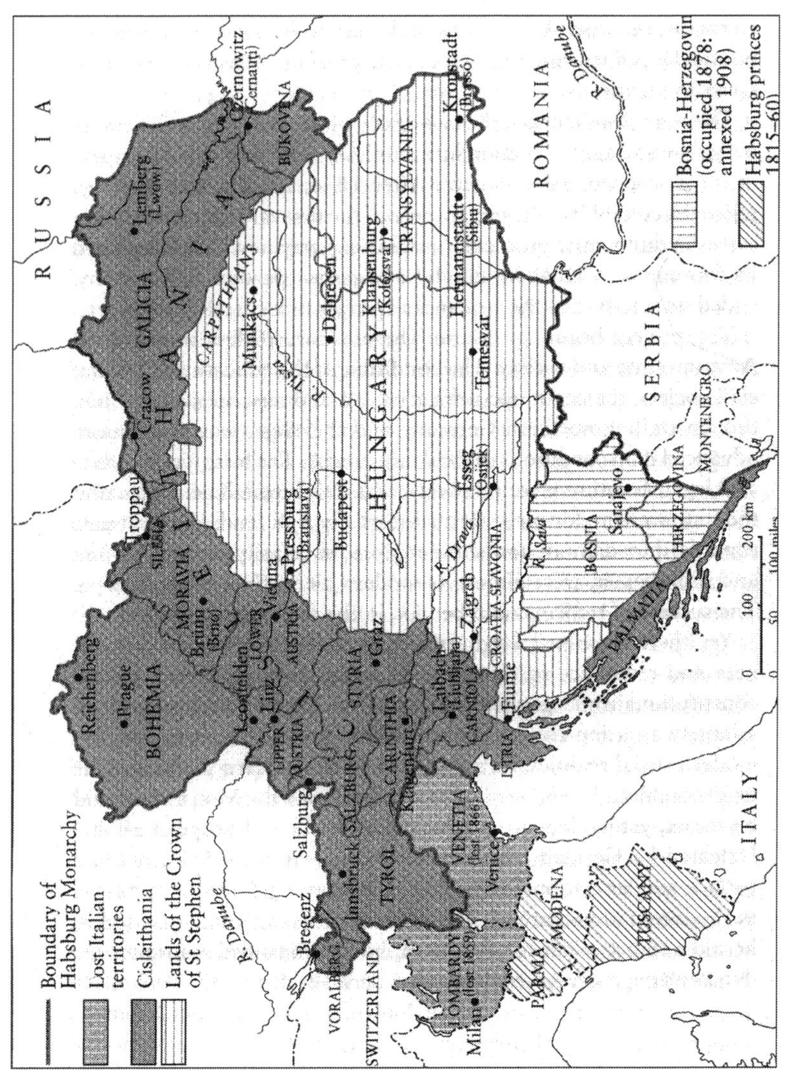


Hungarian Lands in the Hapsburg Monarchy (1815-1918)

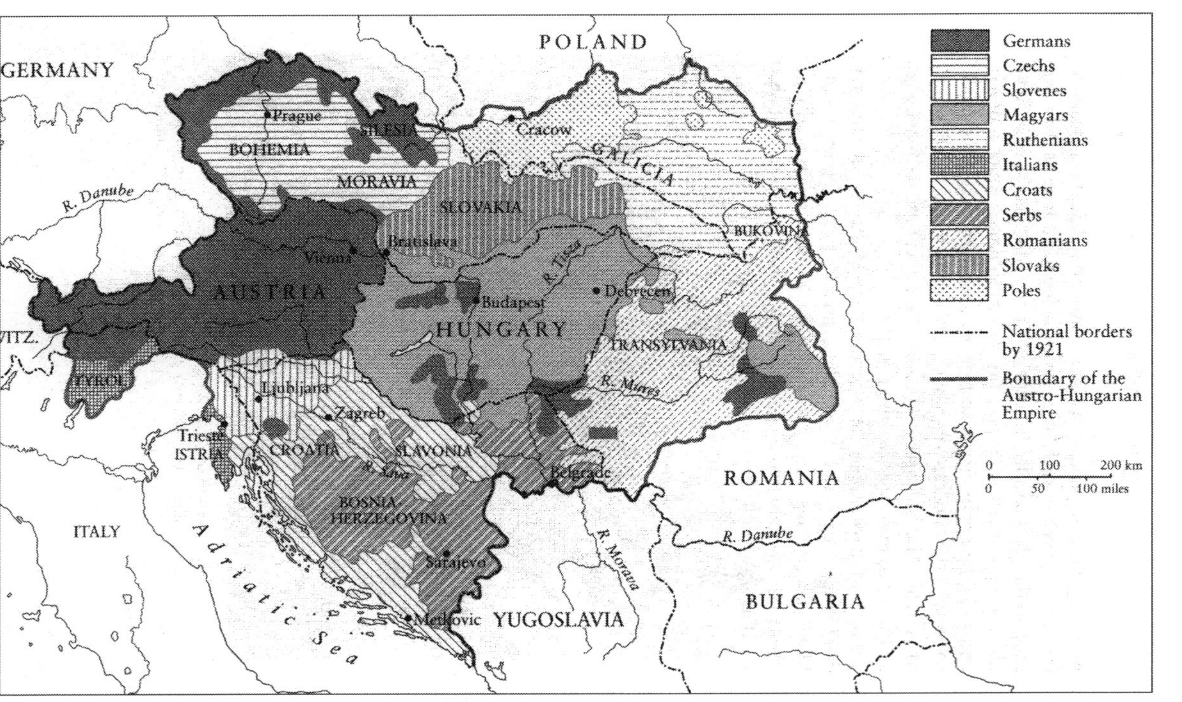


Changes in the make up of Austria-Hungary (1918-1921)

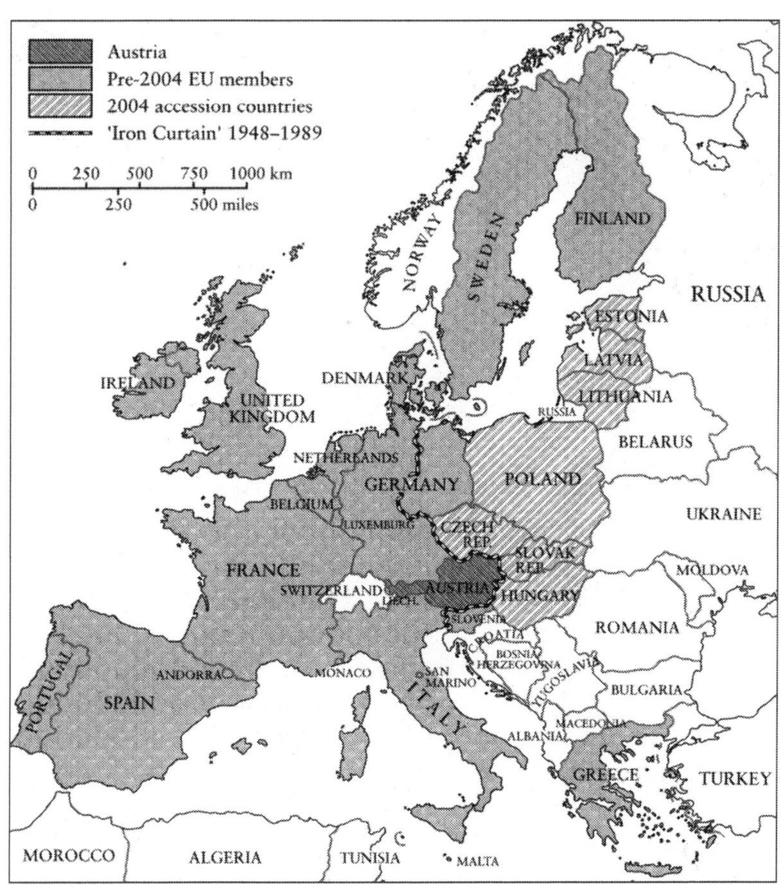


Evolution of Europe post WWII (1955-2004)

# Introduction

On September 7, 1909 a twenty-two year old Slovak immigrant named Ján Kocúr stepped off the ocean liner *Bremen* and onto American soil. Kocúr's journey to the United States, like thousands of immigrants before and since, was based on the prospect of a better life. It was a journey that took him from the small village of Turzovka in what was then the Kingdom of Hungary to Western Pennsylvania, the industrial heartland of America.

Ján Kocúr found the United States to be a place that was thriving. The United States had turned the corner into the new century at full speed. Industrial power was driving the country to new economic heights and a nationalistic energy gave Americans a sense that theirs was a special place in the world. Just as coal powered the blast furnaces and steel mills that dotted the landscape outside Pittsburgh, the U.S. industrial engine of the new century also had to be fueled. More often than not, immigrant labor was that fuel.

Ján Kocúr first settled in Arnold, a small town along the Allegheny River northeast of Pittsburgh. The Pittsburgh area was the final destination for many Slovak immigrants at the turn of the century. It was an area with topography similar to the Slovak lands the immigrants left behind, it contained neighborhoods settled by Slovaks from similar regions of their home country, and it offered the newly arrived immigrants ready opportunity to work. While the whole of American society may not have been ready to accept the immigrants of Eastern Europe, Pittsburgh contained enough Slovaks and enough Slovak neighborhoods to make assimilation easier than in any other part of the country.

Ján Kocúr was a principled person, and America was a place of principles, a country founded first and foremost on principles. American independence and democracy were rooted in the principles of self-determination, freedom, and individual liberty. In stark contrast to the new environment Kocúr encountered in America, the land he left was its mirror opposite—a land historically steeped in concentrated centralized power and little individual liberty.

The history of the people living in the lands of Ján Kocúr's birth, lands now part of modern Slovakia, is a story of conquest and struggles for freedom. As early as the tenth century Slovakia was a battlefield in the struggles among the Slavs, Magyars (Hungarians), and Germans.[1] The eleventh century saw the lands of the Slavs become part of the Kingdom of Hungary and begin an unsteady relationship with the Hungarian throne that would last into the seventeenth century. During that time much of Hungarian political, social, and cultural life was centered along the banks of the Danube in the city of Bratislava, now the capital of the Slovak Republic. While Slovaks seldom suffered from national oppression during this period in their history, they lacked the opportunity to build national institutions because they did not control their own destiny.[2]

As the 1800s began, a wave of nationalism sparked by a spiritual re-birth began to roll through Central and Eastern Europe. As the dominant ruling entity, the Hapsburg monarchy felt the effect of this nationalistic wave from all sides. Political and social reforms sought by the various peoples under their rule, including Czechs, Poles, Slovenes, Croatians, Slovaks, Rumanians, and Serbs ran counter to the monarchy's centralistic approach to governance. As those holding authority, the Magyars in Hungary and Germans in Austria resisted the sharing of power and influence with any of the ethnic elements of their kingdom.

Throughout the second half of the nineteenth century, the Slovak people put forward efforts to gain a degree of political and cultural freedom from the Hungarian monarchy. At first, trying to work within the Hungarian political structure, the Slovaks attempted to create a "Slovak Region," an administrative unit comprised of the counties with traditionally high Slovak populations. This move and others like it, however, were considered by the Hungarian rulers to be the first step on a slippery slope of decentralization and subsequent loss of power.

The immediate response of the Hungarian parliament to the nationalistic rumblings of the Slovak people was *more* centralization of power and authority, not less. In 1868 the parliament of Hungary approved the Nationality Act, an act in which Magyar (Hungarian) was proclaimed the official language of the state administration of the kingdom. In 1874 the activities of the Slovak Institute of Sciences and Arts (Matica slovenská) were suppressed by the Hungarian Minister of Education. One year later, in 1875 the last three Slovak gymnasia (high schools) were closed by the government. By enacting such measures, the rulers in Budapest endeavored to create conditions for the transformation of Hungary into a homogenous Magyar national state.[3]

The effort by the Magyar regime to suppress Slovak ethnic identity, institutions, and history continued through the remainder of the nineteenth century. It was into this environment that Ján Kocúr was born on May 22, 1887 in the village of Turzovka, located in the northwestern portion of modern day Slovakia. Throughout his early life Ján Kocúr no doubt witnessed and experienced first hand the effect of Magyar rule on the Slovak people. The efforts of "Magyarization," however, would only serve to fire a greater sense of Slovak identity for the young Kocúr and propel his work in the future toward the goal of a free and independent Slovakia.

Ján Kocúr's first step toward that goal was the first step on a journey that, ironically, took him away from his own country. It was a step onto the gangplank of an ocean liner in Bremen, Germany bound for America. Like many from Eastern Europe at the time, the prospect of a better life in the United States was a powerful draw for Ján Kocúr. Leaving one's family and friends and starting life over thousands of miles away in a different country with a different language and a somewhat less than tolerant view of those who were different was a difficult but all too necessary decision. It was a decision Ján Kocúr may have made early in life but acted upon in the fall of 1909.

The principles of America that Ján Kocúr found so appealing were also motivating. They truly meant something to him beyond being just words. These principles meant enough for the newly minted American, Kocúr, to voluntarily enlist in the United States

Army in the spring of 1918 and to fight with the forces of the United States against familiar foes on European soil in the Great War.

Principle also helped guide Ján Kocúr in the work he took up after his return from service in the U.S. Army at the close of World War I. This time, however, the work was a labor of love based on Kocúr's desire to see his homeland free and his fellow Slovaks independent. As of 1918 Ján Kocúr had the roadmap that would guide him and his fellow Slovaks in their journey toward freedom, the Pittsburgh Agreement. Signed in May of 1918, the principles in the Pittsburgh Agreement were designed to provide the framework that would guide the Czech and Slovak people in their efforts to form an independent nation while maintaining their respective autonomy. For Ján Kocúr, the Pittsburgh Agreement became the basis of a life's work focused on helping his fellow Slovaks live the "American" dream in the land of their birth.

The instrument through which Ján Kocúr strove to achieve the idea of Slovak independence and bring to his fellow countrymen the same benefits he enjoyed as a free and independent Slovak-American was the Slovak League of America. The league, first formed in 1907, was one of the largest civic and cultural federations of its kind in the United States and acted as the driving force for Slovak-American causes during the first half of the twentieth century. Ján Kocúr served as the organization's national secretary for twenty-six years, longer than any league officer before or since.

The Slovak League contributed to both sides of the Slovak-American hyphenation in good times and in bad. Ján Kocúr served the causes of the league through five United States presidents, the Great Depression, and World War II. He saw the focus of the league turn from immigrant assimilation and acceptance in the United States to the establishment of an autonomous, independent Slovakia to the World War that tested the very idea of both. Throughout his tenure in the Slovak League, Ján Kocúr maintained a steady focus on two goals: the rights and acceptance of his fellow Slovaks in the United States and the establishment of a free and independent Slovak state for his fellow Slovaks still in Europe.

Ján Kocúr's life was one driven by a handful of core principles: fair and equal treatment of his fellow Slovaks in the United States, dedication and devotion to the ideals which made

America great, and freedom and self-determination for his Slovak homeland. Ján Kocúr's story is one that goes well beyond the simple story of an immigrant achieving the American dream. Ján Kocúr's story demonstrates the power of pride, principle, and perseverance and what can be achieved in a life dedicated to the service of others. Ján Kocúr's story is a story worth knowing.

**Endnotes**

1. *Stasko, Joseph: Slovaks in the United States of America, pg 15. 1974.*
2. *Stolarik, M. Mark; The Role of Slovak Émigrés in North America in the Emancipation of the Slovak Nation; pg 75. 1997*
3. *Stasko, Joseph: Slovaks in the United States of America, pg 15. 1974.*

## Chapter 1

# WINDS OF CHANGE

# Chapter 1

In 1909 Bremen, Germany was one of the busiest ports in Europe. Ships from all over the world came into and went out of this historic city located in northern Germany. Bremen provided central and eastern Europe with direct access to the North Sea and then the Atlantic Ocean. Luxury liners, merchant ships, ships of war, and small seafaring craft knew Bremen as an efficient and hospitable port. These ships transported cargo of all sorts and with varying purposes. Bremen's location made it an ideal port head for the transport of goods into the heart of Europe and a point accessible by the population and industries of eastern Europe in order to connect with the rest of the world.

A large part of the cargo in the ships leaving Bremen during 1909 was a new kind of raw material. It was the kind of raw material that the centers of industry in the United States needed to continue their rapid industrial advancement. It was the kind of raw material absolutely necessary to make the mills and mines of the United States run, and run profitably. It was a raw material that was in high demand but in cheap supply, an economic equation that any good industrial capitalist found appealing. It was a raw material found in abundance, easily transported to a distribution point like Bremen and supplied to waiting buyers in America. The raw material, of course, was the plentiful human capital from the villages and towns all over eastern Europe.

While Bremen served as a portal of transport for immigrants leaving the European continent, Germany, the country whose coffers were filled by ship duties and port fees coming and going from Bremen, was leading Europe down a new and dangerous road.

Ján Kocúr's continental home, Europe, had undergone dramatic changes in the first twenty-two years of his life. The "Long Fuse," as the period between 1880 and 1914 was called, was well into a sustained burn by the time 1909 came around and it was, at that point, nearly impossible to extinguish. By 1909 the powers of Europe had positioned themselves for an unavoidable collision. Clouds were on the horizon and they were gathering swiftly. The ensuing storm brought by these clouds would topple rulers, alter boundaries, and rain destruction on the entire continent.

The changes across Europe, which brought about the storm that would become World War I, were not singular. They were more the result of economic and social forces colliding with political systems unwilling and incapable of change.

With thriving domestic economies, countries like England and France sought new sources for economic supply, support, and growth. Throughout the late nineteenth century and into the early twentieth century, colonial expansion in areas like North Africa and Asia met this need. The more traditional monarchies of the day, Germany and Austria-Hungary, were for the most part locked out of any meaningful expansion through the benefits of colonization and thus put at an economic disadvantage. The ruling class of both countries spent considerable time and effort trying not to be outdistanced by their European neighbors.

With a new economic paradigm firmly in place across much of Europe by the early 1900s, citizens with a newfound economic power began to demand greater social change. In Britain, women demanded and received the right to vote. Laborers across industrial Europe fought for a greater share of the industrial spoils they helped to generate. Socialists called for a greater sharing of concentrated national wealth and power in order to aid and benefit all people.

In addition to the demands for social change across Europe, citizens of countries like England, France, and Germany also began to consider the role their respective nations played in the greater European community. Gaining momentum in the later half of the 1800s, the idea of nationalism took on increased significance as Europe entered the new century. Nationalism is the concept in which the goals (economic, social, military) of one's country are believed to be superior to those of any other country. When nationalism is considered on the level of people who share a common language, history and culture, it can be a particularly powerful and unifying force, as it was across much of western and central Europe.

With economic forces driving social change, the political landscape of Europe, and in particular eastern Europe, became increasingly complicated. Germany, in an attempt to maintain a firm place in the pecking order of Europe and to keep pace with England and France abroad, increased its military standing through a buildup of arms, material, and troops. England and France each responded in kind and a military arms race, fueled by nationalistic ideals, was on.

As a result of economic and social factors as well as the governmental and political rivalries of early twentieth century Europe, the powers of the continent began to group themselves through various alliances. Driven by common interests and in an attempt to politically isolate rivals, countries entered treaties, agreements, and secret alliances designed to protect them in the event of military aggression. While designed to protect individual nations these agreements were akin to a complex design of domino rows waiting for the lead marker to fall.

Ján Kocúr's homeland, part of the kingdom of Austria-Hungary during this tumultuous time, was a step behind the rest of Europe in its economic, social, and political development, and in fact across many regions on the kingdom was still mainly a land of peasant farmers still living in much the same way people of past generations had lived. The state of affairs in Austria-Hungary at the turn of the century was due in large part to the complicated patchwork of ethnic, religious, and geographic divisions within the kingdom.

The United States is often referred to as the "melting pot," a unique mix of nationalities, races, religions and ideas that when brought together form the distinct composition of an American. The melting pot description as it relates to the U.S. has it that the citizens, regardless of origin, come together under a common belief in the ideals of freedom and democracy and are thus bound together as Americans. As a citizen of the United States, one can live under the banner of "American" and yet keep the ties to one's unique racial, religious, and national origins. While Americans are not immune to social problems brought on by these differences, they are generally an example to the world of an existence of harmonious differences. During the early part of the twentieth century, about the time that Ján Kocúr boarded the *Bremen*, America's melting pot was adding new ingredients by the day, their differences combining to strengthen and advance the United States' role in the world.

The "melting pot" descriptor could also be applied to Ján Kocúr's country, Austria-Hungary, except with much different results. Austria-Hungary, unlike the United States, approached the idea of differing social, ethnic, cultural, and religious elements in society as weakening rather than strengthening its kingdom. Compared to the United States, Austria-Hungary was a land that practiced a "melting pot in reverse." This social strategy was the result of a long and troubled history that provided the rulers in Vienna and Budapest a unique historical perspective. This perspective drove the Austro-Hungarian throne to act in the manner they did toward their subjects.

Within the borders of Austria-Hungary in 1909 peoples of at least a dozen different national origins could be found. Poles, Slovaks, Croatians, Serbs, Bohemians, and Hungarians all occupied a place in the empire. Geographically, the Austrian portion of the empire was a series of adjoining territories or provinces beginning along the eastern edge of the Adriatic Sea and running in a north-northeasterly ring around the countries of Bosnia, Croatia, and Hungary. This ring of provinces, together with the three aforementioned countries, made up the Austro-Hungarian empire. Slovaks like Ján Kocúr were mostly concentrated in the northern portion of the Hungarian region at the foot of the High Tatra Mountains.

The political organization of Austria-Hungary was nearly as complicated as its geography. The empire was governed by a dual monarchy whose genesis was rooted in an alliance between Austria and Hungary established in 1867. The same ruler was called emperor in one country and king in the other. In 1909 Emperor Franz Joseph presided over this patchwork of provinces, languages, religions and peoples. To the majority of people under his rule, the idea and implementation of the dual monarchy was nothing short of a disaster. The two countries, Austria and Hungary, had in common an army and navy, a tariff, a system of weights, measures, and coinage, and three ministers (war, foreign affairs, and finance). Outside of these matters they stood apart; they had no common legislature, money, or post office system.[1] The dual monarchy of Austria-Hungary, with its political and geographic irregularity, was also beset with divisions driven by nationality, race, and language. In the Austrian portion of the kingdom Bohemians (Czechs) were pitted against Germans, while further north, Jews and non-Jewish Poles were at odds. The situation was no better and in fact worse in the areas of Hungary. Discontent among Romanians, Slovaks, and Germans living in Hungary was driven by arbitrary and sometimes cruel persecution on the part of the Magyar (Hungarian) officials. To the south of Hungary proper in Croatia, religious differences and the overall effect of Magyar policies made it a region rife with constant tension.

Emperor Franz Joseph's throne surely seemed unsteady given the internal discord across virtually every region of his kingdom. Compounding Franz Joseph's problem of unrest and discontent among his subjects was the external pressure exerted on the monarchy by the political, social, and economic dynamic sweeping Europe in the early 1900s. While he could suppress and control his own subjects, brutally in some instances, the Austro-Hungarian emperor couldn't hold back the inevitable pressure on his country generated by these changes.

An inevitable consequence of the dissatisfaction felt among the subjects of the Austro-Hungarian empire was the immigration of its citizens, citizens like Ján Kocúr. The Slovak peoples living in the northern regions of Hungary acutely felt the negative effect of Magyar rule. The Slovak culture, language, schools, and religion was all subject to Magyar regulation and oversight. For this reason and for the reasons that have always motivated peoples to leave one area for another, Slovaks began leaving their homeland in increasing numbers as the turn of the century approached. According to American immigration statistics, a steadily increasing number of Slovaks began entering the United States beginning in the last decades of the nineteenth century. From 1871 to 1914 Slovakia lost 650,000 people through emigration or an average of 15,000 per year.[2] In 1909, Ján Kocúr was one of approximately 22,586 Slovaks to leave their native land and be admitted into America.[3]

This was the complicated landscape of Europe that Ján Kocúr left on an August day in 1909. It was a landscape that would shortly be changed forever when the first domino fell in Sarajevo five short years later. As Ján Kocúr, the twenty-two year old Hungarian subject of Slovak origin, walked up the gang-plank of the ship *Bremen*, bound for America, his final glance backward was to a continent nearing the brink of catastrophe, his own home country a domino in line to fall and to be forever changed as a result.

## Endnotes

1. *Balch, Emily: Our Slavic Fellow Citizens, pg 29. 1910*
2. *Stolarik, M. Mark: Immigration and Urbanization – The Slovak Experience 1870-1918, pg 25. 1989*
3. *Ibid, pg 103, Table 8*

## Chapter 2

# THE SLOVAKS OF HUNGARY

# Chapter 2

Ján Kocúr was born on May 22, 1887 to Jozef and Dorota Kocúr, the second of two male children, in the village of Turzovka located near the northern border of what was, in 1887, Hungary. Young Ján's father, Jozef Kocúr, was a teacher in the government-run schools and his mother tended to the family home. Ján Kocúr's older brother and only sibling, Matej, had been born twelve years earlier in February of 1875. Today the village of Turzovka is included in the adca district of the Žilina region in the Slovak Republic near the border with the Czech Republic and Poland. It is not, by many European standards, an ancient village but is certainly a well established one, founded over four hundred years ago in 1598. The Čadca district is hilly country with Turzovka lying in the Kysuca River valley, surrounded by the mountain ranges of Beskydy and Javorníky.[1] Today, Turzovka is a town of approximately 8,000 people and possesses a mix of the new and the old. An older and somewhat isolated village but set in a now modern country moving quickly to make up lost ground. It was not, however, always this way.

Ján Kocúr's Turzovka, that is the Turzovka of 1887, was a typical Slovak village with people, amenities, and a pace of life more similar with those of fifty years prior than fifty years since. Emily Balch in her book *Our Slavic Fellow Citizens* described the typical Slovak village as such:

> *The Slovak village is typified by long, low houses, neat and clean, ranged with their gable roofs end to end in an even row, flush with the street, the eaves just above the door. The roofs are apt to be of hand made shingles and the houses are generally either of brick, frequently merely sun dried, or of wood. Often the ends of cross laid logs or great squared beams show clearly at the corners. But whatever the materials, it is generally covered with plaster or raw clay, and either whitewashed or painted some pale shade of buff, green, or blue. The houses are generally perfectly plain in their design, though some have pretty woodwork at the gable ends, or patterns painted on the walls or about the windows; a kind of work which is a specialty of the women, who are said to do it freehand.*[2]

More often than not in 1887, the houses of villages like Turzovka still had earthen floors inside. Earthen floors, however, were a necessity and not an indication of any lack of cleanliness. Inside rooms were low but kept neat. Walls were decorated with painted crockery, pots of wall flowers, and pictures of sacred subjects. Of note in many homes was also an ornament hanging over the table. The ornament, made of a blown eggshell and with a tail and wings of pleated paper, was meant to represent the Holy Spirit.

Also of importance to the Slovak villager and prominent in their homes were the loom, spinning wheel, and sewing machine. The Slovak women were known for their skill and creativity with needle and thread. Colorful dress, bright patterns on the skirt, bodice, or apron, and detailed designs of flowers, animals, and the heart were the standards of women's dress.

The economy of villages like Turzovka at the turn of the twentieth century was still squarely based on agriculture. It was, for all intents and purposes, a self-sufficing and stable economy with agriculture augmented by suppliers of basic trades and skills. Each village was almost an economic entity unto itself, with only minimal requirements from outside sources. As time went on, however, the influence and effect of industrialization would begin to chip away at both the village way of life and the men and women who made this economic system run.

The backbone of the economy in Slovak villages near the turn of the century was the peasant. Current-day thinking of a peasant conjures an image of a poor, struggling, lower class person who is in many ways inferior to all those around him. While a peasant in agricultural Austria-Hungary did have a social place, it was not at the bottom of the social ladder. He may have often been a property owner, a tax-payer, and very independent minded. In addition to forming a strong link in the economic chain of the times, the peasant also often produced a world of song, tradition, and culture that influenced generations.

The characteristics that went into making the peasant self sufficient - endurance, persistence, and self-reliance - were counterbalanced by the immobility of the class structure in Austria-Hungary. The wealthy and upper class did consider the peasant inferior, not because of any lack of skill or ability, but as a result of the long standing social structure that existed. The same peasant with the same attitude, skills, and initiative transplanted into the United States and without the inferior social stigma would be one who opened a world of possibilities for himself and his family through hard work and initiative. In the cases of many Slovak immigrants, that is exactly what happened.

Emigration among the Slovaks of Austria-Hungary to the United States began a steady increase over the last part of the nineteenth century. In 1899 nearly sixteen thousand Slovak immigrant aliens were admitted to the United States.[3] That number reached its peak in 1905 with fifty-two thousand Slovaks entering the U.S. In 1909 when Ján Kocúr entered the U.S. he was among twenty-two thousand Slovak immigrants. Even these numbers may be a conservative estimate of native Slovak immigration as American data at the time listed immigrants by country of origin and thus lumped immigrants from Hungary (of which the Slovaks were a part) into the whole group from Austria-Hungary. It wasn't until the second decade of the twentieth century that immigrants were recognized and recorded based on their language as well as national origin. Not surprisingly, the counties of Hungary with the highest percentage of Slovak population contributed the most Slovak immigrants. These counties, mainly located in northern Hungary, included Trencsen, Arva, Lipto, and Zolyom.[4] In some cases Slovak counties in Hungary lost as much as twenty-five percent of their Slovak population due to immigration during the last two decades of the nineteenth century.[5]

So what caused such an outflow of Slovaks from Hungary between the late 1870s and 1910? For Slovaks of Hungary there was no new world to settle, like the English of the 1700s, or catastrophic event, like the potato famine of the Irish in the 1800s. For the Slovaks of Hungary, the wave of immigration was not an avalanche brought on by a singular event, but a slow and steady erosion over several decades brought on by the policies and practices of their Magyar rulers.

For many years, Slovaks were a people whose villages, homes, and appearance reflected their personality: basic, plain, and modest. They were a people with no independent history, having been ruled by various outside factions for hundreds of years. Their lands, (the northern edge of Hungary), their customs, and traditions were the only consistencies in their lives. They were mainly peasants who worked the land and whose self-sufficing economy was based on their agricultural success.

As the nineteenth century passed its half-way point, the successes of industrialization began to emerge at the expense of agriculture across many parts of Europe. Even in the Slovak lands of northern Hungary, where no industry existed, effects of industrialization were still felt. New materials, products, and opportunities made their way into agrarian regions where no form of industrialization had previously existed, and as money became more important to survival than simply the land, the balance of economic importance began to shift. By 1900 in the Slovak lands, as with many places across Europe, the opportunity to make a better life, brought on by industrialization, was a powerful draw and no place had industrial needs like the United States.

In addition to the economic factors exerting pressure on Slovaks to emigrate, the political situation they faced at the turn of the century also played a significant role in their movement out of the Slovak homeland. As early as the mid 1800s, the Hungarian throne recognized the political and social implications of trying to rule a kingdom of widely varying nationalities, languages, and cultures. Instead of providing a degree of political and cultural independence to these various groups and involving them in the political process, the Hungarian monarchy took the exact opposite approach, consolidating their power and increasing their influence over their subjects. Despite the petitions of local Slovak administrators and politicians for an independent, county-based political unit still under the ultimate authority of the Hungarians, the Hungarian rulers began a national policy of "Magyarization," the forced transformation of Hungary in to a homogenous Magyar[6] national state.

One of the first steps on the path to a pure Magyar nation was the passage of the Nationality Act by the Hungarian parliament in 1868. The Nationality Act proclaimed that Magyar (Hungarian) was to be the official language of the state administration in the kingdom.[7] This action had an obvious trickle down effect as it meant that all administrative business conducted in the kingdom had to be in the Magyar language. This pertained to any and all documents of a political nature, legal documents, tax documents, and in some cases church documents.

By natural extension the Hungarian parliament broadened the application of the Nationality Act beyond its administrative business to include uniformity of language throughout the country. In essence, the act mandated use of the Magyar language as the official language of the country. The Nationality Act was a sweeping and dramatic change for a country where the Magyars accounted for only 51 percent of the population and where entire areas of the country and significant portions of the population had never heard or seen the Magyar language.[8]

In villages like Turzovka all across the Slovak lands, Ján Kocúr and his fellow countrymen experienced a number of oppressive measures designed to strip them of their national identity in the name of the "Magyar Ideal." The outright persecution of Slovaks in the name of Magyarization attained world attention, most notably in the work of Seton-Watson in the book *Racial Problems in Hungary*, published in 1907. The world's attention, however, did not stop the Magyars from continuing to force Slovaks to adopt all that was Magyar in nearly all aspects of life.

One of the first Slovak targets for Magyarization was the school system. As part of the nationalization process, the Magyar language was to replace Slovak throughout all levels of the school system. This meant that native Slovaks were forced to learn, speak, and write not their native tongue, not the language of their ancestors, or the language of their homes, but Magyar. As this official government policy was in full force during the late 1800s and early 1900s it is likely that Ján Kocúr and other elementary school age children of his time were subject to learning what amounted to be a foreign language. Those teachers that did not comply with this element of the Nationality Act were simply dismissed while those schools that presented any sort of resistance to the implementation of the act were quickly closed. The policy of forced Magyarization had, by 1905, reduced the number of elementary schools providing any Slovak language instruction to 241, a decline from 1,822 schools in 1869. Only seven percent of Slovak children enrolled in primary schools in 1905 were being instructed in their own language.[9]

Implementing the language policy also extended beyond the Slovak primary schools. The secondary schools, also known as "gymnasiums", also felt the effect of the Hungarian throne's policies. Between 1875 and 1918, there were no secondary schools in Slovakia at all and even the three schools that the Slovaks built and endowed at their own expense were dissolved.[10] The policy of forced Magyarization within the Slovak schools was, as one social commentator of the times wrote, "a machine which from one side is fed by Slovak children and from the other side come out Magyars."[11]

Even in advanced studies such as those for the priesthood, a Slovak had to first pass through a Magyar seminary where the Magyar language formed the basis for his education and subsequent vehicle of communication to his flock. Because of the important role the priest played in the daily lives of Slovaks and the influence he carried, seminarians were closely scrutinized throughout their education. An example of the treatment received by some Slovak seminarians is noted in Seton-Watson's *Racial Problems in Hungary*:

> *Some of the grounds on which three young Slovak theological students were expelled from a Hungarian Catholic College in Vicuna in 1906 are grotesque to the point of the incredible. It was said that they (a) "formed a special group in which they aired their favorite views and drew suspicion on themselves by their somewhat retiring manners;" (b) that they nevertheless propagated Slovak national ideas, and that one of them admitted this so that inquiry was unnecessary, though it*

> *was actually held; further (c) that they were in direct communication with two Slovak nationalists; (d) though in the institution, every foreign language is forbidden, they smuggled in Mr. S and talked Slovak with him." The students were not heard in their defense. One of them is now a priest in America.*[12]

The blow that Magyarization dealt to the Slovak educational system had far- reaching consequences. Forced Magyarization resulted in a decrease in the student enrollment in elementary schools. As a direct result, the rates of illiteracy among younger Slovaks dramatically increased in the last quarter of the nineteenth century. The policy also created a void in the Slovak intelligentsia, as those who were educated left the Slovak lands and took their talents (literary, creative, or otherwise) and their ideas with them. It is surprising given the enforcement of these policies, that Ján Kocúr was able to develop the level of education and eloquence that would mark the expression of his ideas later in his life. One can surmise by Kocúr's later writings, detailed and expressive, as well as his ability to communicate effectively in English, that his early education included learning the English language. As a teacher, Kocúr's father, Jozef, may have contributed to his son's education either formally or informally despite the Magyar regulations.

As if the policy of Magyarization and its negative effects on the Slovak school system and language was not enough, the Magyars also took more direct and sinister steps to complete the homogenization of its peoples. Slovak newspapers were shut down, those who spoke the Slovak language in public, especially educated Slovaks, were branded political traitors and often jailed, the Slovak Literary Association was dissolved and its building seized, Slovak companies found it difficult to obtain the necessary Magyar permits to conduct business, Slovak children were deported from their homes in the north to southern Hungary, the Matica slovenska (a Slovak cultural and scientific organization) was closed, and Slovak villages were given new Magyar names on all official government maps.

The Slovak people, peaceful yet tenacious, objected to Magyarization in all its forms on both practical and sentimental grounds.[13] Without any organized political influence, means for resistance, or economic leverage, Slovaks were confronted with a choice; accept Magyarization, submit to Hungarian rule, and try and maintain their cultural identity on their own or strive for a better life elsewhere. It was a choice faced and acted upon by many Slovaks in the early part of the twentieth century, including Ján Kocúr.

**Endnotes**

1. *www.mestoturzovka.sk*
2. *Balch, Emily: Our Slavic Fellow Citizens, pg 89. 1910*
3. *Ibid, pg 103, Table 8.*
4. *Hungarian counties as of 1900. May not reflect modern names or spellings.*
5. *Balch, Emily: Our Slavic Fellow Citizens, pg 105, Table 9. 1910*
6. *For purposes of definition, Magyar is to mean Hungarian*
7. *Stasko, Joseph: Slovaks in the United States of America, pg 17. 1974*
8. *Balch, Emily: Our Slavic Fellow Citizens, pg 109. 1910*
9. *Alexander, June: Ethnic Pride, American Patriotism, pg 60. 2004*
10. *Stasko, Joseph, et al: Slovaks in the United States of America, pg 26. 1974*
11. *Denis, Ernest: Question of Austria – The Slovaks, pg 201. 1922*
12. *Seton-Watson: Racial Problems in Hungary, pg 213-214. 1907*
13. *Balch, Emily: Our Slavic Fellow Citizens, pg 110. 1910*

## Chapter 3

# THE FELLOWSHIP OF STEERAGE

# Chapter 3

On April 14, 1912 the British ocean liner *Titanic*, speeding to set a new record for the North Atlantic crossing, collided with an iceberg shortly before midnight. The mighty ship was heralded as a technological marvel and took years to design and build. It broke apart and sank in a little over two hours. Nearly fifteen hundred passengers and crew perished on this "night to remember" making it the largest disaster in commercial maritime history. The *Titanic* was constructed as the technological marvel of ocean liners and deemed unsinkable. Six small punctures fatally located in a twelve-square-foot area of the ship's starboard watertight holds proved otherwise.[1]

At the time the *Titanic* sank to the bottom of the frigid waters of the North Atlantic, ocean liners had been crossing the Atlantic for nearly three decades. These ships carried rich vacationers to and from Europe, poor immigrants on a one-way trip to a better life, and cargo of all shapes and sizes. Ocean liners represented the main mode of transportation across the Atlantic and a link between America and the European continent. As the unsinkable *Titanic* proved, however, an Atlantic crossing on an ocean liner no matter what the social status of her passengers was not without risk, hardship, and uncertainty.

Slovaks first began emigrating to the United States in large numbers in 1873, when thirteen hundred immigrants came from Hungary.[2] Over the next forty years Slovaks would seek a better life in the United States by settling in places like Pittsburgh, Cleveland, Detroit, and New York. The decision to emigrate was often a difficult one; not difficult in the sense that making a choice to seek a better life is difficult, but difficult in knowing that one's decision had dramatic effects on those people to whom one is most close. It meant leaving one's home, family, friends, and livelihood for a place where none of those things existed; a place of unfamiliarity; a place with a new culture, new language, new laws, and new traditions; a place where the immigrant was an outsider and was treated as such. In essence it meant trading the certainty and comfort of a life well known for exactly the opposite. Yet they came anyway.

Ján Kocúr set out from Turzovka, likely with only a modest pack of personal possessions and a small supply of food to supplement that which he would be able to acquire during his journey. While the exact details of Kocúr's trip are lost to the past as he kept no diary or record, he left Turzovka either by foot or by horse and wagon and likely headed for Bratislava or Budapest. As a twenty-two year old at the time of his departure, Ján Kocúr was several years younger than the average Slovak immigrant of the time. The average Slovak making the trip to America at the turn of the century was twenty-eight years old, male, and likely traveling alone. Several factors contributed to making the Slovak immigrant nearly thirty years of age before coming to the United States. First and foremost, money to pay for a passage across the Atlantic had to be secured and in the agricultural peasant economy of the day, passage money, or any money for that matter, was accumulated slowly. Second, all men in Austria and Hungary were required to serve three years military service; even being forbidden to marry until their service was completed.[3] As a Slovak living in Austria-Hungary, Ján Kocúr was subject to the constraints of both of these factors although no evidence exists to confirm he served in the Austro-Hungarian army prior to leaving for America.

Once arriving in Bratislava or Budapest and securing the proper government approvals, stamps, and paperwork, Ján Kocúr likely boarded a train bound for larger cities in Germany, ultimately making it to a port city. For most Slovak immigrants the German ports of Bremen and Hamburg were the primary choices for embarkation due to their proximity and access via rail service. Ján Kocúr was headed to Bremen, one of the largest and busiest of all German ports. While most Slovak immigrants leaving Austria-Hungary secured the proper papers, many did not. Those individuals who did not obtain the proper credentials often bluffed their way by German officials by presenting any type of Magyar (Hungarian) document or credential. This often satisfied the request for papers, all Hungarian paperwork being equally unintelligible to those German officials who were responsible for them.[4]

The steamship ticket that Ján Kocúr saved for and purchased to get him from Bremen across the Atlantic cost him approximately fifty crowns or about twenty-five dollars. Kocúr's costs for train transportation from a place like Munich to Bremen was likely another five dollars and additional expenses along the way, such as food, lodging, and miscellaneous expenses, only added to the total. The thought of immigrating to America was cheap, the actual costs, however, required some commitment.

Kocúr arrived in Bremen, Germany in August of 1909. As one of the busiest ports in Europe, Bremen teamed with people, some of them coming, many of them going, and a handful of them looking to take advantage of the situation. The port of Bremen was populated not only with immigrants, merchants, and sailors, but also with agents of all types. Many of these port agents were soliciting workers for American mining and steel companies, promising work and housing in exchange for committed employment; others offered rich financial inducements for railroad construction while some peddled tickets for various steamship lines and promised glowing opportunities available at the immigrant's final destination. There were also representatives of land companies, railroad lines, and a variety of employers.[5] While many of these agents represented legitimate employers in search of desperately needed labor and presented immigrants with genuine opportunities, some were unscrupulously taking advantage of people who, in many cases, had never before ventured ten miles from their own front doors. Schemes and trickery often relieved the immigrants of their extra money before they even stepped on the gangplank. Ján Kocúr already had a plan of where he would go once he reached America's shores. Kocúr also knew that two of his closest friends from Turzovka, Anton Hranec and Juraj Gazak, were waiting for him in a small Western Pennsylvania town, ready to help him with employment. Ján Kocúr wisely avoided all the inducements and temptations that would serve to separate him from what little money he had and patiently waited in Bremen for his departure date to arrive.

Ján Kocúr's voyage to America began when he boarded the vessel that would take him across the Atlantic. His hard-earned savings had purchased him a ticket on the ocean liner *Bremen*, a large steamer of the North German Lloyd line. The ship was originally built in 1897 by Schichau Shipyard in Danzig, Germany and had already made several transatlantic crossings. The *Bremen* was a solid ship, a mainstay in the company's line. Its dual center smoke stacks exhausted the thick smoke produced by its powerful coal- fired steam engines and its twin quadruple screw propellers powerfully pushed the ten thousand-ton ship smoothly through the water. While not the largest ship of its day, the *Bremen* was large enough to carry, in addition to its crew, 230 first class, 250 second class, and 1,850 third class or steerage passengers.

On August 28, 1909 the *Bremen* bustled with activity. The ship's boilers were fired, slowly bringing the roaring engines to life, the low steam whistle bellowed, and the crew busied with the preparations for departure. From afar the *Bremen* looked like an ant hill with its workers busily moving here and there while on the dock, lines of passengers began to form. The neat and tidy lines of first-class and second-class passengers were in stark contrast in almost every way, from their dress and appearance to their luggage, with the throngs of steerage passengers crowding toward the third-class gangplank. Among the first-class and second-class passengers, "Welcome aboard sir (or madam)," was routinely heard. These privileged passengers spoke mostly German or English and were ushered to their cabins by impeccably dressed ship stewards in their crisp white uniforms. Among the third-class passengers, however, no such greeting or amenities were offered. Third- class passengers were directed, or more likely herded, to their place in the cramped quarters below deck. The languages heard among the third-class passengers, nearly all of them immigrants, often included Polish, Hungarian, Russian, Slovak, or any one of many eastern European languages.

Ján Kocúr, like the majority of his fellow Slovak immigrants during that time, boarded the *Bremen* that August day with only the bare necessities. If Kocúr was at all like the immigrants who had put everything into their chance to come to America, he likely carried a small personal bundle or small case containing some clothing items, a few personal effects, an item or two of remembrance from the family and a small supply of food possibly left over from his journey to Germany or purchased at the port prior to departure. These items would have been typical. For the many Slovaks who decided to emigrate, the money saved over the course of months or even years was just barely enough to cover the cost of transit to a port like Bremen, basic accommodations along the way, and their ship's ticket with only a little left over. Because of their economic situation at home, Slovak immigrants could only afford the lowest-priced ticket; a third class accommodation called steerage. All of the major steamship lines crossing the Atlantic in those days carried three classes of passengers, first class, second class, and third class or steerage. Each of these classes of transit came with the appropriate level of service, amenities, and cost. Suffice to say that steerage class had the minimum of each. The steerage-class ticket, despite its lack of any frills, was cheap and Slovaks like Ján Kocúr, used to hardship and little more than basic necessities at home, took the conditions of steerage class in stride.

Steerage space aboard a steamship liner was the kind of space that could not be put to use for freight or for any other profitable purpose.[6] Most liners carried nearly nine hundred steerage passengers often with little space for the passengers to move about. In good weather there wasn't enough space above deck for all the passengers to stand or walk around. In bad weather, with hatches down, the suffering of the passengers packed below like cattle could be unbearable. Sleeping conditions in steerage were equally as unpleasant. In some cases, as many as two hundred steerage passengers slept in one compartment on bunks, one above another, with little light or creature comforts.

Joseph Krajsa, et. al. in the book *Slovaks in America: A Bicentennial Study* describes the other conditions typically found in the steerage compartment aboard a steamship populated with immigrants:

> *Men, women, and children were quartered in the same area where there was minimal ventilation or provision for hygienic facilities. No one was entitled to any degree of privacy or common comfort. Drinking water was sparingly dispensed every three hours but no water was provided for washing. For a small fee passengers were able to obtain a thin mattress and a coverlet as well as a spoon, fork, and a mug in to which their food was apportioned at meal time.*[7]

The food served to the immigrants in steerage class, which was miserable, was dealt out of huge kettles into the dinner pails provided by the ship. When it was distributed, the passengers pushed and crowded so that meals were anything but an orderly procedure.[8] The food was doled out, as one immigrant recalled, with less courtesy than one would find in a charity soup kitchen. For most, the inadequate supply of food provided by the steamship line was supplemented by the small quantities of food brought along from home. All this in contrast to the linen-covered tables, fine china, and well prepared and served food of the second- and first-class dining room.

As the *Bremen* pulled farther from the dock on that August day in 1909 its immigrant passengers like Ján Kocúr must have wondered if their decision to leave family, friends, and home was the right one. The mood of these passengers at this moment, the moment of no turning back, was melancholy at best and at its worst filled with regret and sorrow. For the immigrants on board the *Bremen* the departure was not a celebration with streamers and waving passengers, but a reflective and solemn moment.

Once in the open water, passengers on board became subject to the military-like procedures and rules of the ship. During the day, weather permitting, the steerage passengers emerged from below deck wrapped in blankets, shawls, or coats. Some were hopeful that the fresh air might alleviate their sea sickness while other simply wanted to get out of the crowd below and stretch their legs. Steerage passengers on deck, in their native skirts, babushkas, and jackets and speaking any number of languages, made quite the spectacle for the first- and second-class passengers whose vantage points were the decks above. When the weather was bad or the seas too rough, the steerage passengers were sequestered below, forbidden to come up on deck. Unlike their fellow first- or second-class passengers, the steerage passengers had no well-appointed dining room or parlor room in which they could pass the time by playing cards or listening to music. Regardless, the immigrants in steerage made the best of circumstances.

As with many instances when people of various backgrounds are thrown together, bound by some common thread, kinship eventually surfaces. Ján Kocúr and his fellow steerage passengers were literally all in the same boat together and for the most part they made the best of it. The passengers sought out and found their fellow countrymen. They found fellow passengers who knew someone who was related to someone in their village. They swapped stories, sang, and drank; celebrated birthdays and anniversaries; or simply celebrated being together. Space permitting, they even danced to the sounds of an accordion, violin, or harmonica. No matter their country of origin, the steerage passengers had something in common to share. All of them were headed to America; headed somewhere or to someone for a chance at a better life.

Traveling across the Atlantic in the steerage class of a steamship ocean liner was an experience the immigrants never forgot. But these immigrants, Ján Kocúr included, endured all of it with a faith in the future, a faith that was eventually rewarded as the *Bremen* approached the coastline of the United States.

> *Be patient, this seems like Hell, but it will soon seem to you like Heaven. Yes, this heaven is coming; coming down almost from above, on yonder fringe of the sea, for far away trails the low lying smoke of the pilot boat, and but a little farther off is land...land. None but the shipwrecked and immigrants know the joy of that note which goes from lip to lip as it echoes and reechoes in thirty languages, yet with the one word of throbbing joy, land...land...America!*[9]

## Endnotes

1. *Great Events of the Twentieth Century: Time, pg 86. 1997*
2. *Balch, Emily: Our Slavic Fellow Citizens, pg 100. 1910*
3. *Ibid pg 51.*
4. *Krajsa, Joseph, et. al.: Slovaks in America: A Bicentennial Study, pg 16. 1971*
5. *Ibid.*
6. *Ibid.*
7. *Ibid.*
8. *Steiner, Edward: On the Trail of the Immigrant - The Fellowship of Steerage, pg 32. 1906*
9. *Ibid, pg 35.*

## Chapter 4

# THROUGH THE GOLDEN DOOR

# Chapter 4

After ten days at sea, Ján Kocúr and his fellow passengers on the *Bremen* came within sight of New York City on September 7, 1909. The weather in New York for that early September day was cloudy but warm, the temperature reaching eighty degrees. First greeted by small pilot boats outside of New York harbor but within sight of the coastline, the big ship, its engines now reduced to an idle, slowly made its way towards its termination point. As the ship drew closer to the coastline, the welcoming gaze of the Statue of Liberty and the rising skyline of New York City came into view, confirming to all of the immigrants now crowded on the *Bremen*'s deck that they truly were in America. Most passengers had never before laid eyes on or been in a city the size of New York. There were certainly large cities in the European home of many of these immigrants, Vienna, Budapest, and Warsaw to name a few, but their sights and sounds were only experienced by most immigrants through secondhand stories. Very few Slovaks or Poles had ever been to a large city, even in their own country. The sight of New York with its tall buildings, bridges, and bustling wharfs was unlike anything Ján Kocúr had ever seen. The young immigrant would have to wait a little longer to experience New York, however, because as the *Bremen*'s engines were ordered to stop and the ship was docked on the West Side of Manhattan, one last test awaited only a few short miles away. Before beginning a new life in America, Ján Kocúr and the rest of the steerage-class passengers on the *Bremen* had to first pass through the Immigration Center at Castle Garden, New York, better known as Ellis Island.

Ján Kocúr's journey crossing the Atlantic had lasted ten days and was thankfully now at an end. The ordeal of immigrating to America, however, would last a little longer. Throughout their voyage, the immigrants onboard the *Bremen,* like those on many ships before and after her, knew what awaited them at Ellis Island. Nearly all had heard the stories from family members, friends, or fellow passengers of the poor souls who were so close to their final destination only to be turned away by immigration officials and sent back to Europe without ever setting foot on the U.S. mainland. In reality, about eighty percent of all immigrants who landed at Ellis Island passed through without any difficulties.[1] While the statistics showed that immigrant deportation occurred only on a limited basis, it certainly would have made for riveting conversation while passing the time during the ten-day crossing for immigrants to hear of how the poor Slovak was turned away from America. The prospect of enduring all that an immigrant's journey entailed and yet being sent back across the Atlantic would have only added to the already heightened anxieties of the ship's passengers.

As the *Bremen* sat docked on Manhattan's West Side, it was boarded by U.S. immigration officials. The ship's officers delivered the passenger manifest lists to the inspectors and the process of identification began. Immigrants were given cards to present to the immigration officials that were coded back to a corresponding number and passenger information on the manifest list. The officials who boarded the *Bremen,* immigrant landing inspectors and medical officers, first quickly examined the first- and second-class passengers. Most of these passengers had paid anywhere between thirty and ninety dollars for a second- or first-class ticket and were rapidly passed, free to go through customs. First- and second-class passengers aboard ships like the *Bremen* often stepped out onto American soil within hours of arriving. The cursory inspection and quick approval of these passengers was partially based on the belief by immigration officials that if a passenger could afford a second- or first-class ticket, they posed no risk to America and could be welcomed ashore immediately. For steerage-class passengers like Ján Kocúr, however, the immigration officials took a very different approach.

While still aboard the ship, steerage passengers were divided into groups of thirty according to their manifest list number. The groups of thirty were then loaded on to barges destined for Ellis Island, with a capacity of exactly thirty people, and they would stay together throughout the inspection process. Oftentimes if the Ellis Island inspection station was at capacity with previous arrivals, the passengers would wait aboard ship, sometimes for days, before proceeding. If the immigrant passengers had learned one thing throughout their journey, it was how to be patient. Waiting was not a new experience for these people and most immigrants patiently persevered until it was their turn to board the barge and make the short trip across the harbor to Ellis Island.

The immigrant-laden barges chugged from the lower West Side of Manhattan to the East Side of Ellis Island, a distance of just over one mile. The barges unloaded their passengers in front of the island's administration building and the groups of thirty proceeded to the first-floor entrance. As Ján Kocúr approached the administration building, he looked up to see a castle-like structure with three large glass-paned archways squarely framed by the building itself and bordered by two large domed towers. It's no wonder why the island was given its former name, Castle Garden, when viewing such a structure. Leading up to the middle archway was a covered walk, which led immigrants like the young Kocúr to the building's main entrance and through the "golden door."

After leaving the barge with his fellow passengers, Ján Kocúr stood in the slow but steadily moving line outside Ellis' main entrance, his numbered inspection card pinned to his coat, and gradually made his way to the door. As he passed through the main door and into the building at Ellis Island, Ján Kocúr encountered a large hall buzzing with the din of thousands of people and hundreds of languages that widened to both sides as far as he could see. The entire east end of the first floor was devoted to baggage and immigrants were encouraged to check whatever personal belongings they may have had for the duration of the inspection process.[2] From the baggage check, Kocúr and his group proceeded to climb a long central stairway leading to the Great Hall located on the second floor for their individual medical and legal inspections. The stairway itself served a dual purpose, one fairly obvious to the immigrants about to ascend it and one not so obvious. The stairway connected the first and second floors but it also served as the unofficial start of the medical examination process. As immigrants climbed the stairway to the second floor, medical officers stationed at the top of the stairs carefully watched for anyone that showed signs of difficulty, lameness, or shortness of breath. This came to be known as the "six-second physical" and was used to identify problems for which further examination might be necessary.[3] The Public Health Service doctors who watched the immigrants ascend the steps would chalk a coded letter on a suspicious immigrant's right coat front or lapel to indicate potential problems. An "L" meant lameness, "B" for back problems, "Ft" for feet, and "E" for eyes.

Once Ján Kocúr reached the top of the steps, he was subject to an official medical exam, which lasted anywhere from five to ten minutes. Each immigrant was examined for any physical or mental condition that would make them incapable of earning a living and for any signs or symptoms of communicable diseases. If any immigrant failed the medical exam or aroused suspicion among the medical examiners they were detained for a more comprehensive exam in one of the private exam rooms around the perimeter of the second floor's Great Hall. If the more detailed exam revealed any serious cases, the immigrant would be confined to the Ellis Island hospital ward for treatment and recovery and then likely deportation. In a few cases the sickly immigrant was deported immediately. As a young immigrant in good health, Ján Kocúr passed through Ellis Island's medical exams without incident.

After passing his medical exam, Kocúr proceeded to the main area of the second floor's Great Hall located on the west side of the building for the legal examination. The legal exam consisted mainly of standard questions from immigration officials that verified the information on the ship's manifest. Dividing the space between the medical exam area on the hall's east side and the legal exam desks on the west side was a maze-like series of wire and piping designed to keep an orderly flow between the two stations. The iron-railed channels funneled the groups of thirty toward the legal exam officers at a slow pace. If Ján Kocúr's experience was typical, it likely took him a few hours to make his way across the cavernous Great Hall. Depending on the time of the year, which often dictated how great the influx of immigrants was, the detention time of immigrants at Ellis Island could be as much as three weeks before final clearance was completed.[4]

Once reaching the legal examination area, Kocúr was asked a series of questions. His vital statistics, like height and eye color, his nationality, race, last permanent residence, and final destination were all of interest to the immigration officials. Questions as to his medical history and current condition ensured he brought no communicable diseases to his new country. Answers to questions on his political affiliations and whether or not he was an anarchist helped to put officials at ease as to his political intentions. All of these questions, provided they were even understood by the immigrants, did nothing more than formalize the process by which new Americans entered the United States. The handwritten forms and standard questions were the early twentieth century's version of homeland security.

In response to all the questioning, prodding, and examining, immigration records show that Ján Kocúr provided the following information to officials as he made his way through Ellis Island. His name in full was Ján (Slovak for John) Kocúr. He was twenty-two years of age, male, and not married. He listed his calling or occupation as "laborer," as did the majority of other Slovak immigrants of the time. He was able to read and write, although at what level of proficiency and whether or not that meant reading and writing English was not specified. Kocúr listed his country (of which he was a subject or citizen) as Hungary. At the time, the land of the Slovaks was part of Hungary proper although technically also part of the larger empire of Austria-Hungary. He did list his race, however, as Slovak and not Hungarian. Ján Kocúr's answers to these questions provide particular insight into his attitude towards his ethnic background. He viewed himself not as Austrian or even Hungarian but as Slovak regardless of who controlled his land, made his laws, or presided over his government. Kocúr's city or town and place of birth was recorded by officials as "Turzofkla," the Hungarian spelling and name for the Kocúr's Slovak village of Turzovka. Oftentimes busy immigration officials, impatient with broken-English speaking immigrants, wrote down what they thought to be the phonetic spelling of what they had heard the immigrant say, without concern for proper spelling. This phenomenon applied not only to the names of towns and villages but also to first and last names as well. Many immigrants entered Ellis Island with their given last name and ended up with a derivation of their original last names on official records simply because it was easier and quicker for officials to spell based on what they heard. Such an act, made with an instant stroke of a pen, was then carried forward for generations to come. Ján Kocúr listed Springdale, Pennsylvania as his final destination and indicated that he possessed a ticket to that final destination. He also indicated that he had never before been in the United States and had arrived in his new country with the sum total of thirty-seven dollars.

Apart from the basic background information, immigration officials wanted to know if Kocúr was a polygamist or an anarchist; he answered no to both. Officials also asked if he had ever been in a prison, almshouse, insane asylum, or supported by charity; he answered no. Finally he was asked if he came to the United States because of solicitation of offer of employment; again he answered no.

The officials at Ellis Island also recorded a detailed physical description of Ján Kocúr. The records indicate that Kocúr was five feet four inches tall, had a fair complexion, blond hair, and blue eyes. Kocúr also went through a physical exam, most likely carried out by current or former military doctors and most likely conducted with the rapidity of a typical military physical. Ján Kocúr was found to be in good physical and mental condition with no physical deformities, crippled limbs, or distinctive physical marks of identification.

Of particular interest was the answer to the question of whether or not the young Kocúr was going to join a relative, and if so, who. As someone who had never been to the United States before and by all accounts someone who arrived alone, immigration officials wanted to ensure the twenty-two year old Slovak from Turzovka had some connection in the United States. As noted, Kocúr indicated that Springdale, Pennsylvania was his final destination and went on to tell the immigration officials that waiting for his arrival in Springdale was his brother Matej Kocúr. Matej's wife, Dorota, who was still living in Turzovka, was listed by Ján Kocúr as his nearest relative in the country from which he came. What makes this portion of the immigration record so interesting is the fact that while Ján Kocúr did indeed have an older brother named Matej Kocúr, family records make no mention of Matej ever traveling to the U.S. or living in Springdale. Ján Kocúr may have been more carefully prepared for the questioning at Ellis Island than one would imagine. With the prospect of a longer detention facing those coming through Ellis Island without a connection already here in America, Kocúr may have simply created the connection. It is not unimaginable that as immigrants crossed the Atlantic, stories about what to expect during the procedures at Ellis Island were discussed and analyzed during their small group conversations; and that immigrants like Ján Kocúr prepared and practiced their answers to ensure that immigration officials had no reason to detain them a minute longer than necessary. Having no physical, political, or social reason to deny him admission in to the United States, Ján Kocúr, having satisfied all of the criteria required of newly arrived immigrants, was cleared for entry into America.

After successfully completing the necessary exams, Ján Kocúr was issued a landing card and was free to enter the U.S. Kocúr then left the examination area and descended another large stairway at the west end of the Great Hall back down to the first floor. While the treatment of newly arrived immigrants may be rightfully viewed as harsh, Ellis Island did provide a number of services that aided approved immigrants with the initial steps of entering the country. Located at the bottom of the staircase that descended from the second floor of the Great Hall were a number of courtesy services of which the immigrants could take advantage. Ellis Island officials at the money exchange would change foreign currency to U.S. dollars. Every major railroad line maintained a ticket office on Ellis Island and were more than willing to sell the newly arrived train tickets for departure out of New York City. Many religious and charitable organizations kept offices on the island to assist immigrants in their spiritual and physical needs. There was even a U.S. Post Office and a Western Union office at the west end of the first floor.[5]

Ján Kocúr's experience at Ellis Island was probably typical of thousands of other immigrants arriving in the early twentieth century. Depending on the time of year and number of immigrants being processed on the island, it likely took him about three to four hours to pass though all of the island's stations. Despite all the physical prodding, legal questioning, and bureaucratic processing, Ján Kocúr, his landing card prominently displayed, could now legally enter the United States and begin a new life. He would begin that new life in America, however, not as Ján Kocúr but as John Kocur; the "Americanized" version of his first and last name. An English spelling and pronunciation that he and subsequent generations would carry forward, indicative of his new home.

With the close inspection and formalities of immigrant processing over, John Kocur was now on his own. Along with other freshly approved immigrants the young Kocur proceeded to the Ellis Island ferry for the short trip to New York and the next leg of his journey. Immigrants like John Kocur were easily identified as newcomers once they reached the city wharfs; their clothes, language, baggage, and many other characteristics immediately set them apart from the "natives." The appearance of the newly arrived immigrants also made many an easy mark for the unscrupulous agents, swindlers, and con men who roamed the docks of New York looking for fresh prey. If the immigrants were lucky, they were met by friends or relatives at the docks. The lone immigrant or young family without American connections was sometimes not so lucky. Many were "befriended" by heartless schemers who would soon separate the immigrants from what little money they had by offering bogus railroad tickets, "immigrant taxes," or the promise of employment for a fee.

Many immigrants arrived with nothing more than a slip of paper containing an address to guide them but with no idea how far or in what direction their destination may be. Some simply followed the railroad tracks hoping at some point to find employment in the nearest mine, railroad building, or mill site. Others had pre-arranged employment with company agents before leaving Europe and simply went where they were told.

Although some immigrants fell prey even before they were on American soil for a few hours, the majority persevered and moved on. Approximately half of the Slovak immigrants like John Kocur settled in Pennsylvania, and the rest in the surrounding Northeastern states.[6] The most common destinations included cities like Pittsburgh, Scranton, Passaic, and Cleveland. Over the years, Slovak communities had taken hold and had grown in and around some of the most industrialized areas of the country - in the extensive anthracite mining towns of Northeast Pennsylvania and the steel mills of Western Pennsylvania - places where labor was in demand and jobs were to be had.

John Kocur's trip to America had ended but his journey was only beginning. Kocur boarded a train in New York that, for the next several days, most likely took him through Philadelphia, Harrisburg, and then on to Pittsburgh. From there it was only a short ride to the area northeast of Pittsburgh where he would settle, find employment, raise a family, and undertake the work of not only living the American dream but doing everything in his power to transfer that dream to his fellow Slovaks. John Kocur's two- and-a-half day train ride from New York to Pittsburgh would offer him plenty of time for introspection and thought. Was this the right thing to have done, coming to America? What will the future hold? Will America truly be the land of opportunity? It seemed that John Kocur had more questions than answers in the early fall of 1909 when he arrived in America with only the barest of necessities. What Kocur could not fully realize at the time, but would be revealed over the course of his life in America, was that those necessities included a passion for freedom, a love for his Slovak homeland, and a drive to bring the two together. John Kocur's "opportunity" in America would become the opportunity to literally change the lives of Slovaks, both in the U.S. and abroad, forever. Like the train that carried him away from New York that day, John Kocur's life slowly picked up momentum, moving forward with unstoppable purpose.

## Endnotes

1. *Tifft, William: Ellis Island, pg 84. 1990*
2. *Ibid, pg 85.*
3. *Ibid, pg 86.*
4. *Krajsa, Joseph, et. al.: Slovaks in America: A Bicentennial Study, pg 16. 1971*
5. *Tifft, William: Ellis Island, pg 85. 1990*
6. *Stolarik, M. Mark: Slovak Fraternal-Benefit Societies in North America, pg 11. Slovakia, 1998.*

**Chapter 5**

# LIFE AND WORK IN ARNOLD

# Chapter 5

As John Kocur arrived in New York City via the *Bremen* on September 7, 1909 his world was made up of the short term; what lay directly in front of him, what the next few hours would bring. Given the swirling circumstances of Kocur's first few hours in America he didn't have time to think about the long term. Life in America moved at a rapid pace and immigrants like John Kocur would have to join in and take their chance at success. It was as if the newly arrived immigrant was simply waiting on the bank of a fast moving stream, ready, with some trepidation, to jump in.

When asked by the immigration officials at Ellis Island where he intended to go once in America, John Kocur had answered Springdale, Pennsylvania. Springdale was a small industrial town along the banks of the Allegheny River just northeast of Pittsburgh. Life in and around Pittsburgh on that September day, the proverbial stream into which John Kocur would jump, also moved along at its own pace. The Joseph Horne Company began its September furniture sale featuring an early English desk for twenty dollars. An organized labor parade was a well-attended recent event that, according to the *Pittsburgh Post*, "pleased the women folk." The Pittsburgh Pirates dropped two games to the Chicago Cubs by scores of three to one and six to three but would go on to win the 1909 World Series over the Detroit Tigers four games to three a little more than a month later.[1] The distance that Kocur would cover going from New York to Pittsburgh was around three hundred and seventy miles. The distance between Kocur's Slovak homeland culture and way of life and that which he was beginning to encounter in America must have seemed like a divide of one hundred times that distance.

Although Springdale was John Kocur's intended destination, he would end up settling in the small town of Arnold, Pennsylvania, only a few miles up the Allegheny River from Springdale. What exactly drew Kocur to Arnold instead of Springdale is unclear but the availability of housing and need for labor (Arnold had more) most likely were contributing factors. In addition, a relative and an acquaintance of John Kocur from the Slovak town of Podvysoka, very close to his own village of Turzovka, had also settled in the area. Anton Hranec was related to John Kocur through his mother, Dora's, side of the family; her maiden name was Hranec. Juraj (George) Gazak was a close friend from near Kocur's home village. Both men traveled from Europe together and arrived in the United States only three months prior to Kocur's arrival.[2] Both Hranec and Gazak also headed for Western Pennsylvania and settled in the Springdale area. Like many immigrants unfamiliar with their final destination, John Kocur had to rely on contacts from the old country to help him find housing and work. When Hranec and Gazak arrived in the U.S. both were in their early twenties and both likely sought the same thing that their friend John Kocur did - an opportunity to escape the suffocating economic and social circumstances of their homeland and a chance at the American dream. These two fellow Slovaks from the same village likely provided John Kocur with guidance and help once he arrived. Hranec, Gazak, and Kocur would remain close friends and business associates throughout their lives, bound by their Slovak heritage and their common experience as immigrants to the United States.

Springdale, Pennsylvania would ultimately turn out to be John Kocur's home but not until after he'd lived nearly ten years in the United States. Until that time he would call the small community of Arnold home. The town of Arnold was first settled in 1852 and consisted of a tract of approximately two hundred and twenty-six acres of land situated on the east side of the Allegheny River in Westmoreland County.[3] By the turn of the century Arnold had been transformed from a small and quiet village many considered just an extension of New Kensington, Pennsylvania into a thriving industrial town. As Arnold's population grew, driven by the area's industrialization and swelled by the arriving immigrants anxious to find work, it became more than just a ward of New Kensington; Arnold became a borough unto itself. In the early 1900s, however, its streets were still dirt and its gas street lamps were still lit by hand.

When Kocur arrived in Arnold during September 1909 employment and housing were his first priorities. For nearly all immigrants of the time the two necessities were closely linked. John Kocur's first job after his arrival in Arnold was as a laborer in a large local glass factory, the American Window Glass Company. Kocur's hiring was probably the result of Slovak connections in the community and within the factory. Oftentimes the newly arrived immigrants found work based on the recommendation or connection of a friend or family member who was already employed. Knowing someone on the "inside" who could put in a good word with a boss or foreman was the most common job application. Glass factories were a major industrial fixture, running day and night, along the Allegheny River near Arnold. The Heidenkamp Glass Works, for example, was located near Springdale and had a reputation for manufacturing some of the finest plate glass and mirrors in the region. Shortly after the turn of the century the plant had the capacity of producing 120 thousand square feet of polished plate glass and mirrors per month. The plant was equipped with four blast furnaces with twenty-four pots to each furnace and employed over three hundred men.[4] Due to the lack of housing in Springdale, many of the men employed by Heidenkamp lived on the outskirts of Springdale and in surrounding towns like New Kensington and Arnold. The Heidenkamp factory was a successful regional business and offered immigrants the chance to get on their feet in the new country by earning a living unimaginable in their homelands; not an easy living by any means but a steady paying job none the less. Work shifts were long, as much as sixty hours during a six-day work week, the work hard, and the pay, while seemingly sparse compared to standards of today, was much more than the typical Slovak could earn in the old country. John Kocur earned the typical salary of an unskilled laborer, six to eight dollars a week. As a newly arrived immigrant and inexperienced member of the labor force, Kocur probably started out performing the most basic of unskilled labor; loading or unloading raw materials like sand, necessary for making glass, transferring finished product to the shipping yards, or working maintenance jobs on the mill floor. More important than the type of work he did, John Kocur's entrance into the American work force enabled the young Slovak to take the first steps on the road of opportunity, providing for his own needs and eventually for those of his family.

Industry in and around Pittsburgh had grown significantly in the years just preceding the turn of the century. In order to keep up with the pace of growth demanded by an ever-expanding America, the industrial machine needed labor. Pittsburgh's industrial landscape was dominated by the giant Frick Company, whose mills manufactured coke, and Andrew Carnegie's steel works, which was well on its way to industrial dominance. In addition, the industries that formed the support network for Frick and Carnegie and fed these giants included various coal mines, railroads, iron foundries, and wire mills. These were the engines that were driving America's industrial growth in the early 1900s and the resources that made those engines run were arriving by the thousands at Ellis Island every single day.

Although most Slovak immigrants to the United States came from agricultural backgrounds, they found their livelihood not in farming but in industry.[5] They were traditionally a people closely bound to the soil but they did not attach themselves to farming in their new world.[6] Their love for the land did not decrease with their arrival to America, however, nearly all lacked the funds necessary to purchase even the basic necessities of farming; land, machinery, and livestock. In addition, because many Slovak immigrants initially came to America with the viewpoint that they would work, earn, save, and then return to their homeland, immediate paying jobs were needed. Farming on the other hand was an occupation that implied a longer commitment.

The Slovak immigrants at the turn of the century found ready opportunity in the industrial centers of the Northeast United States. Slovaks, accustomed to the hard and physically demanding work in their homeland, thought nothing of accepting work under similar circumstances. The type of work done by many Slovak immigrants yielded ready pay and gave a man the joy and satisfaction of reasonably quick earnings. For this reason, early immigrants gravitated toward mines, foundries, steel mills, oil refineries, forges, textile plants, factories, and coke ovens.[7] Often groups of Slovaks would together find work in one of these industries and begin the formation of Slovak communities. Growing numbers of other Slovak immigrants would continue to come to these established areas and the settlement grew into a community or even a town composed mainly of Slovaks. This is exactly the pattern that grew Slovak communities in towns across Pennsylvania like Hazleton, Wilkes-Barre, Pittston, Braddock, and Homestead. In some cases Slovaks came to a specific area because they were imported labor and legally bound to do so. In order to secure a labor force, agents of a company would travel abroad, to ports and towns, looking to induce men to emigrate, settle, and work. In many other cases, Slovaks like John Kocur came to a particular town because they had the connection of a friend or family member. The strongest drawing card for Slovaks with even the slightest interest in leaving home, however, was the money sent to a family from one of its members in America.[8] These funds, whether designed to sustain a family in the absence of a breadwinner or pay for the passage of more relatives, showed that there was indeed money to be made in America.

As workers, Slovaks were highly sought after in the hard and unforgiving industries of mining and steel. Slovaks were diligent and efficient and had the capacity to work long hours and endure great physical hardship.[9] They were honest workers who felt the moral obligation to give a full day's work for a full day's pay. Slovak immigrants were also of course motivated by the desire to earn more money and assure a brighter economic future. If a Slovak man earned more money in America and returned to his homeland, he would be able to free himself and his family from the poverty to which he was so accustomed in the old country. Earning more also became a way to facilitate the arrival of a wife, children, mother or brother. Because of this, the Slovaks did not shirk any type of work, provided it meant higher wages; and since jobs were plentiful the newcomer found plenty of work. For that reason the Slovak peasant, now an immigrant worker, willingly worked harder and longer hours so that he might improve his living conditions and those of his family across the sea.[10]

John Kocur's work in the glass factory, like the work of his fellow Slovaks in the mines and mills of Western Pennsylvania, was hard and long. It afforded him, however, something he could only dream of had he remained in Turzovka. Kocur earned more money in a few months as a laborer than he likely could make in a year in the Slovak homeland, he established a foothold in America's rapidly changing society, which respected and recognized an individual for what one did rather than for who one's father was, and began to realize and appreciate the American ideals of freedom, independence, and self-determination. In many respects it was those ideals that became more valuable to John Kocur than any pay he was to receive. Those ideals, not the size of his band account would help to shape and motivate Kocur's life's work in America.

With steady employment secured through Slovak connections in Arnold and Springdale, Kocur needed a place to live. For immigrants who arrived without a family or who lacked relatives in the area there were two choices for housing and accommodations: company housing or boarding.

Company houses were designed for the work crews and were typically plain, identically dull houses constructed with the barest of materials, containing only the minimum necessities and at the lowest possible expense. Designed strictly for the company's workers, these houses lacked nearly all creature comforts except heat, usually by way of a coal-burning stove, and in some cases running water. Bathroom facilities were almost always constructed separately and consisted of a long, multi-station outhouse.

The company houses were not really houses at all in the sense one may imagine a house but more like bunk houses. In many instances these quarters were designed to accommodate up to thirty workers. Sometimes the workers occupied the boarding space in shifts so that if a boarding boss had five beds or cots for boarders, he could take in ten men who worked on alternating shifts.[11] Men housed in these conditions not only had to deal with the featureless surroundings of their houses, but also suffer the houses' location. Efficiency in all things drives industrial production. Houses located close the mill lessened the distance men had to travel, reduced the likelihood they would be prevented from getting to work on time, and enabled the company more control over their labor force. For the men living in the row upon row of company houses, this proximity meant suffering the ever-present noise, dust, fumes, and waste of the mills and factories around the clock.

Not only would the company provide the housing accommodations for their labor force but would also provide meals for the men. A worker who boarded in a company house would take his meals not at home, but in "free lunch cafes." These establishments, also owned and operated by the company, provided various kinds of basic foods for each meal with the laborer expected to pay out of his pocket for drinks. This seemed like a very liberal arrangement but in reality it had many disadvantages and bred much evil.[12] While the food was "free" to workers, their pay was adjusted accordingly, either weekly, monthly, or as part of their up-front pay scale with their employer. The cost of the labor pool's housing, even in the poorest condition, was also accounted for in a similar manner. Managed and controlled by the company, the laborer's housing and food costs were nothing more than a ledger entry deducted from the weekly or monthly pay. The only thing the workers "paid" for in this arrangement was their drink. For much of the immigrant labor, that meant alcohol; for the company-owned bars and dining halls that meant cheap alcohol at exorbitant prices. If there was one stereotype associated with unskilled Slovak labor, one weakness in character of an otherwise hardworking people, it was their affinity for alcohol. Free-pouring bartenders were careful to account for every drop of whiskey or beer they provided to their customers. If cash was not on hand to pay for the drinks at the end of one's shift, and in most cases it was not, credit would be happily extended. It would all be settled at the end of the week in the form of a lighter pay envelope.

A prime example of the typical labor-management arrangement in the early twentieth century was found in the same industry in which John Kocur worked, glass, and was located only a few miles from Arnold in Springdale. As the Heidenkamp Plate Glass Company expanded during the early twentieth century it too had a need to accommodate its labor force's housing needs. Since there was little in the way of private affordable housing for laborers in Springdale, Heidenkamp constructed numerous dwellings for the employees to rent. The duplexes were constructed on either side of Standard Avenue and came to be known as "Yellow Row" due to the fact that they were all painted yellow. A row of brick houses was also constructed on Colfax Street.[13] Although John Kocur initially worked in the glass industry as a laborer after his arrival to the area around Springdale in the autumn of 1909, he never lived in "company houses." In order to put a roof over his head and food on his table, John Kocur relied again on connections with his fellow Slovaks.

The company housing provided to those laborers who either couldn't afford or couldn't find any other place to live was at best a short-term, convenient solution to an immediate problem and at worst a method by which some companies held their labor force captive. John Kocur was fortunate in the sense that he was able to establish a connection to the growing Slovak community in the Arnold area. Whether these connections were aided by Anton Hranec and Juraj Gazak or some other Slovak compatriot is difficult to say. Regardless of the source of the connection, John Kocur's solution to the question of what to do for housing was one of the most common practices for immigrants of the early twentieth century. Kocur became a boarder.

Boarding was not a new practice in 1909. In one way, shape, or form it has been present in the United States since the country's earliest days. An individual or family rents boarding rooms to those needing a place to live, providing beds, regular meals, and other services like washing and cleaning. In return the boarder pays his housekeeper an agreed-upon fee each week or month. In this arrangement, a young family could make extra money, helping to improve their economic situation and standard of living. Approximately 36% of all Slovak households in America operated boarding houses in 1911 and 29% continued to do so in 1920.[14] Through money made by boarding, some families earned enough to return to their homeland, open their own business or move to a more desirable part of town.

Kocur, without family or relatives in the area, became the boarder of John and Elizabeth Tarrabey of Arnold and lived in their house on Fourth Avenue. A typical boarding house of the time usually contained about ten boarders. In the case of the Tarrabeys, they boarded a total of nine men including John Kocur. The boarder usually paid the housekeeper between eight and twelve dollars per month for the boarding room, which was likely shared with up to three other men. The monthly fee also included laundry, mending, and one cooked meal per day. Besides preparing the stipulated cooked meal each day, the housekeeper also provided bread and coffee for breakfast and prepared each man's lunch pail for work.[15] This meant that the housekeeper had to rise well before dawn each day to begin the preparations for breakfast, baking bread and brewing coffee, as well as preparing the lunch pails for up to ten men. Because the head of the household often worked in the same place as the boarders, the housekeeper had to tend to her husband's needs for food and clothing as well.

Joseph Krajsa, et.al. in the book *Slovaks in America: A Bicentennial Study*, describes how the lady of the house managed the needs of the boarder's food requirements.

"She did all the shopping and the general practice was to buy all foods and groceries except meat on one account. At the end of the month, the total food bill was divided by the number of men in the house and each one contributed an equal share of the expenses. The housekeeper was not expected to contribute any part of this expense. Meat was a separate item. It was bought to suit each man's individual preference, marked with a colored cord or in some other way to identify the portions when they were served so that each one enjoyed his particular cut at supper, and at the end of the week each man paid for his own meat bill." [16]

With meals made and boarders out of the house for work, unless they worked a later day shift, the housekeeper began the home chores and other duties associated with caring for boarders. Laundry was done on nearly an everyday basis given the condition of the clothing after a day's work and the limited number of changes that each man had. Without modern appliances in the early 1900s laundry was done outdoors, often in large kettles, and dried outdoors regardless of the season. When the men returned from work they often removed their dirty, sweat-soaked clothing and cleaned themselves in an outside building, the clothing left for the next day's wash. A typical laborer had three sets of clothes, two sets of work clothes and one set of everyday clothes. If the workers were lucky or had some disposable income to spend on clothing, they may also have owned a suit for occasions like church (if they attended), weddings (if they were invited), or funerals (if they had to attend).

Also typical in the boarding business was the selectivity with which boarders were chosen. In many instances, boarders were of similar ethnic backgrounds and often came from the same area or village in the old country. Boarders often worked in the same location, factory or mill, even in the same work crew. Before a boarder was taken on, something of his character must be known and references, preferably from an existing boarder in the house, would need to be secured. It was not uncommon for a boarder who may be perpetually late in paying or a known regular at the local tavern to quickly gain a reputation among the boarding houses in the area and have difficulty moving from one to another. In close-knit ethnic communities where friends and relatives speak often and gossiping is an art form, there were no secrets.

John and Elizabeth Tarrabey, originally spelled Taraba when John passed through Ellis Island, were typical of the type of Slovak family that enhanced their income and bettered their lives by taking in boarders like John Kocur. At the time of the 1910 Federal Census in April of that year, John Tarrabey was twenty-three years old, his wife Elizabeth was twenty-seven, and their daughter, Helen, was three. John and Elizabeth had been married for nine years, since each was 14 and 18, respectively. Helen had been born in 1907. The Tarrabeys, however, like many families at the turn of the century had also experienced the loss of children. In fact Helen was the only child still living of the five that were born to the Tarrabeys,[17] a stark reminder that even in the early twentieth century, infant mortality was significant for many immigrant families.

John Tarrabey arrived in the United States from the Slovak lands of Austria-Hungary in 1903. Elizabeth arrived in a few years later in 1906, likely after John had worked and saved enough for her passage. Both were considered "alien" because neither had formalized U.S. citizenship. Only their daughter Helen was a United States citizen, as she was born in the United States in 1907. Tarrabey worked as a miner in one of the local Western

Pennsylvania coal mines and Elizabeth busied herself with the tasks of caring for their young daughter and the nine men whom she boarded.

The common bond for John and Elizabeth Tarrabey and their nine boarders was that they were all Slovaks, born in Austria-Hungary, immigrants to the United States and settlers in Arnold, Pennsylvania. John Tarrabey had an additional link to one of his boarders, Martin Rebel. Rebel, originally spelled Wrabel when he passed through Ellis Island, was John Tarrabey's brother-in-law. The practice of utilizing connections to those who were fellow countrymen or relatives often aided new immigrants like John Kocur in the important tasks of finding work and housing. Living in the Tarrabey house with Kocur was a mix of men as old as fifty-five and as young as eighteen. Three were married with wives back in the old country, five were single and one was widowed. Eight of these men, including John Kocur, worked in the local glass factory as laborers; the remaining man was a coal miner. It's likely that it was this common connection, the glass factory, that enabled the young immigrant Kocur to find housing among those with whom he worked. Kocur and five other boarders spoke both English and Slovak, the rest spoke only Slovak. It's also likely that within the walls of the Tarrabey house and in the area of Arnold where these men lived, shopped, drank, and socialized only Slovak was spoken. In addition to John Kocur, the men who regularly paid the Tarrabeys for the luxury of a roof over their heads, meals, and laundry were named Martin Rebel, John Linhart, Joe Gohesk, Frank Curmara, Mike Smoker, Edgar Hourt, and two other immigrant laborers simply listed as John.[18]

It's possible that as the standard of living among immigrant Slovaks like the Tarrabeys improved, their need to take on boarders was no longer necessary. In general the improvement of one's economic situation lead to a more stable family life for many Slovak immigrants and less of a need for and reliance on the practice of boarding. For much of the early time spent in the United States by John Kocur, however, the need for people like John and Elizabeth Tarrabey was absolutely critical. Slovaks in Western Pennsylvania relied heavily on one another to provide economic and social support. Already facing barriers of language and social discrimination, Slovak immigrants welcomed the sense of security and comfort brought on by having neighbors, friends, and business owners who looked like them, spoke like them and had the same beliefs and cultural background that they had. John Kocur's assimilation to America was enabled by the Arnold Slovak community into which he entered, fellow Slovaks who helped him find work, and Slovak families like the Tarrabeys. The help Kocur received from fellow Slovaks would not be forgotten. The notion of Slovaks helping Slovaks, learned through real-life experiences, would stay with Kocur for the rest of his life and become a centerpiece of his beliefs and work.

## Endnotes

1. *Pittsburgh Post, September 7, 1909*

2. *Passenger Manifest – S.S. Kaiser Wilhelm; May 18, 1909*

3. *Arnold: Proud City of Proud People 1896-1996, Arnold Centennial Committee, pg 6*

4. *Springdale: A Walk Down Memory Lane 1906-1981, pgs 12-13*

5. *Stolarik, M. Mark: Immigration and Urbanization – The Slovak Experience 1870-1918, pg 110. 1989*

6. *Krajsa, Joseph, et. al.: Slovaks in America: A Bicentennial Study, pg 17. 1971*

7. *Ibid.*

8. *Ibid.*

9. *Jankola, Matus: News Items from the Catholic Slovak Parish in Pittston, Pa. pgs 301-306. 1900*

10. *Hrusovsky, Francis: American Democracy and Slovak Life: Sixty Years of the Slovak League of America, pg 10. 1967*

11. *Krajsa, Joseph, et. al.: Slovaks in America: A Bicentennial Study, pg 18. 1971*

12. *Culen, Constantine: History of the Slovaks in America, Vol I, pg 62. 1942*

13. *Springdale: A Walk Down Memory Lane 1906-1981, pgs 13*

14. *Stolarik, M. Mark: Immigration and Urbanization – The Slovak Experience, 1870-1918, pg 114. 1989*

15. *Krajsa, Joseph, et. al.: Slovaks in America: A Bicentennial Study, pg 19. 1971*

16. *Ibid.*

17. *1910 Federal Census, E.D #104, Sheet 4, Line # 26.*

18. *1910 Federal Census, E.D #104, Sheet 4, Lines 29-37.*

## Chapter 6

# “SLOVAK SOM” (I AM SLOVAK)

# Chapter 6

The journey of John Kocur from the village of Turzovka in northwest Slovakia to America was, in reality, a series of journeys. Some were steps in the physical journey, like the trip from Turzovka to Bremen, Germany to New York to Western Pennsylvania. The larger and more significant part of Kocur's journey, however, was not physical, not aboard a boat or train and not to a specific location on a map; it was a mental and emotional journey that lasted for the next forty years. Simply arriving in New York aboard the *Bremen* was not the end of John Kocur's journey, nor was his arrival in Arnold, Pennsylvania. Kocur's journey as a young Slovak-American continued throughout his life in America. The destinations in this lifelong journey included finding employment, housing, friends and acquaintances, becoming a citizen, defending America's principles, championing the causes of others, and ultimately becoming a contributing member of society in the United States. In essence Kocur embarked on two journeys once he made the decision to leave his home in Turzovka; one that brought him to Western Pennsylvania and another that brought him full and equal standing in his new country and the fulfillment of his life's work.

John Kocur's early existence in Arnold settled into a fairly predictable routine. The cycle was simple for at least six days per week: work, eat, and sleep. Ten hour days at the glass factory left little time for much else. Kocur likely became a part of the local Slovak social network through any one of the many places where the Slovak people of Arnold gathered - one of the taverns located near the glass works, with his fellow boarders at the Tarrabey home, at the Slovak church, or through Slovak fraternal organizations. Finding themselves in the United States, Slovak immigrants were drawn together by several key factors. The early Slovak immigrants had very little understanding of or proficiency in the English language. As such, these immigrants needed to find fellow Slovaks with whom they could communicate. The need to be with those who understood one's customs, traditions, and language and had shared experiences drew Slovaks together in to tightly knit communities. Slovaks are known to be a sentimental people and so while America represented endless opportunity which would never have been available in the old country it also caused nostalgic longing for their homeland, friends, and family. Continuing their "village" lifestyle in small communities in the United States helped to compensate for the homesickness. No matter their village of origin in the old country, there was one additional factor that drew Slovaks together. They all came to the United States with the same goal: a better life.

Drawn together by the need to be with fellow Slovaks, mutual understanding, and common goals, Slovak immigrants often came together and organized societies, parishes, and social clubs. These organizations enabled them to protect their mutual interests and promote worthwhile social activities.[1] It also gave them a sense of community and cohesion, a sense of identity; something they never had and were never permitted to work toward in their native lands. The congregation of Slovaks in communities across areas of America like Western Pennsylvania gave them the sense of their own national origin. In the United States, John Kocur and the Slovaks in his work crew or in his boarding house were not merely individuals but were men who belonged to a distinct ethnic group and had a distinct national origin. Here, in the United States, these men could proudly proclaim, "Slovak Som:" roughly translated to mean, "I am Slovak". Ironically, "Slovak Som" was not something that Slovaks could claim in any sort of official or meaningful way within the borders of their own home country. It was only once these proud Slovaks were in the United States, far from their homeland, that the claim "Slovak Som" actually carried an inherent meaning. In the United States, "Slovak Som" was not a claim needing the official recognition of the government, it was never out of place, never needed to be uttered in secret, or required to be legislated. In America anyone, Slovaks, Italians, Irish, or Chinese, could freely organize amongst themselves, speak their native language, practice native customs, and act in the best interests of their national origins without restriction. In direct contrast for Slovaks, however, was the fact that in their own native country nothing of the sort could be done. In the lands of Slovakia, though the Slovaks were what they were and nothing else, the words "Slovak Som" had no recognizable meaning. Slovaks were not Slovaks; they were subjects of Magyar overlords and, as such, feudal peasants who were officially listed as "Hungarian inhabitants." Their real national origin was to be denied and ultimately erased according to the designs of their Magyar masters.[2]

Slovaks like John Kocur who came to the United States in search of a better life worked diligently to achieve their goals. Along the way they also came to realize that in addition to economic opportunity, America gave them a sense of themselves that they could not find anywhere else, even in their own homeland. Even as a full-fledged citizen of the United States, John Kocur never lost his identity as a Slovak. America, in fact, taught Kocur how to summon his ethnic identity and harness its power. John Kocur learned that critical lesson early in his new country and would actively put that concept into practice for his fellow Slovaks both in the United States and abroad for the rest of his journey.

By early 1913 John Kocur had been in the United States for nearly four years and in that time had gained a foothold as a member of America's workforce and within the Arnold and Springdale communities. Through a focused and tireless work ethic, a trait which would continue to be a part of his personality throughout his life, Kocur saved and prepared for his future life in America. A large part of that future included the woman who, later in 1913, he would wed.

The village of Podvysoka, Slovakia is located only a few kilometers to the north and east of Turzovka, John Kocur's home village. Both villages lie in the Kysuca River valley, surrounded by the mountain ranges of Beskydy and Javornicky. In the late 1800s Turzovka was a larger village surrounded by small clusters of homes and farms, which served to make up a number of smaller villages, Podvysoka being one. Inhabitants in both villages worked very hard to wring out a meager existence in the near feudal peasant economy of the then Austria-Hungary. It was in the village of Podvysoka on June 10, 1893 that John Kocur's future wife, Margeta Zbojkova, was born.

While John Kocur had the opportunity to receive an education while growing up as a boy in Turzovka, Margeta Zbojkova had no such chance. The young Kocur benefited from the position of his father, Jozef, who was a teacher in the government-run schools. John Kocur learned to read and write not only Slovak and Hungarian, the state language, but also English. As a young boy, Kocur was one of a decreasing number of Slovaks at that time to receive any semblance of a higher-level education. The policies of the Magyar rulers, bent on creating a homogenous, Hungarian-focused society, limited the number of educational opportunities available to Slovaks. By 1905, the policy of forced Magyarization had purposefully reduced the number of elementary schools providing any Slovak language instruction and with it the opportunity for Slovaks to pursue formal education in anything other than the Hungarian language. Margeta Zbojkova was doubly affected by the time into which she was born. First, as a woman she was born into a society of limited educational opportunity for all Slovaks, but especially for women. Second, as soon as she was old enough, her focus turned not to education but to the more critical need of contributing to the economic survival of her family. Margeta's was a situation, however, not unlike many of her fellow villagers. Margeta Zbojkova was likely provided a basic elementary education by the government schools with any additional learning attained through the aid of her parents, Jozef and Anna, and through her life experience.

While it is not known how these two came to know each other and eventually commit their lives to one another, it is likely that the connection was facilitated through the marriage of Kocur's older brother Matej to Margeta's older sister Dorota. With the families already connected by the marriage of the couple's older siblings, John Kocur and Margeta Zbojkova were married in Turzovka on June 10, 1913, Margeta's twentieth birthday. By the time of the wedding ceremony in 1913 John Kocur's parents,

Jozef and Dorota, were deceased. Margeta's parents, Jozef and Anna, however, were present at the ceremony. In addition to the small wedding party, the service also included two witnesses, Mikalus Jurikovsky of Podvysoka and Jakub Virobina of Olesna (a village located north of Podvysoka on the opposite bank of the Kysuca River).

John Kocur was twenty-six years old when he married Margeta and had returned home to Slovakia to do so after four years of working, planning, and saving in America. Kocur came back to his homeland to marry with a new perspective on what it meant to be a free man in a free country. The ideals of liberty and self-determination are universal and motivating whether one is in the city streets of Arnold, Pennsylvania or the dirt roads of a Slovak village.

A considerable number of Slovak immigrants who went to America in search of work and higher earning power returned to their native land.[3] They returned with the money they had accumulated in America in order to upgrade their lives. The American way of life had been ingrained in these men and women and this, combined with the economic boost America had given them, enabled the returning immigrants to in turn stimulate Slovak economic progress. Hard-earned American capital in the hands of Slovak immigrants who returned to their homeland proved to be an essential factor in rebuilding their lives in their homeland. These returning immigrants were able to acquire land with their savings and this alone strengthened their power through ownership.[4] Even into the early twentieth century, land ownership in Slovakia was equated with power. With land and title the Slovak man could apply the same strong work ethic he brought to an American mine or factory to the land that *he* owned, the products of his labors serving *his* interests, and the economic success of his family under *his* control. In addition to acquiring land, the returning immigrants also possessed the financial resources and newly acquired experience necessary to start new enterprises in their native land. Stiff competition for the new enterprises greeted their founders but this did not deter the Slovaks who had returned from America, for they had learned through experience that competition was not to be feared but rather it was what stimulated progress and was an added incentive to success. Against their non-Slovak competitors, therefore, the new business men succeeded in breaking up what was considered somewhat of a monopoly by the old owners and directors in various businesses. Their experience in America served them well as they met every challenge with confidence and generally with success.[5]

John Kocur was not among the Slovaks who made their time in America temporary. Kocur returned to the United States after his marriage to continue the new life he had started four years previous. John Kocur's new wife, Margeta, however, would not accompany her new husband back to America following their wedding. John returned to the U.S. to continue working and living in Arnold, Pennsylvania, establishing himself as a part of American society, while Margeta would stay in Podvysoka.

The ties that bind Slovak families are very strong, perhaps stronger than most. Many Slovak immigrants to the United States left behind wives, children, parents, and siblings. As soon as the immigrant saved enough to bring the family members to America to join him, he did so. The years of separation, however, were often very difficult. This difficulty was compounded by slow and, in the case of their Slovak homeland, inefficient means of communication. Letters crossing the Atlantic to America often brought news of events that had long since happened. The death of a parent or marriage of a sister would reach the Slovak immigrant in Homestead or Wilkes-Barre weeks after it actually happened, leaving him to wonder and imagine the events beyond the words on the page of the letter. The ability to return to one's homeland after a few years with newfound economic power or enable a reunion with a wife and children in a new homeland, America, made the immigrant's work and sacrifice worthwhile. There would be, however, no such quick reunion for John and Margeta.

Margeta Zbojkova Kocur's ties to her family were equally strong. While John returned to Pennsylvania after their marriage in 1913 Margeta remained in her village. The young bride's motives were simple; she would remain in Podvysoka to help support her family financially and care for her mother, Anna, for as long as support and care was required. Anna Zbojkova suffered from a heart condition which required help and support; her daughter Margeta would stay in Podvysoka with her for as long as she was needed. The actions of the twenty-year-old newly married Margeta Kocur at the outset of her marriage were typical of the type of person she was throughout the remaining eighty-three years of her life. Family and religious devotion were at the center of all Margeta did. In order to help support her family and make ends meet in the difficult rural setting of Podvysoka, Austria-Hungary, Margeta held jobs typical of many young Slovak women. She helped tend and care for the small area of land the Zbojek family lived on and served as a housekeeper for a Jewish family who lived near the village. The work performed by the young Margeta Kocur in her housekeeping job was a means not only to earn much needed money, but also an opportunity to provide food for her family and for herself. Margeta found her time in the services of this family to be some of the most rewarding of her life as the family treated her very well, kept her well fed, enabled her to care for her mother, and provided a source of savings for her eventual new life in America. Margeta's income and the money supplied by John as he worked in America proved invaluable for the subsistence of the Zbojek family.

It is doubtful that either John or Margeta expected to be separated for an extended period of time when they were married in 1913. Margeta's mother's health was, at the time, the determining factor for the length of their separation; or so they thought. Not far on the horizon, however, the clouds of a powerful storm were gathering, clouds that would build and swirl and gather strength until they darkened the skies all across the European continent. The storm would strike close to home in Podvysoka and Turzovka and as far away as England, France and Russia. Not more than a year after John and Margeta were married, the storm's first bolt hit in the provincial town of Sarajevo, Yugoslavia and didn't let up for five years. World War I would wreak havoc on Europe until the close of the decade, cost hundreds of thousands of Europeans their homes or their lives, and keep John and Margeta apart for the next ten years.

## Endnotes

1. *Hrusovsky, Francis: American Democracy and Slovak Life: Sixty Years of the Slovak League of America, pg 13. 1967*
2. *Ibid.*
3. *Ibid, pg 17.*
4. *Ibid, pg 18.*
5. *Ibid, pg 20.*

## Chapter 7

# CITIZEN KOCUR

# Chapter 7

When John Kocur returned to America following his marriage in the summer of 1913, the United States was continuing to move ahead in all aspects of life; and the opportunities to move ahead with it seemed endless. The principles that made America great had already taken root in John Kocur. In stark contrast to the conditions in Kocur's Slovak homeland, an individual in America had the opportunities, the avenues, and the means to make a better life for himself. Self-determination and opportunity went hand in hand in determining one's success in America. Through hard work in the glass factory, John Kocur was making more money in America than could ever be imagined by his fellow countrymen in Turzovka. Kocur also realized that the key to improving one's life in America was tied closely to economic opportunity. John Kocur was about to take a small step forward in realizing the American dream, a step upward. It involved stepping out of the hot, noisy, and sometimes dangerous glass factory and stepping into private business with his friend and fellow countryman Juraj Gazak. For John Kocur, it was a step behind a barber's chair.

John Kocur may have learned the skills necessary to be a barber long before coming to America or he may have picked them up through the local barber shop or though a friend. It's unclear why or when Kocur traded the long leather apron of the glass works for a barber's smock, but by 1915 his new occupation afforded him the luxury of working indoors, surrounded mostly by fellow Slovaks, and making a reasonable living.

Being a good barber, much like a good bartender, has as much to do with being a good conversationalist as it does with being an expert with a pair of scissors or an expert pouring a drink. Kocur was an intelligent man, able to speak, read, and write English even as he arrived in America as a younger man. He was well versed on subjects of the day, especially those that affected or influenced events in his homeland. In the ethnic populations of Arnold, New Kensington, and Springdale, Kocur likely found a regular cliental of Slovaks who discussed, debated, and disputed events in America and in Austria-Hungary day after day. The clientele of a barbershop is also varied, often representing a cross section of young, old, native, immigrant, well-read, or uneducated. John Kocur's exposure to men from all backgrounds and educational levels likely opened his eyes and helped form his views on many subjects. It also made him a number of friends and contacts throughout the area as he provided shaves and haircuts to his customers.

As Kocur worked in the barbershop through the mid-teens in America's new century he continually prepared himself for his future, economically and socially. By establishing contacts throughout the Slovak community and working and saving with focused determination, John Kocur was preparing to take advantage of the unbounded opportunity that America offered those willing to put forth the effort. Part of this self- determined effort took the form of more education, an avenue by which Kocur continued to learn skills that enabled him to take advantage of opportunities open to all Americans. Unlike many of his fellow Slovak immigrants, John Kocur was not satisfied with only the slight improvement in working and living conditions the local mills and factories offered versus those in his homeland. Kocur advanced his knowledge and skill set by taking classes at the Pittsburgh Academy, studying bookkeeping and typing.[1] Slovaks in the early 1900s formed the backbone of America's, and especially Western Pennsylvania's, unskilled labor force. While the conditions were at times deplorable, the work hard, and the hours long, it was night and day compared to living in the Slovak lands under Magyar rule. Many Slovaks were satisfied to work in the mills and factories, make a little extra money on the side by boarding their newly arrived countrymen, and provide a better life for their families. The early Slovak immigrants laid the ground work for their children and subsequent generations through their hard work and self-sacrifice.

Having moved out of the glass works by 1915 and behind the barber's chair, John Kocur had taken that important first step upward in terms of his social and economic life in America. With the importance of education to his family and in his own life, Kocur's studies provided him an additional boost. Economic self-reliance and the benefits of additional education were keys to success for anyone in realizing the American dream. There was a third part to the equation of the American dream, however, that John Kocur and nearly every other immigrant who came to the United States needed in order to truly belong. It was a piece of the American dream that no native-born American ever needed to be personally concerned about and it was another step in the journey on which John Kocur found himself. John Kocur wanted and needed to become a citizen of the United States of America.

The early part of the twentieth century brought hundreds of thousands of immigrants to America's shores, many from central, eastern, and southern Europe. This wave of immigration came on the heels of the previous fifty years that brought immigrants to the United States from many parts of western Europe. In the early 1900s, the mood of native-born Americans as well as many of those who had already made it to the United States was much like those having gained entrance to an exclusive party. Once safely inside, enjoying the benefits, one is reluctant to let anyone else in. Some in the United States, much like those party goers, were beginning to grow tired of more and more guests seeking entrance.

The subject of immigration, however, needed to be addressed carefully. At the time John Kocur arrived, industries like steel, iron, and glass were booming. The product of the nation's coal mines, required to feed the industrial giants, had to be procured and delivered. The nation's railroads, necessary for rapid and efficient commerce and travel, had to be manned. All of these required the one thing America had little to spare; cheap labor. Immigrants from Slovakia, Russia, Hungary, and Poland stepped in to fill that void. Shutting off immigration all together was not something the industrial powers-that-be, or the U.S. government for that matter, wanted. Advocating a totally open border policy, however, was not a position that went over well with many of the American electorate either.

The other side of the immigration issue had to do with the process by which those who were already here or who would arrive would be naturalized. The complex question of what exactly was an "American" and how one could achieve that status was also a subject hotly debated from the halls of American government to churches, corner saloons, and even in barbershops. A balance had to be struck. Congress, not wanting to throw out the baby with the bathwater, eventually took the approach that immigration to the United States was appropriate and would be continued. It would only be continued, however, under a system of quotas allocated by native country of origin. With allotments based on country, not ethnic group, Czechoslovakia's puny allocation was shared by Slovaks, Czechs, Carpatho-Russyns, and a few other nationalities.[2] This served to reduce the number of immigrants entering the United States without completely shutting off the faucet.

The process by which foreign-born residents of the United States would become full citizens would go hand in hand with changes in the immigration law and become more structured and rigorous. The legislative approach to immigration and naturalization that the U.S. government set forth attempted to strike the balance between the needs of the country and the attitude of many of its citizens. While this approach did strike that balance, the debate among the American people with regard to immigration and naturalization would go on for decades and never really be over.

To John Kocur, becoming an American citizen was a necessity. It would be, however, a long and drawn out process lasting nearly five years. Kocur would have to follow steps toward naturalization that had been set into law only three short years before his arrival in the United States, a result of the Naturalization Act of 1906. The Act of June 29, 1906, creating a Bureau of Immigration and Naturalization, had as its purpose, "to provide for a uniform rule for the naturalization of aliens throughout the United States." The resulting agency had authority for rule making.[3] Within the Division of Naturalization's rule of August

25, 1906, a system to give "dignity, uniformity, and regularity" to the naturalization procedure began effective September 27. Its method was through the management, design, and control of forms.[4] As with any government-created entity, the bureaucracy created by the Naturalization Act perpetuated itself through changes in the naturalization law, process, procedures, and forms. The forms required for naturalization were supplied exclusively by the Bureau of Immigration and Naturalization, Department of Commerce and Labor. Only by using those forms could an immigrant living in the U.S. become a naturalized citizen. By regulating the distribution of those forms and records, the agency could control the number of courts able to naturalize.[5]

As a result of the Naturalization Act of 1906, immigrants in the United States wishing to become naturalized citizens had to follow a pre-defined, specific process. This process required a series of records to be created applicable to anyone who filed a declaration of intention or petition for citizenship, regardless of age or time of arrival in the Untied States, unless the individual met some exception.[6] The entire process was managed through state courts and the paperwork was standard for everyone. The management of the naturalization process through the court system helped to streamline and standardize the necessary steps for an immigrant to become a United States citizen. In the end, however, the act and the bureaucracy it perpetuated provided the necessary mechanism for the U.S. government to carefully control the number of courts able to naturalize and ultimately the number of immigrants who could become naturalized.

John Kocur's path to naturalization began with the paperwork that documented his arrival and processing through Ellis Island. The form capturing this information was called "The Certificate of Arrival." The Certificate of Arrival showed the date, place, and manner of the alien's arrival into the United States and was required of all aliens who arrived after June 29, 1906.[7] John Kocur's Certificate of Arrival (no. 2774 d) documented some very basic information. It simply read: "This is to certify that the following named alien arrived at the port indicated on the date and manner described below."

The form went on to spell out:

*Name of alien: Kocur, Jan*

*Port of entry: New York, NY*

*Date of arrival: Sept. 7, 1909*

*Name of vessel: Bremen*

Once the Certificate of Arrival had been secured, John Kocur went on to file his "Declaration of Intention." Under the Naturalization Act of 1906, the Declaration of Intention was made before the clerk of court by the alien, who had to be at least eighteen years old.[8] Three copies of the Declaration of Intention were made and were then filed in the court's permanent record, the Bureau of Naturalization, and the final copy remained with the applicant. The applying alien's copy remained with him until he petitioned for citizenship, at which time the form was surrendered, attached to, and made part of the Naturalization Petition.[9] In most cases, the applying alien had seven years to make a formal petition for naturalization. After that time, the Declaration of Intention expired and had to be made again in order to keep the naturalization process moving. The majority of immigrants applying for naturalization, John Kocur included, moved quickly to petition the court for naturalization rather than let the Declaration of Intention expire and risk losing ground in their bid for citizenship.

John Kocur's Declaration of Intention (No. 30317) was made before and filed in the District Court of the United States, Western Pennsylvania District on July 21, 1915. The Declaration was received and signed by J. Wood Clark, the Clerk of the District Court of the United States, Western Pennsylvania District and filed that day. In the declaration, John Kocur was asked a series of questions designed to document aspects of his background, his current residence, and his intention to disavow all foreign allegiances.

On his Declaration of Intention, John Kocur, at age 28, was described as white with a fair complexion, blonde hair, and gray eyes. Kocur stood five feet six inches tall and weighed one hundred twenty-two pounds. John Kocur also indicated that he was born on May 22, 1887 in Turzovka, Hungary; that his current place of residence was Box 25, Arnold, Pennsylvania, and that he immigrated to the United States on the vessel *Bremen*, arriving in New York in September of 1909. Kocur further went on to pledge that, "It is my bona fide intention to renounce forever all allegiance and fidelity to any foreign prince, potentate, state, or sovereignty, and particularly to Francis Joseph, Emperor of Austria and Apostolic King of Hungary, of whom I am now a subject." It is interesting to note that the name and title of Francis Joseph is stamped rather than written on John Kocur's Declaration of Intention. Given the great number of Slovaks who went through the immigration process in Western Pennsylvania, this would not be unexpected. It probably made sense from an efficiency point of view to keep on hand stamps of the common foreign rulers of ethnic groups located in the area served by the District Court. In Western Pennsylvania, the stamp for Francis Joseph most likely had to be replaced several times over given the number of Slovaks becoming naturalized. Lastly, before John Kocur's Declaration of Intention could become official, he had to sign a pledge that he was not "an anarchist, a polygamist nor a believer in the practice of polygamy; and it is my intention in good faith to become a citizen of the United States of America and to permanently reside therein SO HELP ME GOD." (The capitalization of these words reflects the form in the actual document.) John Kocur took that oath and signed his Declaration of Intention, "Subscribed and sworn to"... in Pittsburgh on July 21, 1915. Kocur's next step on the path to naturalization would have to wait, by law, at least two years.

Before taking up the next requirement in the process of naturalization, the Petition for Naturalization, aliens like John Kocur had to meet certain criteria. Among these were that the alien's Declaration of Intention had to be at least two years but not more than seven years old. He or she must have had five years of continuous residence in the United States and must have filed a preliminary petition with the Immigration and Naturalization Service, which performed a preliminary examination.[10] The Immigration Service sought to discover certain facts about the person applying, including marriage history, how many children, and the residence of any spouse and or children. In addition to this information, witnesses were also called upon in court to testify as to the validity of the information provided and the standing and character of the applicant. Upon completion of all these steps, there was a final hearing in open court at least ninety days after filing the petition. As the last step, the petitioner took the oath of allegiance and renunciation of the former head of state.[11]

At the time of John Kocur's Petition for Naturalization, he listed his address as 1614 Fifth Avenue, Arnold, Pennsylvania and his occupation as barber. Much of the same information from the Declaration of Intention appears in the petition, especially the date of birth, place of birth, arrival date in the United States, and vessel of arrival. The additional information that begins to appear on the petition has to do with marital status. John Kocur indicates that he is married to Margaret Kocur who was born in 1893 (Kocur was either unsure or didn't know his wife's birthday so it is listed as XX), in the town of Padvisoka, Austria-Hungary; (the town name is correctly spelled Podvysoka and is likely the result of the clerk's attempt at spelling). The petition also includes the statement renouncing allegiance to Charles, Emperor of Austria and Apostolic King of Hungary, (Francis Joseph had since been replaced by Charles as emperor and the petition reflected this fact). In addition to the renouncement of allegiance, the petition also once again asked for John Kocur's affirmation of his belief in organized government, the principles of the Constitution of the United States, and his intention to become a citizen of the United States.

John Kocur's Petition for Naturalization included references to the past documents submitted in the naturalization process, the Certificate of Arrival and the Declaration of Intention. Additionally, the Petition for Naturalization also included a requirement for witnesses. The witnesses were sworn under oath and attested on behalf of the petitioner. In Kocur's case, two men accompanied him to petition the court and act as his witnesses. These men were Joseph Booth, a laborer from Arnold, Pennsylvania and John Timko, a bartender from New Kensington. Both men swore to the following:

> *That he has personally known John Kocur, the petitioner above mentioned, to have resided in the United States continuously immediately preceding the date of filing of this petition, since the 13$^{th}$ day of September 1910 and in the State*

*in which the petition is made, and that he has personal knowledge that the said petitioner is a person of good moral character, attached to the principles of the Constitution of the United States, and the petitioner is in every way qualified in his opinion to be admitted a citizen of the United States.*

Both men's signatures follow this statement.

The final portion of the Petition for Naturalization hearing involved the oath of allegiance of the petitioner and the order of the court admitting the petitioner. On December 13, 1917 John Kocur raised his right hand and swore an oath of allegiance to the United States. It read, "I hereby declare, on oath, that I absolutely and entirely renounce all allegiance and fidelity to any foreign prince, potentate, state, or sovereign, and particularly Charles, Emperor of Austria and Apostolic King of Hungary of whom I have heretofore been a subject; that I will support and defend the Constitution and laws of the United States of America against all enemies foreign and domestic; and that I will bear true faith and allegiance to the same."

Having satisfied all the requirements of the law, completed all the required forms, and waited the required time, the court issued Certificate of Naturalization number 901043 to John Kocur and ordered that he be permitted to become a citizen of the United States of America. Although laws and paperwork formalized the process on December 13, 1917, the process of becoming an American had begun much earlier for John Kocur. The longer he lived in the United States the more he came to realize what "American" truly meant. Kocur had already become actively engaged with the principles of America, liberty, independence, and self-determination; he had already taken advantage of the opportunities America offered, finding gainful employment, making and saving money to improve one's standing; and shortly, he would demonstrate his commitment to these principles through his participation in America's involvement in the Great War. John Kocur didn't really need a piece of paper to make him feel like an American. The principles by which he lived his life and the pride he took in being a Slovak living in America, to him, were all that mattered.

## Endnotes

1. *The History of Pittsburgh, Volume V – Biographies, pg 353. 1923*
2. *Alexander, June Granatir: Ethnic Pride, American Patriotism, pg 89. 2001*
3. *Newman, John J.; American Naturalization Records 1790-1990, pg 17. 1999*
4. *Ibid.*
5. *Ibid.*
6. *Ibid, pg 37.*
7. *Ibid.*
8. *Ibid, pg 40.*
9. *Ibid.*
10. *Ibid.*
11. *Ibid.*

**Chapter 8**

# EUROPEAN DOMINOS

# Chapter 8

On June 28, 1914 John Kocur had only recently celebrated his one-year wedding anniversary to Margeta Zbojkova. Kocur began his day like he had done hundreds of times before since arriving in the Western Pennsylvania town of Arnold in 1909; he rose early, ate breakfast, and prepared for work. As the sun rose higher on that early summer day and the townspeople of Arnold and New Kensington made their way through the streets to their jobs in the shops, mills, and mines, none could have imagined the dramatic events that had already occurred half of a world away. Events whose consequences would boggle the mind, stagger the senses, and take America and Americans into places and situations that, at the time, seemed unimaginable. Events that would stir the feelings of nationalism among many of America's new arrivals and thrust the Slovaks' struggle for freedom and independence to the forefront. Events that would challenge America's foreign policy assumptions and perception of itself as a player on the world stage. Events that would serve to inspire John Kocur and at the same time leave lasting effects.

On June 28, 1914 as the townspeople of Arnold, like John Kocur, went about their daily routine, a nineteen-year-old Serbian named Gavrilo Princip, standing in a crowd of people in the small Bosnian town of Sarajevo, pulled a pistol and fired two shots in to a slow-moving, open motor car, killing both passengers. Moments before, Archduke Franz Ferdinand of

Austria, heir to the Austro-Hungarian throne and the picture of a bygone age of European aristocracy in his military uniform and plumed hat, and his wife, Sophie, Duchess of Hohenberg, had climbed into the open car to the cheers of the crowd around them. Minutes later both were dead and the powder keg that was Europe in 1914 exploded.

Not since the days of Lexington and Concord had gun shots created such an impact on the world. In the days and weeks that followed the assassination of Archduke Ferdinand the line of European alliances and treaties began to fall like rows of dominos. The European powers of the day, allied by everything from the blood lines of their rulers to their own economic self interest, became entwined in the first truly global conflict. In an opportunistic response to the assassination of their heir, Austria-Hungary served Serbia an ultimatum threatening war, convinced that the Serbian government was behind Princip's actions. Not satisfied with Serbia's response, Austria-Hungary formally declared war on Serbia in July 1914. Russia, a long-time ally of Serbia, then mobilized her armies in order to defend the Serbs. This action by the Russians caused the next domino in line, Germany, allied to Austria-Hungary, to declare war on Russia. France, at the time bound by treaty to Russia, found itself as a consequence at war against Germany and Austria-Hungary. The last remaining European power, Great Britain, fell into line as a result of treaties with France and Belgium and with it brought her worldwide colonies to the conflict against Germany and Austria-Hungary. In addition to the major European powers, many other smaller countries also became entangled in the conflict, having aligned themselves at a previous point in time with one side or the other by choice or by force.

By August of 1914, less than two months after the assassination, German forces pushed into Belgium and later into Northern France. The French army mobilized quickly and set into motion military defense plans that had been in place for years; such was the state of trust between the European neighbors at the turn of the century. Germany's plans for a quick strike at France and drive to Paris quickly slowed and the lines stabilized. The conflict then morphed into a new horrible mode of war, trench warfare, which would persist until nearly three years later when American soldiers, fighting on the European continent for the first time, tipped the scales in favor of the allies. In the summer of 1914, however, the war raging in France and America's entry into "Europe's problem" seemed distant, as distant as Sarajevo was from Arnold.

Although the battlefields of Europe were far from America's shores, the conflict began to take on greater meaning in America as time wore on. As war engulfed Europe, many of America's immigrants turned their attention to events in their homelands. This interest among the immigrant population stirred fears among America's "native-born" and within some elements of the U.S. Government that the country's foreign inhabitants had not only a sentimental attachment but perhaps a loyalty to their native lands. The concern immigrants displayed about happenings in Europe bothered many Americans.[1] The early twentieth century saw perhaps the greatest influx of eastern European immigrants to America's shores. These immigrants were distinctly different in so many ways from the western and northern European immigrants of the last half of the nineteenth century that many "native-born" Americans reacted negatively toward their presence. The growing intolerance of the foreign born, while not an official position of the U.S. government, was present in a segment of public opinion. The idea of distrust of foreigners was smoldering among many Americans in 1914-1915. The events in Europe only served to fuel that fire.

Many prominent political leaders of the time, reflecting public sentiment, spoke out against the idea of a "hyphenated American." Among these leaders were Theodore Roosevelt and Woodrow Wilson. Wilson even went so far as to define what he believed to be a "genuine American," calling him a person who, "when he votes or when he acts or when he fights his head and his thought are nowhere but in the center of the emotions and the purposes, and the policies of the United States."[2]

After war broke out in Europe, many of America's new immigrants began to take an increased interest in the events of their homelands. This included Slovaks like John Kocur whose native land, then under control of Austria-Hungary, now seemed to have the potential to be pushed, by virtue of a military defeat, into self- rule. This was one fact on which the Slovaks, as well as the other multi-national minorities of Austria-Hungary, could agree. The attention that America's immigrants paid to events in their homeland concerned many private citizens as well as the U.S. government. Both entities were concerned that certain immigrants' attachment to their native land went beyond the sentimental; even calling into question the loyalty of the immigrant population. The confluence of events in Europe and the existing attitudes in America only served to heighten the awareness of the conflict and bring the subject more and more to the forefront in the discussion of America's foreign policy. During the interim of declared neutrality, being disloyal was not limited to overt or even covert acts of treason. From the standpoint of those insisting on national unity, disloyal could merely entail trying to influence American foreign policy or taking positions that diverged from the official line.[3]

If the definition of disloyal could be extended to merely taking a position divergent from the official line, then many ethnic immigrants in the United States, Slovaks included, were disloyal. Kocur and his fellow Slovaks saw the European conflict as an opportunity to dissolve the old Austria-Hungary Empire and begin a new age of self rule and self determination; and they were not alone. As the war dragged on, many of the ethnic minorities still in Europe sought the support of their American immigrant brethren to bolster their claims of being legitimate governmental bodies. Many even sent representatives to America to seek the recognition of American ethnic immigrant groups. Dawning the mantle of spokespersons, immigrants in America claimed to represent their European compatriots stifled by the war.[4]

They say that politics makes strange bedfellows. This was never more true than in the resulting cooperation among American ethnic groups in their efforts to hasten the breakup of Austria-Hungary. The dream of separating Slovakia from Hungary caused Slovak religious groups to project a unified front. Equally important, Czechs and Slovaks, two separate Slavic peoples with separate histories and cultures, joined forces to work on behalf of their respective homelands.[5] The opportunity for freedom and self determination, after years of subjugation, was a very strong draw.

As the war dragged on and the youth of France, England, and Germany continued to be cut down in alarming numbers, President Wilson steadfastly adhered to America's declared neutrality. Most Americans of the day believed this was the correct course and supported their president. At the start of World War I a significant portion of the American population could still vividly remember the horrors of the Civil War, fought only a generation ago, with its epic battles and long casualty lists. Most Americans wanted no part of a conflict that was slaughter on a scale equal or greater to what was still for many a fresh memory.

As time progressed, however, Wilson faced increasingly intense diplomatic pressure from France and England. It was also becoming ever more apparent that despite several years of intense war and nearly a generation of English, French, and German youth, neither side had a decided edge toward victory. Ever the diplomat, Wilson assumed the mantle of the leading voice in attempting to negotiate a settlement of the conflict. After the presidential election in 1916, Wilson's position of "peace without victory" became the central theme of his approach to the European war. President Wilson's idealistic rhetoric also contained a theme that caught the attention of many of America's immigrants; that being the principle of self-determination. A peace without victors, Wilson reasoned, would lead to a reorganization of Europe's nations based on the desires of its people. Wilson's idealistic rhetoric motivated America's other ethnic groups to organize efforts aimed at persuading the administration to expand self-determination to include Eastern Europe's other subject nations.[6] These groups included Slovaks in the U.S. who viewed the potential break up of Austria-Hungary as a result of "peace without victory" to be a golden opportunity to establish freedom and independence. Wilson's approach to ending the conflict in Europe, supported by the principle of self-determination, clashed with the anti hyphened-American sentiment directed toward immigrants over the previous two decades. The president's policies and position with regard to the European conflict actually produced an effect that ran counter to many of his previous statements. For ethnic groups like the Slovaks, Wilson's policies served to encourage even more work on behalf of their homelands. The resulting effect was a greater emphasis on the ethnic portion of the hyphenated American and not a move toward full "Americanization" of immigrants.

It became increasingly clear as time wore on that the United States could not maintain its neutrality in the hope that the rest of the world would come to its senses and end the conflict.

Militarily and diplomatically, Europe's powers had dug in their heels. The final act that drew America into the conflict actually took nearly two years to play out. With concern already heightened in the U.S. over Germany's policy of open submarine warfare in the Atlantic, the sinking of the RMS Lusitania in May 1915 and the subsequent loss of American lives started the United States down the path of entering the World War. Despite several diplomatic protests, Germany was unmoved in its stance towards open submarine warfare. This stance combined with the stalemate of events on the European battlefields led America to come to the aid of the allies.

On April 2, 1917, President Woodrow Wilson appeared before a joint session of Congress to ask for a declaration of war against Germany and her allies. Wilson accused the German government of, "a reckless lack of compassion or of principle" and even referenced "the rights and liberties of small nations." The president finished his address with the now famous line, serving to justify America's leap from neutrality to war, stating that, "The world must be made safe for democracy." On April 4, 1917 the U.S. Senate voted to adopt Wilson's declaration of war. Two days later, the House of Representatives also approved the bill and it was immediately signed by the president.

John Kocur, still living on Fifth Avenue in Arnold, Pennsylvania and working as a barber in the spring of 1917, had followed the events leading up to America's declaration of war as closely as any of his fellow Slovak-Americans. The prospect of America playing a role in tipping the scales against Germany and Austria-Hungary must have been an appealing idea to anyone who spent time living under Hungarian rule, as Kocur had. The mobilization of the American army would unfold over the coming months and rely heavily on a mix of the professional army (at the time woefully small), draftees and volunteers. Given the growing size of America's immigrant population, they too would contribute heavily to the war effort by being a large part of the latter two groups. Perhaps some felt a sense of duty to their new country while some simply needed a change from the mills and mines and saw military service as the way out. For Slovaks, Czechs, Serbs, and other Eastern Europeans, however, service in the American army meant an opportunity to rid their former countries of the yoke of oppression that many had experienced personally. These men, John Kocur included, had a stake in the game.

The declaration of war against Germany set into motion the call for men under arms and the organization of the National Army. According to the laws put in to place for registration with the Selective Service, men of military age were required to complete a registration card with their local draft boards and be on call for military service should their number come up. On June 5, 1917 three months after the declaration of war, John Kocur followed through on his duty as a male American citizen of military age and completed a draft registration card. He was thirty years of age at the time, on the older side of those required to register, having celebrated his birthday less than a month earlier on May 22. As he completed his registration card, Kocur listed his occupation as a barber and his address as 1614 5$^{th}$ Avenue, Arnold, Pennsylvania. At the time John Kocur completed his registration card he was a naturalized citizen, had been married for four years and indicated he had no prior military service. Kocur went on to answer the other few basic questions on the registration card such as birthplace (s.p. Turzofka) and if any father, mother, wife or children under twelve were solely dependent on him (no, no, yes, and no). Kocur then placed his signature on the bottom of the card. The registrar taking John Kocur's information, John J. Thomas, Sr. also provided some basic data for the card. The registrar listed John Kocur as having a medium build, slender appearance, gray eyes, light colored hair, and no obvious physical disabilities. John Thomas also signed the registration card and by virtue of his role as the registrar for the Arnold precinct, Westmoreland County, state of Pennsylvania, assigned John Kocur draft number 262. Kocur was now registered and available to be drafted for military service; all he would have to do now was to wait.

By the fall of 1917, the first half-million men came into American military service.[7] This first group of soldiers included both men who had voluntarily enlisted as well as those who were called as a result of the draft. In the spring of 1918, however, events in France led to a more rapid call-up of soldiers. The Germans had begun their great spring offensive and France urgently needed help. Over a period of several months, the numbers of new men brought into the service mounted and reached their highest point in July 1918.[8] Throughout that time, however, the local draft board had not pulled draft number 262, John Kocur. During the first half of 1918 and especially following the German spring offensive, the U.S. government pressed for more volunteers. The idea of America's involvement in the European conflict had been fully turned from neutrality to full engagement in a geopolitically and morally justifiable cause. The full flavor of patriotism and duty became a part of America's drive to fill the ranks of the National Army. The Wilson administration was also fully aware of the powerful combination that patriotism for America and the interest in events of one's homeland could have on mobilizing immigrants to respond to America's needs. President Wilson viewed the participation of America's ethnic immigrants, especially those from Eastern Europe, as a demonstration of their "Americanism." Wilson also conveniently knew that the immigrant's own nationalistic interests could be leveraged in order to help fill the ranks. The anti-immigrant rhetoric of only a few years earlier faded, drowned out by the call for more American troops.

There is no doubt that John Kocur was pulled by both of these forces, American patriotism and a vested interest in the defeat of Germany's main ally and his former ruler, Austria-Hungary. Kocur was, after all, a naturalized U.S. citizen at the time, but he was also a Slovak not that far removed from living in his homeland and with an intimate understanding of the oppressive effects of Hungarian rule. Since registering for the draft, Kocur had continued to follow the events in Europe for nearly one year. With the final push for ending the war at its height in early 1918 it appeared to be time for a decision; continue to wait for draft number 262 to be called and possibly not be called to help defeat Germany and Austria-Hungary, or volunteer. On May 27, 1918 John Kocur chose the latter; he traveled the short distance from Arnold to the neighboring town of New Kensington, entered the local recruiting office and volunteered for the United States Army. Kocur's personal motivations for doing so at the time can only be surmised by examining the circumstance he found himself in during the spring of 1918. On one hand John Kocur had already registered for the draft and fulfilled his obligation under the law. By luck of the draw, Kocur's draft number hadn't been called; this was no fault of his. The United States would fight in Europe and most likely help defeat Germany and Austria-Hungary with or without John Kocur as a draftee. On the other hand, Kocur's love for his Slovak homeland and his wife, Margeta, still residing there, as well as an opportunity to play a part in bringing an end to Hungarian domination over the Slovak people appeared to be a more powerful draw. It's likely that those forces are what drove John Kocur to enter the recruiting office in New Kensington in late May, 1918 and voluntarily enlist in the U.S. Army.

As John Kocur prepared for his departure from Arnold and entry into the army, another event in late May 1918 would serve as a reminder for what he would fight for and have a lifelong impact on Kocur's life. On May 30, 1918, one of the largest political gatherings in the history of the city of Pittsburgh formalized the Slovaks fight for independence and put to paper the principles that would guide the Czech and Slovak peoples in their effort to form an independent nation. The document became known as the "Pittsburgh Agreement." The simple, one-page agreement, signed by representatives of various Slovak, Czech and American organizations, formally declared the intention of Czechs and Slovaks to form a federal state and outlined how the two nations and peoples would cooperate yet maintain their autonomy. Among its core points, the Pittsburgh Agreement stated that the Slovaks would have an autonomous legislative assembly, its own free local administration, its own courts and judicial system, its own schools, and its own official language. The Pittsburgh Agreement, in essence, was the declaration of independence for a Slovak state fully responsible for its own destiny in a political union of equals with the Czechs. If John Kocur needed any further motivation for wanting to become a willing participant in the crusade to defeat Germany and her allies, he now had it on paper. The Pittsburgh Agreement, sometimes considered the Declaration of Independence of the Slovaks, was something that Kocur would fight for. He would fight for its principles beginning in 1918 and would continue the fight for the next thirty years.

## Endnotes

1. *Alexander, June G.; Ethnic Pride, American Patriotism, pg 18. 2004.*
2. *Ibid, pg 17.*
3. *Ibid, pg 18.*
4. *Ibid, pg 23.*
5. *Ibid.*
6. *Ibid, pg 22.*
7. *Beamish, Richard J.: America's Part in the World War, pg 76. 1921.*
8. *Ibid.*

## Chapter 9

# DOUGHBOY

# Chapter 9

When John Kocur's orders for duty came through he was assigned to report to Camp Greenleaf, a special army cantonment located in Fort Oglethorpe, Georgia. Camp Greenleaf was considered a special camp due to the type of training conducted there and nature of the forces which it housed. As with Camp Greenleaf, most of the National Army camps at the time of the United State's entry into World War I were located in the southern and western states of the U.S. in order to take advantage of the more favorable weather conditions necessary for year-round training. While Camp Greenleaf was named for the nature of the surrounding countryside, the names of most army camps charged with the training of American forces prior to their deployment to Europe reflected the fresh memory of the last great American military conflict. Names like Camp Meade, Lee, Hancock, Shelby, Stuart, and Sheridan were the training destinations of hundreds of thousands of newly minted American soldiers.

The task of organizing and training the new National Army was a mammoth undertaking but as the American forces grew, training camps sprung up across the sixteen divisional areas of the United States. Within three months from the time ground was broken, the men were drilling on the parade grounds of the camps.[1] The task was really the erection of sixteen cities, each with accommodations for forty thousand inhabitants.[2]

Acting in much the way an independent city would, each camp had its own sewage system, fire department, bakeries, ice plants, and hospitals.[3] The construction of these camps and cantonments was a logistical marvel and feat of building efficiency, all accomplished at a time when the need for trained and prepared fighting men was the greatest.

Before being deployed to France, the average American soldier received six months of training in his country.[4] In John Kocur's case, training would be condensed to only two months of intensified instruction. The instruction Kocur received would be of a dual purpose, part field training typical of the American infantryman and part specialized training in the services his assigned unit would perform. John Kocur would go in to the Great War carrying not only a rifle but responsible for carrying stretchers as well. Kocur was assigned to the Seventh Infantry Division, Seventh Sanitary Train, Ambulance Company 36.

The Seventh Infantry Division, Regular Army, was organized by order of the War Department on December 6, 1917. The Seventh Division, whose unit insignia was two black triangles with apexes touching on a red circular background, was made up of four Infantry Regiments ($34^{th}$, $55^{th}$, $56^{th}$, and $64^{th}$), three Machine Gun battalions ($19^{th}$, $20^{th}$, and $21^{st}$), three Artillery regiments ($8^{th}$, $79^{th}$, and $80^{th}$), one Trench Mortar regiment ($7^{th}$), one Field Signal battalion ($10^{th}$), and four distinct Divisional Support Trains (Supply, Ammunition, Engineer, and Sanitary). The medical support personnel of the Seventh Division were organized within the Ambulance Companies and Field Hospitals, falling under the Sanitary Train organizational structure. In June of 1918, John Kocur was one of the thousands of men in the Seventh Division and a part of one of the largest contingents of new enlistees and draftees to join the division. As with many aspects of military service, luck often plays a role in the type of duty one performs, how likely it is that one could be placed in harm's way, and may ultimately mean life or death. For Kocur, his assignment to Ambulance Company 36, Seventh Sanitary Train, Seventh Division was one that would enable to him to contribute to the American war effort while serving his fellow soldiers, often in their time of greatest need at the front. The experience would also physically scar John Kocur and remain with him the rest of his life.

The duties that John Kocur would perform as a member of Ambulance Company 36 were, in some aspects, more dangerous than that of the front line soldiers. The function of the ambulance company is to collect the sick and wounded, to afford them temporary care and treatment, and to transport them to the next sanitary unit in the rear. In camp, the ambulance company operates an ambulance service between camp infirmaries and field or other hospitals. On the march ambulance companies are distributed among the marching troops, usually one company to each regiment for purposes of supplying transportation to those who become unable to march. In combat the ambulance company operates in two parts. The first establishes and operates a dressing station and collects the wounded, the second operates the wheeled transportation in evacuating the wounded.[5] The intricacies of the duties within an ambulance company as well as the everyday duties of an American soldier would be drilled into the new recruits arriving at Camp Greenleaf throughout the hot summer of 1918.

John Kocur's train ride to Camp Greenleaf, Georgia offered him the opportunity to see a different part of the American landscape. Left behind were the smokestacks and blazing furnaces of the industrial cities of the North, like Pittsburgh. As it made its way south the train now rolled though green farmland bordered by wood lots, fence rows, and stone walls, and through open spaces. Also gone in this part of the country were the ethnic enclaves and neighborhoods that provided a haven to Slovaks, Poles, Italians, and other immigrant groups who had settled in the cities of the North. The train now rolled through areas of the county where the only two parts of town were white and colored. For many on that troop train from the North, this would be their first exposure to the still recovering South and the defiant attitudes towards race and ethnicity. Given the circumstances in June 1918, however, free time for John Kocur and his fellow soldiers to explore the surrounding countryside and interact with the local population was extremely limited.

During the months of May and June 1918, the Seventh Division received twenty thousand new men.[6] Some of these men were members of regular army infantry units who were reassigned to the division. Many men, however, were newly drafted or enlistees from the states of Illinois, Iowa, Michigan,

Missouri, and Pennsylvania. When John Kocur arrived at Camp Greenleaf in June 1918, the Seventh Division was nearly at its full complement of men and taxing the capacity of the camp. By June in Georgia, summer heat and humidity and all that goes with it is in full swing. Weather conditions being what they were and given the strained capacity of the camp, the men of the Seventh Division, including John Kocur, were housed in large, square field tents instead of the long wooden barracks. Living conditions during the first few weeks at Camp Greenleaf were most likely not ideal for many of the inhabitants, who may have been accustomed to more comfortable spaces and a higher standard of living. Kocur, however, probably took the conditions were in stride. Conditions in Kocur's native country as he grew up were far more primitive and harsh; his early living conditions when he first came to the United States, from the steerage compartment of the ship in which he crossed the Atlantic to the crowded boarding house in Arnold where he first came to live, were not all that different from those he encountered at Camp Greenleaf and in fact may have been worse on some levels. The routine of an army camp, its rigid discipline, work, and lack of free time may have been a significant adjustment to some. John Kocur and many other immigrant soldiers, however, had already experienced a routine of work, eat, and sleep via their jobs in the mills, mines, and factories of their hometowns. Free time was a foreign concept to many immigrants, so what one never had one never missed. In many respects, soldiers like John Kocur, given their background, experiences, and attitudes, made a quicker adjustment to army life than did many native-born Americans. For certain, John Kocur had a personal stake in the outcome of the war and was motivated enough to volunteer. This motivation also likely served him well as he made the adjustment from civilian to soldier in the United States Army.

When Kocur and his fellow troops arrived at Camp Greenleaf they were first processed, issued clothing and equipment, examined and inoculated, and assigned quarters. The following weeks would consist of intense training, physical activity, and mental preparation for the duties the soldiers were expected to perform in France. Every minute of every day of every week was scheduled. The schedule provided for both work and recreation but rarely gave the soldiers leisure or free time. It was thought that leisure time would give the recruits an opportunity to brood over whatever problems or grievances they might think they had and make them a less productive member of the squad, company or regiment.

During that first week at Camp Greenleaf, the member of Ambulance Company 36 studied subjects such as the "school of the soldier" and "school of the squad," learning the intricate movements of gradually larger groups of men and the basics of open order drill. The initial days were also taken up by regular physical fitness activities, designed to strengthen the green troops, as well as scores of lectures on military discipline and courtesy. Officers drilled elements of personal hygiene into the soldiers' heads and provided valuable instruction on the care of one's feet, as infection or injury was one of the most troublesome problems a soldier was called upon to solve, particularly when in active service at the front.[7]

The second week of training for soldiers in the ambulance company consisted of "real soldiering." The men learned the intricacies of their Springfield .30 caliber rifles, including how to aim, fire, and more importantly clean and care for this important tool. The soldiers also were taught how to lunge and rip at an opponent with a bayonet attached to their weapon. In addition, the men also learned about other implements of war including lectures, training, and practice with hand grenades, chemical warfare, and close-order combat. Camp Greenleaf was also similar to other camps of instruction in that it also required soldiers to attend lectures with subjects like "Why We Are At War," helping to motivate soldiers and provide justification with a patriotic spin. It is difficult to imagine, however, for immigrant soldiers like John Kocur that a patriotic approach to motivation was as relevant as some of the personal causes that motivated them to enlist in the first place.

After mastering the basics of infantry drill, their weapon, and other standard army practices, the members of the ambulance companies were instructed in a very comprehensive course of training for medical troops. This included long hikes, during which emergency rations were cooked by each soldier using field equipment. At this time, the soldiers also received some valuable instruction in the proper manner of handling the wounded and practical experience in the different methods of tying patients on litters as well as carrying them with and without litters.[8]

Over the course of the weeks of training, the men gradually became accustomed to the routine of army life and the specific duties and requirements of an ambulance company. In a few weeks time the men's health in general was much improved; men who had been overweight lost pounds regularly and safely; men who had been underweight gained pounds; endurance was increased and in some instances it appeared the mind became keener.[9] Given the rigors and routine of army life in camp and the desire to continue to provide structure, the War Department also recognized the need for the amusement of the troops. In many army camps across the country the Commission on Training Camp Activities sought to provide the diversions of civilian life that soldiers were used to in their own hometowns. Activities and diversions such as movie theaters, stage plays, and athletic leagues became a part of U.S. Army camps. Other normalizing influences came from the many volunteer organizations like the Red Cross, YMCA, Knights of Columbus, and Jewish Welfare Board that routinely visited the army camps. Even actors, singers, and entertainers of the day contributed their time and talents in events and shows throughout the country's training camps in order to raise morale and provide a sense of normalcy.

For Ambulance Company 36 and John Kocur, the month of June at Camp Greenleaf was devoted to a thorough course of instruction in the duties of an ambulance company.[10] According to records of the Seventh Sanitary Train, Seventh Division, on June 25 Captain Dana E. Monroe was relieved of duty as commanding officer of Ambulance Company 36 and was succeeded by First Lieutenant Richards E. Amos. On July 4, the company had enlisted personnel of one hundred and twenty-two men, the number required by the War Department's Table of Organization for an ambulance company at war strength.[11] What then followed were strenuous days of final preparation for overseas duty, which included numerous physical inspections as well as inspections of equipment. Before the company was ready to leave for its embarkation point and eventual trip to France, John Kocur did something that many of his fellow soldiers most likely did prior to leaving for the front. He bought an insurance policy. Kocur's policy covered him in the sum of $10,000 for, "total permanent disability and from and after death." As the beneficiaries of this insurance policy, John Kocur named his wife Margaret and Anton Hranec (listed on the policy as his step-brother). Margaret Kocur and Anton Hranec were each to receive $8,000 and $2,000, respectively and the Insurance Policy certificate was sent to Hranec in Springdale, Pennsylvania for safe keeping. At the time, Kocur's wife Margaret still resided in Podvysoka, Austria-Hungary. The policy premiums were paid for by monthly deductions from Kocur's army pay. The insurance policy was a stark reminder for the soldiers about to depart Camp Greenleaf that their training and preparation was for something real, something that would, for some, truly mean life or death.

Ambulance Company 36 left Camp Greenleaf on July 22 and boarded a train at Lytle, Georgia. They traveled for two days and on July 24 arrived at Camp Merritt, New Jersey to await their embarkation orders, and wait they would. After nearly three weeks of more drill, training, inspections, and preparation at Camp Merritt the embarkation orders for Ambulance Company 36 finally arrived on August 13. The next day the nearly one hundred and thirty men of Ambulance Company 36 proceeded to Hoboken, New Jersey where they boarded the U.S.S. *Matsonia*. John Kocur was, for at least the second time since his arrival in the United States some nine years ago, boarding a ship that would take him back across the Atlantic. Kocur's first return trip, occurring in 1913 when he returned home to marry, was for a happier purpose. Given the purpose of that trip, John Kocur may have been nervous but for a much different reason. It's likely that this trip produced much more anxiety. Kocur traveled now not as a passenger on a pleasure tip, but as a part of a great body of men with a more serious destination and purpose. The loaded troop ship carried John Kocur and many of the Seventh Division to France with a singular mission: become engaged in fighting the enemy and help the allies end the war. For some in the division, the insurance policy purchased at Camp Greenleaf would become a necessity.

## Endnotes

1. *Beamish, Richard J: America's Part in the World War, pg 73. 1921.*
2. *Ibid.*
3. *Ibid.*
4. *Ibid, pg 77.*
5. *Brockmann, Felix E; Here, There, and Back, pg 14. 1925*
6. *United States Government; Order of Battle of the U.S. Forces in the World War, pg 101. 1931*
7. *Smith, Harry L, MD; Memoirs of an Ambulance Company Officer, pg 8. 1940.*
8. *Fell, Edgar T; History of the Seventh Division, pg 227. 1927.*
9. *Smith, Harry L, MD; Memoirs of an Ambulance Company Officer, pg 9. 1940.*
10. *Fell, Edgar T; History of the Seventh Division, pg 227. 1927.*
11. *Ibid.*

## Chapter 10

# OVER THERE

# Chapter 10

The transport of American troops to the battlefields of France began in earnest during the early spring of 1918. During the summer of that year more than two hundred thousand soldiers were crossing the Atlantic each month. August of 1918, in particular, saw nearly three hundred thousand men cross, among them the soldiers of Ambulance Company 36, Seventh Division, whose ranks included the now thirty-one-year-old volunteer John Kocur.

By August of 1918, Kocur had been in the United States less than ten years and yet this was his third trip across the Atlantic Ocean. The first trip, made as an immigrant in 1909, brought him from the oppression of Hungarian rule in his native land to the opportunity of America; his second trip, a round trip, took him back to his homeland in 1913 for the happy occasion of marriage to Margeta Zbojkova. During this most recent trip in August of 1918, John Kocur was counted among soldiers in the United States Army.

In the short time between arriving in New York in the early fall of 1909 and leaving New York in the summer's heat of 1918, John Kocur had already accomplished much. After landing in the U.S., Kocur had established himself in the small town of Arnold, Pennsylvania, become gainfully employed at a local glassworks and then independently as a barber; he saved enough to return home for the purposes of getting married; he become a United States citizen, and had voluntarily enlisted in the United States Army. Kocur embraced all that America had to offer, including economic, political, and social freedom and he found companionship among fellow Slovaks, which fostered and grew his strong sense of ethnic pride. Through these life experiences John Kocur came to realize that the principles that were at the heart of America, individual freedom and self-determination, were the same principles that he and his fellow Slovaks yearned for in the old country and that only by leaving that homeland could they access a platform to fight for those principles. As the U.S.S. *Matsonia* left Hoboken on the fourteenth of August, 1918, John Kocur had achieved the type of life many Americans took for granted. Kocur would now put the principles he had come to learn and live by into practice. Instead of steaming toward the outstretched, welcoming arms of Lady Liberty, John Kocur was moving slowly away from her watchful gaze and into more uncertain waters. As the soldiers of the Seventh Division watched from the rail of the ship, the lighted torch of liberty and the skyline of New York slowly sank on the horizon. Kocur would soon have the chance to demonstrate his loyalty and commitment to the principles of his new country and in doing so aid in the defeat of the principles of those who held his old country prisoner.

By the time Ambulance Company 36 left Hoboken on August 14, some of the other units of the Seventh Division had already sailed or were en route to France. Given the size of an army division and its equipage, more than one transport was necessary to transport the troops across the ocean. Crossing the Atlantic in a convoy of ships during wartime was a nerve-wracking and potentially dangerous journey. One of the primary reasons the United States was in the war with Germany and her allies was the German policy of unrestricted submarine warfare in the Atlantic. Now that war with Germany had been declared and the U.S. was sending ships filled with the troops and equipment that would ultimately be brought to bear against Germany, the enemy submarines stepped up their activity. Earlier in the year, during the beginning of the push to send troops to France, the U.S.S. *Moldavia*, which had been carrying men of the 58$^{th}$ Infantry of the 4$^{th}$ Division, had been torpedoed and sunk by a German submarine. The *Moldavia* sank slowly and most of the crew and soldiers were taken off easily but fifty-six men lost their lives in the tragedy.[1]

A typical convoy of ships making the Atlantic crossing consisted of twelve to fifteen vessels, including transports, destroyers, and cruisers. The ships traveled in a formation of three lines of vessels, four to five ships in each line, with the troop transports in the middle lines. The convoy was preceded by an auxiliary cruiser for about one-third of the way across the Atlantic.[2] While a large group of such formidable ships would have been some comfort to the men of the Seventh Division, it only took one torpedo from one lone German submarine smashing into the side of one of the transports to effectively end the war for some soldiers before it even began.

Given the large-scale nature of troop movements to France during the spring and summer of 1918, the conditions on board the U.S.S. *Matsonia* for members of Ambulance Company 36 and the others in the Seventh Division were uncomfortable at best and unbearable at worst. Because of the sheer numbers of men and the physical size of the ship there wasn't enough room for all the soldiers to be on deck at once. Companies would alternate in spending time during the day on deck.[3] Below deck, packed, as one soldier described, "like sardines in a can," conditions could be much less desirable especially in bad weather. Harry L. Smith, MD, a veteran ambulance company officer described the conditions aboard a troop transport:

"Ten days on a transport was misery. The men crowded into the hold with bunks jammed the ceiling; when the ship rose, swayed and fell, seas-sickness became contagious, epidemic, the quarters almost unbearable. Officers forbade smoking on deck and ordered all lights covered. There was nothing to do but shoot craps or play poker until entering the war zone, when one could look for submarines."[4]

Passing the time during the transport became the soldiers first battle. During the daytime the soldiers either spent time on deck in their assigned shifts, weather permitting, or in their bunks. Officers continued the routine inspection of personnel and minor equipment but given the limited real estate of the ship, no close order drill could be performed. Lifeboat drills and submarine drills were held regularly, preparedness for the very real circumstances of trans-Atlantic travel during war time. So seriously did the officers on board take the threat of submarine attack that no lights of any kind were allowed on deck at night, not even the glow of a lighted cigarette, shades were drawn tight over all portholes and windows, men ate and slept in their life belts (a smaller version of the life jacket) and most men were not permitted to undress to go to bed.

It is likely that the conditions experienced by the soldiers bound for France on board the transports were not unlike those that John Kocur experienced crossing the Atlantic in the opposite direction as a young Slovak immigrant passenger traveling steerage class aboard the *Bremen*. The limited space, the restrictions on movement, the less-than-appetizing food, and hours of boredom probably brought back some unpleasant memories for Private Kocur. In this case, however, there was one big difference. At the end of the *Bremen*'s journey, Kocur reached the shores of America. When the *Matsonia* would land, it would be on the shores of a country already damaged by war. France would welcome John Kocur, but for a very different reason than had America.

Fortunately for the troops on the U.S.S. *Matsonia*, the men never saw any signs of a German submarine and their ten days aboard ship passed by uneventfully. On August 25, 1918 the ship arrived at the port city of Brest, located in northwest France. The following day members of Ambulance Company 36, including John Kocur, disembarked and marched to a rest camp near Pontanezon Barracks where they pitched their small shelter tents and remained until August 30.[5] Sleeping in tents in the open, late-summer air of Pontanezon must have been a welcome relief for the men after nearly two weeks of cramped stuffy conditions below the decks of the transport ship. On August 30, the company boarded a train at Brest and moved across the heart of France to the city of Nievres, arriving there August 31. After a short rest in Nievres, the men in Ambulance Company 36 marched northeast to Pimelles where officers and men were assigned their first billets (housing) in France.[6] Not surprisingly, the officers were housed in a chateau and private homes whereas the enlisted men were housed some in homes but most in barns and outbuildings.

According to army practice it was not unusual for a newly arrived unit to spend time in a training sector prior to being placed in the war zone and Ambulance Company 36 was no exception. From September 1 to 26, the company was given a full and intensive course of training in the duties of an ambulance company in action.[7] The training was done in accordance with the prescribed role of an ambulance company as outlined by the Medical Department of the United States Army thus:

> *The evacuation of wounded begins on the field, when members of the regimental medical detachment apply first aid dressings and direct, assist, or carry the wounded men to aid stations. These regimental medical officers apply dressings and splints to prepare the patient for transport. Litter bearers from Ambulance Companies take the patients from aid stations to ambulance heads or collecting stations, ordinarily the most advanced points which could be reached by ambulances; although whenever possible these went all the way to aid stations and thus reduced the heavy labor of litter bearing. The headquarters of the ambulance company, where the bulk of its ambulances were stationed, was usually about a mile to the rear of the ambulance head. When a loaded ambulance passed these on its road to the field hospitals, an empty one started forward to replace it, and constant circulation was thus kept up until the field was cleared.*[8]

In practice, about ninety percent of the duties of an ambulance company, like that of John Kocur's unit, would entail the evacuation of wounded men and about ten percent would entail the administration of first aid. Wounded men were taken from the scene of their injuries to the aid station and then back to various hospitals. Theoretically, ambulance companies were to take wounded men to field hospitals but as it was to happen, men were evacuated to improvised field hospitals that ambulance companies conducted themselves.[9]

The ambulance companies of the First World War were placed in harm's way every bit as much as front line troops. Liaison must be maintained among all combat units of the army, even in the thickest part of the battle, for where there is a battle, there are certain to be wounded soldiers.[10] An ambulance driver is nearly always in mortal danger. He threads his heavy machine over mud and water, swampland and rutted roads. He has double responsibility in that his life and the lives of several others whom he may transport are frequently threatened by shell, aerial bomb, or rifle fire. The litter bearers, also, are subject to as much jeopardy as are the soldiers in the trenches for an active litter bearer is always in the midst of the fight. He must carry out a wounded soldier when the same projectiles that lay the soldier low are whistling and roaring about his own ears. He cannot dodge or swerve or fall to the safety of the earth, as the soldier can. He has to save his own life and the life of the man he is carrying on his litter.[11]

On September 27 Ambulance Company 36 left Pimelles, entrained at the railhead the next day and detrained at Chaligny, nearly two hundred miles to the northeast, on September 29. By this time, having traveled across France and now within a stone's throw of the war zone, John Kocur and his fellow soldiers had been trained both in the United States and in France as to the duties of an ambulance company. Kocur was one of eighty privates listed on the roster of the company as of midnight September 30, 1918. In addition to those eighty men, the company also consisted of fourteen private first class, sixteen wagon drivers, two corporals, five sergeants, one sergeant first class, and five officers including the company commander, First Lieutenant Richard E. Amos. The company was also supported by three cooks and one mechanic. Ambulance Company 36 possessed twelve General Motors-made ambulances, each with a capacity of eight sitting patients and four litter patients.

At the start of October, 1918, Private Kocur of Ambulance Company 36 found himself on the front lines of the Great War. Kocur didn't know at the time that the war would only last for another thirty days but he was now fully trained and prepared to fulfill his duty in removing and aiding the wounded of the Seventh Division. For John Kocur, the next thirty days would be like those of nearly every soldier who has ever seen combat, hours of boredom punctuated by moments of sheer terror. Kocur would do his duty admirably, he would perform under extreme circumstances helping to evacuate and transport wounded from the front lines and would bring home more than just a memory of his service on the front lines of France.

## Endnotes

1. *Smith, Harry L, MD; Memoirs of an Ambulance Company Officer, pg 16. 1940.*
2. *Ibid, pg 17.*
3. *Ibid.*
4. *Ibid.*
5. *Fell, Edgar T; History of the Seventh Division, pg 227. 1927.*
6. *Ibid.*
7. *Ibid, pg 228.*
8. *Medical Dept., United States Army. Duties of Ambulance Companies in the Field.*
9. *Smith, Harry L, MD; Memoirs of an Ambulance Company Officer, pg 22. 1940.*
10. *Ibid.*
11. *Ibid.*

## Chapter 11

# FIGHTING WITH THE SEVENTH

# Chapter 11

At dawn on September 12, after four hours of violent artillery fire of preparation, and accompanied by small tanks, the infantry of the American First and Fourth corps advanced against strong German positions surrounding the French town of St. Mihiel. This was the first operation of an independently operating American army known as the Allied Expeditionary Force, commanded by General John J. "Black Jack" Pershing.

According to Pershing's official report of the St. Mihiel operation, "The reduction of the St. Mihiel salient was important, as it would prevent the enemy from interrupting traffic on the Paris-Nancy Railroad by artillery fire and would free the railroad leading north through St. Mihiel to Verdun. It would also provide us with an advantageous base of departure for an attack against the Metz-Sedan Railroad system which was vital to the German armies west of Verdun, and against the Briey Iron Basin which was necessary for the production of German armament and munitions."[1]

The St. Mihiel salient was a bulge in the German lines on the Western Front that had been in the enemy's hands since September of 1914. The Germans had every reason to want to maintain this position as it afforded them many advantages. The St. Mihiel position was one of the strongest sections of the German lines in France, made even stronger by the natural defensive nature of the terrain in the surrounding area. The western face of the salient extended along the rugged, heavily wooded eastern heights of the Meuse; the southern face followed the heights of the Meuse for eight kilometers to the east and then crossed the plain of the Woevre, including within the German lines the detached heights of Loupmont and Montsec, which dominated the plain and afforded the enemy unusual facilities for observation.[2]

The Americans attacked all along the lines that early September morning with four army corps in concert with French forces numbering approximately 70,000. The combined forces at Pershing's disposal totaled nearly 500,000 men. The American divisions quickly overwhelmed the German defenders and by the afternoon of September 13 Pershing's objectives for the attack had been achieved. The St. Mihiel salient had been pushed back some eighteen kilometers. In the course of two days the American army had captured nearly 16,000 German prisoners, 443 guns and large stores of material and supplies all the while suffering less than 7,000 casualties during the advance.[3]

The American Seventh Division did not participate in the battle of St. Mihiel during mid-September 1918. The Seventh had just recently reached the French countryside and during the battle had been engaged in training and preparation. St. Mihiel, it can be argued, marked the beginning of the end for Germany. That did not mean, however, that the dangers of war did not still exist. The German army, while reduced and pushed back in this area of the Western front, still represented a formidable foe for the American army; and while the sands in the hour glass were quickly slipping by for the Germans, there was plenty of action left for the Seventh Division and Ambulance Company 36.

By early October, 1918 the Seventh Division had been assigned a portion of the front line in the Purvenelle Sector, a section of front line to the northeast of St. Mihiel. Private John Kocur and the other members of Ambulance Company 36 occupied a portion of the field near the town of Montauville. The thirty-sixth relieved Ambulance Company 359, already on duty at this station, and commenced operations on October 9. Kocur and his fellow service men of the Thirty-sixth were responsible for supporting and evacuating men from the 55th and 56th infantry, 5th Engineers, 19th Field Artillery, and 20th Machine Gun Battalion.[4] Ambulance Company 36's duties in evacuating for the various divisional units kept them on the far right of the Seventh

Division line. As such, the company organized its men so that two ambulances with a sergeant in charge were stationed at Fey-en-Haye; four litter bearers with a corporal in charge were stationed at the Advanced Battalion Aid station of the 55$^{th}$ infantry; two runners were stationed at the Regimental P.C. (Command Post) of the 56$^{th}$ infantry and a dressing station was opened at Montauville.[5] Fey-en-Haye and Montauville were approximately three to four miles from the front lines of the 55$^{th}$ and 56$^{th}$ infantry.

The sector of the front occupied by the Seventh Division was generally quiet. Following the battle of St. Mihiel, the Germans did little in terms of actively engaging the infantry of the Americans in their front. This did not stop them, however, from continually bombarding the American lines with artillery and harassing the front and rear of the lines with aerial bombs. The German batteries sent over an average of 720 shells per day during the remaining days of October.[6] While the sector was, for the most part, free from constant engagement with the forces on the ground, the fighting had taken its toll on the surrounding countryside occupied by the Seventh. The war-torn nature of the area required the division to reconstruct virtually all telephone lines, a particular necessity for the ambulance companies. Another impediment faced by John Kocur's ambulance company was the nature of the roads on which they traveled in order to transport the wounded. Transportation of casualties via ambulance was extremely difficult due in part to the fact that the roads had been badly shelled and torn up during the St. Mihiel drive.[7] The shelling combined with the rainy fall weather made the roads a sea of mud. According the official record of the Seventh Division, "It was almost impossible to reach the P.C. (command post) of the 55$^{th}$ Infantry north of Fey-en-Haye on this account."[8] The muddy, shell-torn roads were only a part of the devastation now all around the men of the Seventh Division. At one time, this area of French countryside was a picturesque patchwork of green fields, wood lots, and small farms. In its present state, it more resembled a landscape devastated by a natural disaster like a fire or earthquake. The green of the fields had long been replaced with thick brown mud as far as the eye could see, churned up by constant explosions. Trees, or at least those that still remained, were nothing more than blackened stumps, twisted splintered trunks and barren branches. Even the small provincial towns like Villers-de-Haye, Pont-a-Mossaun, and Jaulny, once filled with quaint wood and stone houses, were reduced to piles of stone and timber. Josh Billings, a private in the Seventh Division summed it up best when he said, "War sure do change things a heap."

Throughout early October, the Germans kept up an intermittent artillery fire on various points of the Seventh Division lines. For members of the 55th and 56th Infantry and Ambulance Company 36, however, the enemy shelling was more than just intermittent beginning October 12, 1918. According to official records of the Seventh Division, October 12 marked the beginning of two days of intense German activity. Enemy airplanes were very active in the afternoon of October 12 locating targets and adjusting artillery fire for the German batteries. While the German infantry occupying the lines in front of the Seventh Division was slightly outnumbered and outgunned, the German air and artillery supremacy was pronounced.

For most of the day on October 12, the artillery fire from the German lines was light, having sent over approximately four hundred shells during the day. This equates to about fifty shells an hour from nine in the morning to five in the afternoon. Strange how this was viewed as "light" by the men in the lines. For the most part, however, the men of the Seventh remained in their dugouts and trenches during the shelling and passed the time as best they could.

The artillery barrage picked up after five in the afternoon and increased in volume and intensity throughout the evening of October 12. At approximately 8:15 p.m. the bombardment intensified yet again with this artillery attack mixing high explosives with lethal gases. The outposts of the 55th and 56th Infantry, the regiments being served by Ambulance Company 36, bore the brunt of the German attack. A total of 317 men were gassed as a result of the more than two thousand mustard, phosgene, and sneezing gas shells delivered in the German's deadly attack.

The 317 men of the 55th and 56th Infantry who were gassed during the evening of the twelfth had to first be evacuated from the lines, treated at the aid station if possible, moved to the dressing station at Montauville and then on the division hospital further to the rear. These men were cared for by soldiers like John Kocur and others in Ambulance Company 36. Many times, their initial contact with members of the ambulance company came in the trenches or portion of the front lines where they were wounded. If the wounded men could not walk or needed assistance moving to the aid station, it was the ambulance company men who carried them on stretchers. After initial aid and comfort, or what little of it could be administered a few hundred yards in the rear of the front lines, the wounded were loaded on ambulances and driven to the dressing station or directly to the division hospital. The stretcher bearers, ambulance drivers and ambulance attendants would continue this loop of care until all the wounded were secured.

On October 13 due to the great concentration of mustard gas in the woods in which the outpost of the 55$^{th}$ Infantry was located, companies I, K, and M were withdrawn back from the outpost line approximately seven hundred meters to the vicinity of the position occupied by the support company in the outpost zone.[9]

As more U.S. forces were deployed in France, the American army quickly become accustomed to dealing with poison gas attacks. For new soldiers on the line, however, poison gas was a fearful thing. Having little practical experience with gas many soldiers believed the faintest whiff would kill them instantly if inhaled without wearing a gas mask. It was well known that many of the larger German artillery shells contained poison gas, either mustard, phosgene, or chlorine gas. It was also not uncommon for the gas to be delivered in grenades thrown by the enemy. The clouds of poison gas produced during an attack could often be seen rolling toward the U.S. lines and had a tendency to linger in low lying areas of the battlefield, such as dug-outs or trenches. The Germans first employed poison gas as a weapon in the early part of the war, using chlorine gas in an attack against the French and British lines on the upper Ypres salient.[10] Despite the soldiers' initial fears, the gas masks issued to the American troops were, for the most part, adequate in protecting soldiers from the effects of these toxic weapons.

The alarm system used in the event of a gas attack consisted of a series of loud Klaxon horns, which were sounded whenever the cry of "Gas!" was heard. If an attack rolled forward, or if anyone saw the yellowish-white clouds of gas at a distance, the alarm would be relayed far back of the Allied lines from one outfit to the next.[11]

In addition to the lingering effects of the previous day's gas and artillery barrage, two German patrols attempted to penetrate the lines in the 55$^{th}$ and 56$^{th}$ Infantry's front but were driven off by rifle and machine gun fire. Two hundred more enemy gas shells were fired on the U.S. lines and fifty-three new gas casualties were reported. Some of these, however, were cases just developing from the gas attack of the day before.[12] In total, nearly eight hundred German shells were fired in to the American lines during the day and evening of October 13.

For most of the remaining days in October 1918, the area along the lines being supported by John Kocur and Ambulance Company 36 remained relatively quiet. The Germans had shifted their attention to other areas of the line occupied by the Seventh Division further to the west. Enemy artillery, however, continued to rain down all along the Seventh Division lines in sporadic but sometimes heavy doses.

At some point in mid-October (official records do not indicate exactly when), Private John Kocur was treated for gas inhalation and spent time in the field hospital to the rear of the Seventh Division lines. Kocur, later in life, applied for compensation as a veteran disabled in the World War and cited "... disorder of respiratory organs" as his condition. On his paperwork, John Kocur was unable to recall the exact date of his wounding or location other than to cite "...in the vicinity of St. Mihiel and Toul, France," areas of the St. Mihel line occupied by Ambulance Company 36.

Kocur was not unlike many individual soldiers who see the battlefield not in the larger picture played out on a map at headquarters, but as their own little corner of the world; the area directly in front, to the sides, and behind him. The names of towns, roads, and hills are often lost to the years but the experiences and memories never leave. In that context it is understandable that nearly two decades later when applying for compensation that private citizen Kocur could not recall the exact details of time and locations when army Private Kocur received his wound. It is also likely that given the slowly developing symptoms of gas exposure, Kocur may not have even realized he was exposed at levels capable of doing any damage until days after the actual event.

John Kocur's time in the field hospital lasted until late October when he rejoined Ambulance Company 36. Some documentation points to October 21 as the date Kocur came back to the company, while another other notes October 28. First Lieutenant James S. Knowles, in his daily field report for Ambulance Company 36 remarked on October 28, "Pvt John Kocur, 2582413, transferred from Hospital to Division." Kocur was subsequently listed as active on the monthly roster of Ambulance Company 36 as of midnight on October 31, 1918. The monthly roster was taken at the end of each month and listed all those active for duty as of the end of that particular month. Private Kocur had been listed on the September roster, as of midnight September 30, and was now on the October roster as well.

Further documentation regarding the nature of the wound John Kocur received during his service and its effects throughout the remainder of his life is found throughout his medical records in the Veterans Administration. The exposure to poison gas damaged his lungs and led to their progressive deterioration. With each subsequent physical examination by army doctors, as well as his family physicians, the condition of John Kocur's lungs became worse. Kocur's application for disability compensation was approved by the Veterans Administration in 1930 with the notation, "...all medical history of treatment for disabilities tending to support a disability allowance claim."

With the combination of circumstances surrounding the location and placement of Ambulance Company 36 in early to mid October 1918, the duties they routinely performed, the action that took place in that part of the line with respect to periods of intense German attacks with poison gas, the reports of Kocur's stay in and return from the hospital, and the disability compensation awarded, a potential scenario of how Private John Kocur received his wound from poison gas comes into focus. It is likely that given this circumstantial evidence, John Kocur was doing his duty in responding to one of the German gas attacks on the 55$^{th}$ or 56$^{th}$ Infantry as a member of Ambulance Company 36. Kocur was not an ambulance driver but more likely a stretcher bearer or serving in the aid station directly behind the lines. In the course of evacuating the wounded during one of the gas attacks, Kocur was exposed to poison gas at either a relatively low level over time or more intensely for a short period of time. Such exposure and the initial symptoms may not have been severe enough or occurred quickly enough to warrant immediate treatment and evacuation to a hospital. Over time the effects of the gas took hold and forced Private Kocur to seek medical attention at one of the locations so familiar to those in Ambulance Company 36. John Kocur would eventually find himself in the hospital where, over the course of several days, he would receive medial treatment for exposure to poison gas and eventually be pronounced fit enough to rejoin his unit. Only later in life would the true effects of the gas begin to manifest themselves and contribute to the decline in Kocur's health, eventually leading to his death.

Ambulance Company 36 left Montauville about October 27 and moved west to Bouillonville on the far left of the Seventh Division line to relieve Ambulance Company 111, which was on duty at this station. Here the unit evacuated for the $34^{th}$, $64^{th}$, and $55^{th}$ Infantry, as well as $340^{th}$ and $342^{nd}$ Field Artillery. Dressing stations were opened at Bouillonville and at Thiaucourt. Two ambulances were stationed at Thiaucourt, one at Jaulny, and one at the Battalion Aid Station of the $64^{th}$ Infantry.[13] On November 1 the ambulance stationed at the $64^{th}$ Infantry aid station was withdrawn.

The movement of Ambulance Company 36 in late October was a part of a larger scale movement of the entire Seventh Division. By orders of the commanding General of the Fourth Army Corps, the Seventh was to sideslip from its previous location to the left (west) and take over part of the sector then held by the U.S. $28^{th}$ Division. During the day of the 27 things were very quiet on the front. Evidently the movements were not known to the Germans as their artillery fire fell way below normal with only two hundred twenty enemy shells being reported.[14] The only other activity of note for the division during that "moving day" was the contact with a German patrol armed with machine guns. The enemy patrol was quickly dispatched and retreated through the woods, never to be seen again.

On October 28, following the movement of the Seventh Division, including Ambulance Company 36, the German activity picked up. The day was marked with heavy machine gun fire from the enemy's positions in the $34^{th}$ Infantry's sector. Enemy aircraft were also very active. Four planes engaged in a battle at low altitude and one of the German planes was brought down in front of the 55th Infantry lines. The German artillery also was active with a total of 573 shells fired into the Seventh Division lines.[15] All the while, John Kocur and the men of Ambulance Company 36 continued to treat and evacuate the wounded of the 34th, 55th, and 64th Infantries from their positions at the front to the dressing station at Thiaucourt and beyond to the hospitals in the rear. The ambulances found the roads barely passable due to constant shelling and constant rain. Getting to the wounded at the front was also becoming more difficult as a result of the thickness of the trees and undergrowth in this part of the line. For the litter bearers of the ambulance company this meant more distance to cover when evacuating the wounded to the aid station, since their vehicles could not travel as close to the front, as well as increased danger of rifle and machine gun fire from a well-hidden enemy. Three patrols of the 34th Infantry, men supported by Ambulance Company 36, left the lines of the Seventh Division in an attempt to occupy and hold positions along the ridge of a spur known as 310. The right patrol encountered machine gun fire from the ridge as well as very heavy and close barbed wire entanglements and were forced to withdraw, suffering casualties. The center patrol also encountered heavy wire and while cutting through were under machine gun, rifle, and hand grenade fire forcing them to withdraw. The patrol on the left encountered an enemy patrol and also had to withdraw.[16] The Germans had been at war now a little over four years and showed that while the Americans may be on the advance they had no intention of making it an easy advance.

The next two days on the front were quiet with the exception of German planes flying over the Seventh Division sector and several artillery rounds being fired into the American lines. Things began to change, however, on the evening of October 30. From eight p.m. to midnight the German artillery gassed the Bois-de-Bonvaux and the woods northeast of Jaulny, sending over a total of 312 gas shells of mixed mustard and phosgene. The bombardment caused 37 casualties. A total of one thousand shells of all kinds were received in the American lines during the day.[17]

The last day of October found more of the same from the Germans. The German airplanes continued flying throughout the sector all day and dropped, according to Seventh Division records, "...great quantities of propaganda." What the Germans thought they could accomplish at this point in the war with propaganda is a puzzling question. The German artillery also became more active as the day progressed and in fact an almost continuous bombardment of the western portion of the Bois-de-Rappes and the north of the Foret-des-Vencheres had been going on all day. Seven hundred shells were thrown in this area, nearly all of which were gas shells, mostly mustard gas. The Americans suffered a total of fifty-nine gas casualties.

For men of Ambulance Company 36 the last several days of October were a busy time. The almost constant German shelling, gas attacks, and aerial bombs provided the backdrop for the activities for which ambulance companies were responsible; retrieving, aiding, and transporting the wounded. The Germans provided the wounded, Ambulance Company 36 provided the rest. This period of activity for Kocur and others in the ambulance company continued as the calendar changed from October to November. The men of the company had established a route of evacuation in a triangle between the towns of Jaulny to the northeast, Thiaucourt to the south, and Bouillonville to the west. As of November 9, two ambulances were stationed at Jaulny and a shuttle service was operated between the three towns. Two runners were placed a Jaulny and two runners at the regimental aid stations. On November 10 nearly half of Ambulance Company 36 was stationed at Jaulny and on the following day the reminder of the company moved from Bouillonville and Thiaucourt to Jaulny and resumed duties at that station.[18]

When Private John Kocur retired to his blanket roll in a barn or cellar in Jaulny France on the evening of November 10, 1918 he had most likely heard, like many of his fellow soldiers, that the war was coming to a close the next day. November 11th dawned cloudy and gray as had nearly every other morning that fall of 1918. If the rumors were true, then the war would be over at precisely 11 a.m. on November 11, 1918, the eleventh hour of the eleventh day of the eleventh month. As the watch hands touched eleven, some American troops recalled, "...a second of expected silence, and then a curious rippling sound which observers far behind the front likened to the noise of a great wind. It was the sound of men cheering from the Vosges to the sea."[19] While that might have occurred, it is more likely that the end of the war was enjoyed in quiet reflection and exhaustive relief. Brigadier General Charles Dawes, in Paris when the armistice was signed, probably summed up most soldiers' feeling of that day when he wrote in his book, *Journal of the Great War*, "I could not cheer to save my life, but I have to try hard all the time to keep from crying."[20]

The men of the American Seventh Division, including Private John Kocur of Ambulance Company 36, did not have a lengthy service in the Great War. The statistics of the division's activities confirm this. Since landing in France, the men of the Seventh spent only about eight weeks engaged in actual combat, far less than most other American Divisions. Only four other American divisions suffered fewer casualties than did the Seventh who accounted for only 0.6 percent of American battle deaths with 302 and 0.6 percent of American wounded with 1,516.[21] During the operations of the division, one officer and sixty-eight men, twenty-eight machine guns and numerous supplies were captured from the enemy.[22] The Seventh Division also stayed relatively stationary during their time at the front compared to other units. The Division made a total advance into enemy territory of three-fourths of a kilometer.[23]

For John Kocur and his ambulance company colleagues the war was also short, the movements also limited. What these men saw of the conflict, however, was nearly always the worst of what a war can offer, the wounded and the dying. Ambulance Company 36 evacuated a total of 1,001 cases during the period of its active operations.[24] Most of these casualties were treated and lived but some ended up making the ultimate sacrifice. All of the wounded, however, who were aided, treated, and evacuated by men like John Kocur and others in Ambulance Company 36 were someone's brothers, sons, fathers, uncles, or friends.

Kocur's part in the war may have started as what he saw to be an opportunity to demonstrate his American patriotism and play a part in the downfall of the oppressors of his native land. Given the role he ended up playing in the Great War, it was all those things and much more. It was a demonstration of his caring and compassion for his fellow man and his willingness to sacrifice his own health and safety for others. He would carry these principles throughout the reminder of his life and put the lessons he learned as a thirty-year old private into constant practice. John Kocur would also carry forward not only the memories of the battlefield but the scars of battle as well. Through exposure to poison gas, the war's most toxic weapon, Kocur's lungs were permanently damaged. While he was well enough to rejoin Ambulance Company 36 after a brief stay in the hospital, the damage done to Kocur's lungs would get progressively worse through the years, contributing to ongoing health conditions like chronic bronchitis, shortness of breath, and ultimately to his death years later.

## Endnotes

1. *Pershing, General John J.; Official Report of November 1919 on the battle of St. Mihiel, pg 2. 1919*

2. *Ibid, pg 4.*

3. *Ibid, pg 5.*

4. *Fell, Edgar T. ; History of the Seventh Division, pg 228. 1927.*

5. *Ibid.*

6. *Ibid, pg 65.*

7. *Ibid.*

8. *Ibid.*

9. *Ibid, pg 66.*

10. *Beamish, Richard J.: America's Part in the World War, pg 316. 1921.*

11. *Smith, Harry L, MD; Memoirs of an Ambulance Company Officer, pg 30. 1940.*

12. *Fell, Edgar T. ; History of the Seventh Division, pg 68. 1927.*

13. *Ibid, pg 228.*

14. *Ibid, pg 81.*

15. *Ibid, pg 82.*

16. *Ibid.*

17. *Ibid, pg 85.*

18. *Ibid, pg 228.*

19. *Smith, Harry L, MD; Memoirs of an Ambulance Company Officer, pg 80. 1940.*

20. *Dawes, Charles; Journal of the Great War. 1920*

21. *Beamish, Richard J.: America's Part in the World War, pg 228. 1921.*

22. *Ibid, pg 560.*

23. *Ibid.*

24. *Fell, Edgar T. ; History of the Seventh Division, pg 228. 1927*

**Jan Kocur**
**May 22, 1887—July 14, 1948**

Crest of
Austria-Hungary,
1915

Devin and the Danube River, Southwest Slovakia

Slovak folk art

Janosik, the Slovak "Robin Hood"

Slovaks blocking and thinning beets near Corunna.
Library of Congress

S.S. Bremen

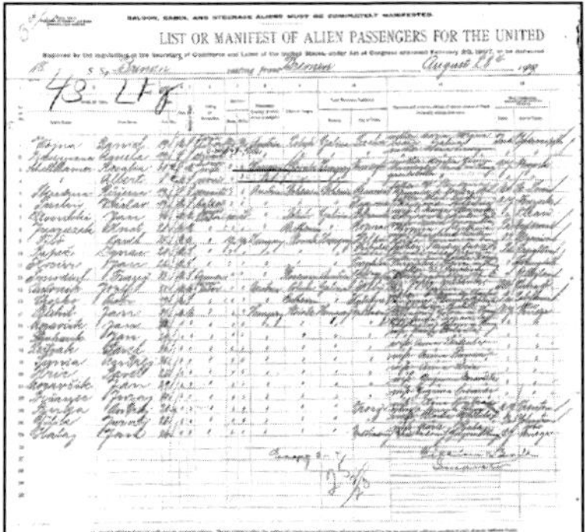
LIST OR MANIFEST OF ALIEN PASSENGERS FOR THE UNITED

Manifest, S.S. Bremen, September 1909
Jan Kocur, line 11

LIST OF UNITED STATES CITIZENS

Manifest, S.S. America, December 1923
Margaret Kocur, line 26

Ellis Island Great Hall circa 1907.
"National Park Service: Statue of Liberty National Monument"

Plate Glass Factory Tarentum, PA.
Carnegie Library of Pittsburgh

Camp Greenleaf, GA May 1918

WWI troop ship circa 1918

U.S. Ambulances at the front

U.S. Ambulances loading the wounded

Jan Kocur circa June, 1918

Memorial Day Parade. Jan Kocur 2nd from right

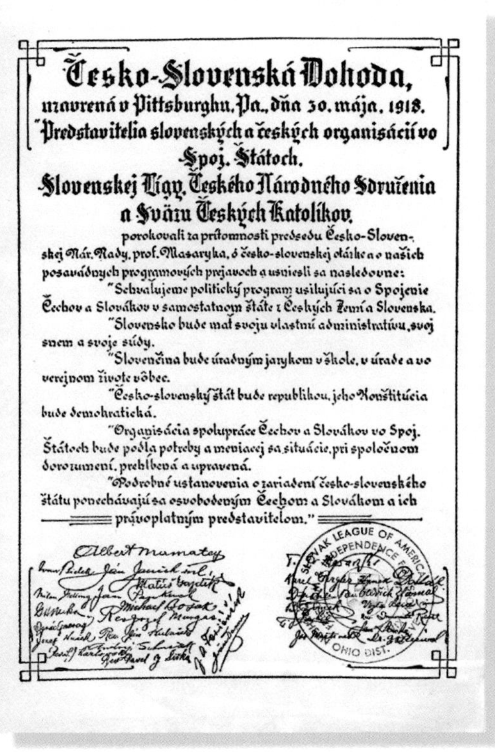

Česko-Slovenská Dohoda,

uzavrená v Pittsburghu, Pa., dňa 30. mája, 1918.

"Predstavitelia slovenských a českých organisácií vo Spoj. Štátoch.

Slovenskej Lígy, Českého Národného Sdruženia a Sväzu Českých Katolíkov,

porokovali za prítomnosti predsedu Česko-Slovenskej Nár. Rady, prof. Masaryka, o česko-slovenskej otázke a o našich posavádnych programových prejavoch a usniesli sa nasledovne:

"Schvalujeme politický program usilujúci sa o Spojenie Čechov a Slovákov v samostatnom štáte z Českých Zemí a Slovenska.

"Slovensko bude mať svoju vlastnú administratívu, svoj snem a svoje súdy.

"Slovenčina bude úradným jazykom v škole, v úrade a vo verejnom živote vôbec.

"Česko-slovenský štát bude republikou, jeho Konštitúcia bude demokratická.

"Organisácia spolupráce Čechov a Slovákov vo Spoj. Štátoch bude podľa potreby a meniacej sa situácie, pri spoločnom dorozumení, prehĺbená a upravená.

"Podrobné ustanovenia o zariadení česko-slovenského štátu ponechávajú sa osvobodeným Čechom a Slovákom a ich právoplatným predstaviteľom."



Pittsburgh Agreement May 30, 1918

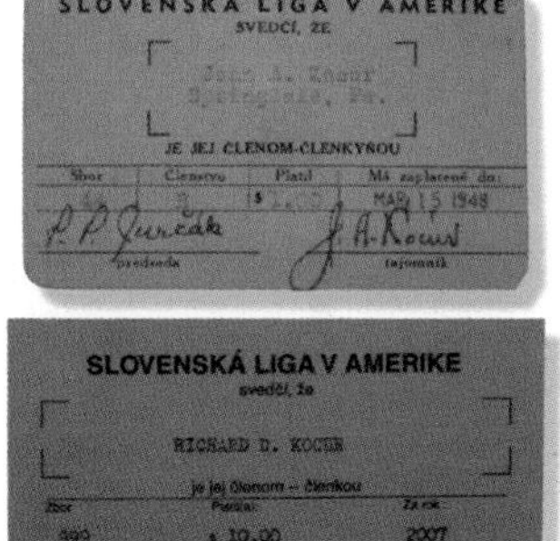


Slovak League Membership Cards
Jan Kocur 1948 (top), Richard Kocur, Jr. 2007

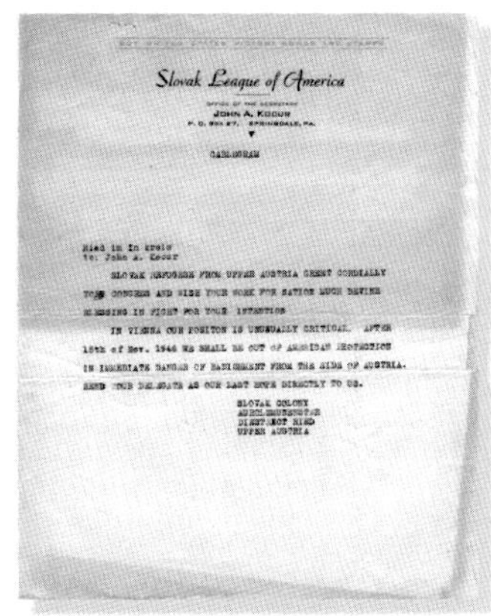

Slovak League of America

JOHN A. KOCUR

CABLEGRAM

Ried im Innkreis
to: John A. Kocur

SLOVAK REFUGEES FROM UPPER AUSTRIA GREET CORDIALLY YOUR CONGRESS AND WISH YOUR WORK FOR NATION MUCH DEVINE BLESSING IN FIGHT FOR YOUR INTENTION

IN VIENNA OUR POSITON IS UNUSUALLY CRITICAL. AFTER 15th of Nov. 1946 WE SHALL BE OUT OF AMERICAN PROTECTION IN IMMEDIATE DANGER OF BANISHMENT FROM THE SIDE OF AUSTRIA. SEND YOUR DELEGATE AS OUR LAST HOPE DIRECTLY TO US.

SLOVAK COLONY
[illegible]
DISTRICT RIED
UPPER AUSTRIA

Cablegram concerning Slovak refugees from Upper Austria

Slovak League Members, Washington DC circa 1925
Jan Kocur, Back row, 3rd left

Slovak League Congress Detroit, Michigan 1926
Jan Kocur, Front row center

Jan Kocur (left) Father J. J. Lach (right)

Jan Kocur
June 1918

Margaret Kocur
June 1918

Kocur Family circa 1944 L to R (Back) Margaret, Jan, Amelia, (Front) Richard, Vera. Missing John Jr.

Kocur children clockwise Amelia (Standing), Vera, Richard "Teddy" the dog

Margaret and daughter Vera

Kocur children clockwise Amelia, John, Richard, Vera

## Chapter 12

# HOMEWARD BOUND

# Chapter 12

November 12, 1918: the Great War was over. For the American troops involved in the conflict, World War I had been an intense but relatively short affair, lasting a little more than a year for most. For the rest of Europe, however, the end of the war marked the close of nearly five years of continuous killing and bloodshed that cut down nearly a generation of young men from France, England, Russia, and Germany. The past five years had changed the way wars were fought, introduced new and more deadly means of killing, and had taken the national structure of traditional European powers and turned them on their ear. The war had destroyed countless cities, villages, and homes and had left a swath of destruction and millions of dollars in damages across half of Europe. In addition to the human cost, political upheaval, and material damage of the war, the political and social consequences of the peace helped to set the stage for the next act in Europe's destructive play with the curtain set to rise on a new stage of players some twenty years later.

For the men of the American Seventh Division the end of the war triggered the immediate thought of any soldier in any era. When will we be going home? The good news for the Seventh Division, Ambulance Company 36, and John Kocur was that, luckily, they would not be part of any army of occupation called upon to enter and secure Germany. The bad news was that for some in the ambulance company, the wheels of army efficiency turned slowly and plenty of time would pass before the army saw fit to return them home.

For the rest of the month of November 1918, the men in Ambulance Company 36 remained in Jaulny, France, the same place they occupied when the armistice was signed. Private John Kocur and his fellow soldiers were housed in the Chateau de Jaulny and surrounding outbuildings. The chateau had been used as a German hospital before it was taken by the American army and a large amount of refuse was found all over the grounds and in the dugouts and rooms of the chateau.[1] At this station, Jaulny, Ambulance Company 36 evacuated men from the 64th Infantry, although at a rate that paled by comparison to the pre-armistice days of October 1918.

Ambulance Company 36 would remain in France for nearly six more months, until the mid-summer of 1919, performing support roles for the division's infantry units, salvaging and organizing equipment and material, and conducting standard training exercises. Private John Kocur, however, would not be among those in the company who remained on foreign soil. According to the December 1918 monthly roster of Ambulance Company 36, Private John Kocur was transferred to another assignment on December 13, 1918. Kocur was to join the 15th Company, 4th Training Battalion, 153rd Depot Brigade. Christmas came early to Private Kocur and his transfer meant that he was to immediately return to the United States and take up his new assignment with his new unit at Camp Dix, New Jersey.

John Kocur began his journey back to the U.S. where he started his European war experience, from the port of Brest, France and once again made his way back across the Atlantic, the fifth such trip of his life. Kocur was likely aboard a troop transport ship heading for the states, but unlike his journey to France a few months earlier, the ship was most likely not packed with soldiers. With only a month since the official end of the war, the army had not had the time to completely re-assign all the troops required for occupation and it is unlikely that troops in any large number would have already been bound for home. John Kocur was one of the lucky soldiers assigned to duty back in the United States well before most other American troops, including those in his own ambulance company. It could be that this was the result of a simple luck of the draw, it could be that John Kocur was selected to participate in a brigade that, as a part of the Camp Dix troop compliment, helped to train other medical units, or that he was selected to return to the states for reasons that related to his health. No records exist which specify why the transfer occurred but only that as of mid-December 1918, Kocur was on a ship bound for home.

The Atlantic crossing from France to the United States was one in which ships often encountered some stretch of bad weather, especially in the winter months. Given that Kocur's crossing occurred in late December and early January the weather most likely kept the men below deck where they engaged in activities like playing cards and telling stories. The experiences the soldiers shared provided them with an endless supply of material from which to spin their tales; and their memories were just clouded enough to stretch even the most mundane service into gallant and heroic acts.

After a ten- to fourteen-day Atlantic crossing and landing in Philadelphia, Private Kocur entrained for the short ride to Camp Dix, Jew Jersey. Camp Dix was named in honor of Maj. Gen. John Adams Dix, U. S. V., who served as Secretary of the Treasury under President Buchanan.[2] The camp was established in the summer of 1917 to serve as a training camp for the 78th Division, National Army. After May 1918 it was used as an embarkation camp, organizing men prior to their shipment overseas. In 1919 Dix was turned into a demobilization center and out-processed service personnel from the army back to civilian life.

Camp Dix had a troop capacity of 42,806, contained 1,414 buildings and covered an area of 6,848 acres.[3] Among the camp's permanent compliment of troops, including medical, ordinance, engineer, and supply troops, was the 153rd Depot Brigade, John Kocur's new outfit. The 153rd Depot Brigade was composed of nine separate training battalions; John Kocur's being the 4th Training Battalion. As part of the camp's permanent contingent of troops, the depot brigades performed various functions including demobilization processing of troops arriving back in the United States, training functions, and standard camp administrative duties. When John Kocur arrived early in 1919 the bulk of the troops who passed through Camp Dix on their way out of the army had not yet arrived. Kocur likely took part in performing routine duties associated with the depot brigades' role in the camp. Regardless of the duties performed, one thing was for certain, John Kocur was back in America away from the theater of war. No more would Private Kocur be called to the front to help wounded and dying American soldiers, aid the wounded in an ambulance bouncing over rutted French roads, or be exposed to enemy artillery fire or exploding gas shells. No longer would he spend his days in a muddy, water logged trench or his nights in a drafty barn or bombed out building. John Kocur's duty now, however strenuous, was always concluded at day's end with a hot meal in a mess hall and under a warm blanket with a roof over his head.

Private Kocur's stay at Camp Dix only lasted a few months. As the winter months neared their end and spring was just on the horizon, Kocur was discharged from his service in the United States Army. On March 31, 1919 at Camp Dix New Jersey, John Kocur once again became a private citizen as he was mustered out of the service by Captain W.E. Maddux, commanding officer of the 15th Company, 4th Battalion, 153rd Depot Brigade. Upon discharge it was noted that Kocur had enlisted on May 24, 1918 in New Kensington, Pennsylvania; he was listed as being five feet, four inches tall with light brown hair and a medium complexion. Kocur had not qualified as a marksman, or received a gunner rating, not surprising given the role he played during the conflict; he had not received any specific horsemanship training but had received his Typhoid and Paratyphoid prophylaxis. John Kocur's discharge papers also confirmed his participation in the St. Mihiel offensive during the fall of 1918; his character was noted as "Excellent" with the remarks that his "Service was honest and faithful." Also of importance to John Kocur as he prepared to return to home to Arnold, Pennsylvania was that he was paid in full in the amount of $152.00 and was allotted his rifle. Even through World War I, soldiers often kept possession of their arms as well as their uniforms and in Kocur's case both accompanied him home.

The train ride from New Jersey back to Pittsburgh most likely gave John Kocur the time to think and reflect on the events of the previous year. The past twelve months had included Kocur's enlistment in New Kensington, training in Georgia, and service in France. In that short span of time John Kocur had traveled more, seen more, and experienced more than he had in all the previous years of his life; he had seen the effects of war on the individual soldiers he tried to help as well as on the French civilians and their towns and villages across the countryside. Private John Kocur's service, like the service and sacrifice of thousands of Slovaks in the United States, had demonstrated his pride and patriotism in being an American. Kocur had played a part in the defeat of Germany and more importantly Austria-Hungary, nations which played a part in the oppressive rule of his native land and fellow Slovaks for centuries.

Although John Kocur had accomplished much during his service in the United States Army it is clear that some uncertainty still remained. First and foremost, what would be the immediate or long-term effect of the wound Kocur sustained as the result of being exposed to poison gas? Would his ability to work, earn, and support himself in the coming years be affected? What would become of his wife, Margeta Kocur, still at home in Podvysoka, Slovakia? Austria-Hungary, the former ruler of the Slovak lands, had been defeated in the war but would the new rulers, whoever they might be, be worse? Would the living conditions for Margeta and her family in an already impoverished area be made worse by the post-war disorganization and lack of government leadership and national infrastructure? Back in the United States, would the Slovak immigrants be given more of a voice or shown more respect as a result of their participation in the U.S. Army? Would causes like immigration, job conditions, and the independence of the Slovak native land be given serious attention? John Kocur could only wonder; he did not have the answers to these questions as only time would reveal their course. Kocur would travel home to Western Pennsylvania and pick up his life where he left off. The barbershop would be waiting. Given John Kocur's accomplishments and contributions in life up to that point, most outside observers would say that he had done his part and achieved much. Kocur's principles, however, not only continued to serve as his guide on living his life but they would also push him to a new level of contribution. Over time Kocur's exposure to the principles of American independence and self-determination had lifted him from being a laborer in a glass factory to an independent businessman; he had fought to rid the world, and by extension his homeland, of the Austro-Hungarian empire and thus bring freedom and independence to his fellow Slovaks. Realizing what he had as a citizen of the United States of America and what his fellow countrymen across the ocean lacked, John Kocur's return from the army marked the beginning of a new battle. Kocur's life would now become focused on the support of the Slovak people here in the United States and in their continuing struggle for freedom and independence in their native land. That battle would begin when John Kocur's train pulled into the station at Arnold.

**Endnotes**

1. *Fell, Edgar T. ; History of the Seventh Division, pg 228. 1927*
2. *U.S. Government; Order of Battle of the United States Land Forces in the World War, pg 723. 1931.*
3. *Ibid, 724.*

# Chapter 13

# ARMISTICE AND OPPORTUNITY

# Chapter 13

Nearly fifty years before the end of World War I the pendulum of an historical conflict between France and a then-confederation of German territories led by Prussia had clearly swung in favor of the Germans, and they were determined to make the French pay. As the decade of the 1870's began, the Franco-Prussian war was going badly for the French. By late October 1870, with the siege of Paris dragging on, the Prussian army chose a site outside of Paris as its headquarters. It was once the traditional seat of the French government, occupied by kings, queens, and the multitudes of the royal court. Its halls once housed priceless art and ornate décor. Its grounds were immaculately groomed and its gardens impeccably cared for. What once was the focal point of French aristocracy was now the center of power for the French adversaries, the Prussians. It was the Palace at Versailles and it would come to hold significant symbolic value to both the French and the Germans for the next fifty years.

The French King Louis XIV officially established the royal court and the center of the French government at Versailles in 1682. Once a royal hunting lodge, Versailles became one of the largest palaces in the world and served French monarchs until the French Revolution. King Louis XIV's motives for the palace were both selfish and practical. First, he wanted a personal legacy and what better symbol of power than the largest palace in Europe. Second, by moving the court and French government to Versailles he could gain greater control of the government from the nobility and distance himself from the population of Paris. The palace contained all government offices as well as the homes of thousands of courtiers and all the attendant functionaries of court. Nobles were required to spend time each year at Versailles which, the king believed, prevented them from developing their own regional power and kept them from countering his efforts to centralize the French government in an absolute monarchy. No French palace or king, however, could resist the will of the people forever. In July of 1789, the Palace at Versailles was stormed by angry crowds from Paris who ended not only the lives of their monarchs, but also put an end to the symbolic nature of Versailles as the center of the French monarchy.

In 1871, nearly a century after the destruction of the French monarchy, the Palace at Versailles was used by the Prussians in a way which left an indelible mark on the French psyche. Not only was it the headquarters of the Prussian army, but in the famous hall of mirrors on January 18, 1871 the Prussian King Wilhelm I was proclaimed German emperor and the German Empire was founded. Following the end of World War I the palace would again play a central role in establishing the terms of peace and the French would be motivated by the memory of the Franco-Prussian war as well as the still- smoldering memory of World War I. It is no coincidence, then, that forty-eight years to the day after the ascension of Wilhelm I to the German throne in the hall of mirrors that on January 18, 1919 the Palace of Versailles played host to the opening of the Paris peace conference. The hall also played host to the signing of the Treaty of Versailles on June 28, 1919 exactly five years after the assassination of Archduke Franz Ferdinand. The French had an eye for symbolism.

When the Paris peace conference began in early 1919, John Kocur was still stationed at Camp Dix, New Jersey serving with the 153rd Depot Brigade. By the early stage of the peace negotiations in March 1919 Kocur was on his way back to Arnold, Pennsylvania and civilian life. John Kocur had completed nearly a year in the U.S. Army fighting to help defeat Germany and, more importantly to Kocur, Austria-Hungary. By joining the fight against the Austro-Hungarian Empire, John Kocur contributed to the downfall of rulers who had oppressed him and his fellow native Slovaks in their own homeland. Upon his return to Arnold, however, Kocur soon realized that while the military fight may have ended, the fight for Slovak independence and self-determination was just beginning; and just as in the case of his military service, John Kocur would not wait to be "drafted" for this fight either. Within a year of returning to the United States, Kocur was back on the front lines fighting for his countrymen; this time in the legions of the Slovak League of America, using his intellect as his ammunition and the pen as his weapon.

The world was watching as the peace negotiations began in January 1919 on French soil. The difficulties in negotiating a peace that was acceptable to all parties involved quickly became apparent. With Germany excluded from the negotiating table the task ultimately fell to the main allied partners of France, England, and the United States. The main objective of the French, having lost some 1.5 million military personnel, an estimated 400,000 civilians, and millions of dollars of property, was to impose a settlement that was deliberately meant to cripple Germany militarily, politically, and economically. The English supported reparations for military and economic losses but to a lesser extent than the French. The British Prime Minister, Lloyd George, was aware that if the demands made by France were carried out, France could become the most powerful force on the continent, and a delicate allied balance of power could be unsettled. In addition, Germany was once England's largest trade partner, so the destruction of the German economy was not in England's best interest. Finally, the Americans took a more conciliatory view toward the issue of German reparations and wanted to ensure the success of future trading opportunities in order to collect on its European debt. In addition, President Woodrow Wilson had put forth terms which would, he believed, help to prevent future wars. These policies were known as Wilson's Fourteen Points, which he delivered in a speech to the Paris peace conference.

The difficulty the three allied powers faced was that their objectives for a lasting peace were at odds with one another: France, focused on exacting revenge and reparations from Germany; England, wanting to preserve her powerful empire and position in Europe; and America, looking to take the opportunity to install higher level political principles into practice. The final agreement, while containing a portion of what each party wanted, was not seen by any of the three as having gone far enough toward what each originally had set out to accomplish. Under the terms of the Treaty of Versailles Germany would be forced to accept full responsibility for the war and be held accountable for all the damage done to the civilian population of the allies.[1] The German military, including its navy, was drastically reduced. German industry was also prohibited from the ongoing manufacture, import, and export of weapons and poison gas. Germany was also ordered to pay reparations to the allies in the form of hard currency (gold), as well as in a variety of other forms including coal, steel, intellectual property and agricultural products. Reparations included these industrial items due in no small part to the economic impact of draining Germany of her currency supply. The Treaty of Versailles also provided for the creation of Wilson's League of Nations, designed to arbitrate international disputes and thereby avoid future wars. A final term contained in the Treaty of Versailles, and one which was closely watched by a number of ethnic populations in the United States, including Slovaks, was the cessation of colonies and European territory forced upon Germany and Austria-Hungary. The reorganization of Europe had been a particularly important topic among Slovaks, Czechs, Poles, and others being ruled by Germany and Austria-Hungary. The Treaty would remove the control these former rulers had over ethnic lands, but the reorganization would not turn out to be the ideal solution for all peoples involved.

Even before the World War had officially come to a close it had become increasingly clear that Germany and Austria-Hungary would be defeated by the allies. Germany would certainly be affected by the negotiated peace in both land and treasure, but what of her ally Austria-Hungary? Prior to and during the war, the Austro-Hungarian Empire included Austria, Hungary and the lands of smaller ethnic groups including the Czechs and Slovaks. For Slovaks in the United States the defeat of their former masters was thought to represent a golden opportunity to gain the independence and self-rule they had sought for years. This effort was bolstered by statements from none other than the president of the United States who in his a message to

Congress in early 1917 emphasized, "the rights of nations, great and small, and the privilege of men everywhere to choose their way of life and obedience." Slovaks in Hungary, due to years of oppression and systematic dismantling of their culture, lacked even the smallest degree of political and social organization necessary to facilitate the creation of their own state. It was left to the Slovaks in the United States then to bring about the change so long desired by their countrymen.

In anticipation of the end of the war and an allied victory, the liberation of the Slovak people began to command the focus of Slovak-Americans. As the movement for liberation became more certain, the more vociferously did the adherents of Czechoslovakism push Slovaks and Czechs together.[2] The interests of the Slovak peoples, both in the U.S. and in the Slovak homeland, were represented by the Slovak League of America. The interests of the Czechs were represented by organizations like the Bohemian National Alliance and led by Thomas G. Massaryk. As Massaryk positioned the cause of the creation of a Czecho-Slovak state he came to the United States to galvanize the support of Czechs and also of Slovaks. In order to ensure that Slovaks were supportive of his plans, he reached out to the Slovak League as a necessary partner. As a way to formalize the commitment of the Czech and Slovak people to establish a new independent nation, Massaryk and his colleagues drafted and signed the Pittsburgh Agreement on May 30, 1918 in Pittsburgh.

The Pittsburgh Agreement was to have guaranteed to the Slovak people a separate administration, judiciary, and parliament; and Slovak was to be the official language in the schools and in public offices throughout the Slovak homeland. The details of organization were left to the Slovaks and Czechs in Europe.[3] To millions of Slovaks the words of the Pittsburgh Agreement were sacred and amounted to the definition of their principles of freedom and self-determination. Counted among these was John Kocur, who had fought for the deliverance of these principles through his service in the U.S. Army during the Great War and through his service in the Slovak League.

The importance of the Pittsburgh Agreement and its principles in the formation of a Czecho-Slovak Republic to John Kocur are clear as he wrote, "The formation of the Czecho-Slovak Republic was received by the people of Slovakia with great joy. It meant the severance of the ties of vassalage which held them bound to the autocratic and feudalistic Hungarian Kingdom for more than a thousand years. It was the promise of a new free life within a state in the building of which they were to be co-partners with the Czechs."[4]

As the allied powers deliberated during the spring of 1919, the issue of the new nation, Czecho-Slovakia, was addressed and settled in a manner benefiting the more politically astute Czechs. The Slovaks were not represented at the Paris Peace Conference by any Slovak politician or committee designated to speak on behalf of their needs. Instead, the Slovak people were drawn in to the new nation in the wake of the Czech politicians' actions in establishing a Czechoslovak nation. One only needs to look at the spelling of the name Czechoslovak to note the difference in how the political union was brought into being by the Czechs versus how Slovaks believed it should be established; Czechoslovak, one word, versus Czecho-Slovak, with the hyphen consciously and deliberately added. On the one hand the Czechs saw the political union of the two countries as a melding of two into one. The Slovaks saw the union as a relationship between two distinct and separate entities bound by the need for political and social cooperation. Slovaks had to look no further for evidence as to how the new political arrangement would work than the principles outlined in the Pittsburgh Agreement.

Unfortunately for the Slovak people the overriding needs of the "Czechoslovak" people were first and foremost at the Paris Peace Conference. Edvard Beneš, a Czech, and his colleagues spoke on behalf of the new nation while the interests of Slovaks fell to the wayside. The Slovaks were not mentioned in the constitution of the Czechoslovak Republic, which referred only to Czechoslovak people.[5] At the time of the formation of the new republic, Czechs greatly outnumbered Slovaks and represented a majority in all government organizations. The government denied the existence of a separate Slovak nationality, claimed that the Slovak language was only a dialect of the Czech language, and sought to absorb the Slovaks in to a Czech-centered culture. As it looked to many Slovaks in their homeland and in the United States, the Slovak people had simply traded one master, the Hungarians, for another, the Czechs.

There is no doubt that John Kocur, now back in the United States after serving in the U.S. Army and helping bring freedom to his homeland, watched these events unfold with great interest. Since returning to Arnold, Kocur had become more actively involved in the Slovak League of America, the singular voice of Slovaks in the United States and, increasingly, abroad. John Kocur's passion for the cause of Slovak freedom, independence and self-determination was no doubt born during his youth in a land then under Hungarian control. It was manifest in his U.S. military service, which helped to defeat the Austro-Hungarian Empire, and it would now continue in his service to the Slovak League.

John Kocur was elected secretary of the Slovak League of America in 1920, only one year after returning from the military. At age 33, the newly appointed secretary wasted no time in establishing himself as a forceful proponent of Slovak independence. The principles of the Pittsburgh Agreement were, to him, *the* guideposts to the freedom of those still in the Slovak homeland. If theses principles were to be ignored by the new Czechoslovak government, Kocur would use his position in the most influential Slovak organization of the time to ensure that the rest of the world not let the promises made to his people be forgotten. In addition to his position as secretary, responsible for all official League communication, Kocur would also use his intellect and communication skills to help get the message of Slovak freedom out to the public.

It was during the Paris Peace Conference in 1920 that events began to unfold that would prompt John Kocur to issue, on behalf of the Slovak League of America, the first of his many public statements on the rights of the Slovak people. As the negotiations went on, the Council of Ambassadors of the Allied Supreme Council put forth a decision that two Slovak districts, those of Orava and Spiš, were to be awarded to Poland in exchange for the industrial district of Tesin, which the Czechs gained. When a Slovak representative named Andre Hlinka failed to even be admitted to the Paris conference to plead the Slovaks' case, the only champion left to voice concern over this injustice was the Slovak League of America. The newly appointed secretary, John Kocur, along with the league's president, Ivan Bielek, were charged with appealing for justice. Kocur and Bielek did so in a memorandum written in September 1920 and their appeal went directly to the president of the United States. As secretary, it is likely that Kocur penned most of the document. Rational in argument, clear in purpose, and using the previously stated positions of the president himself as justification of the Slovak position, the memorandum is an eloquent example of John Kocur's ability to communicate his passion for the idea of freedom for his homeland. The following is the memorandum from the Slovak League of America to President Woodrow Wilson on the issue of the Slovak lands annexed to Poland and in a larger sense the issue of Slovak freedom and independence:

*To His Excellency, Woodrow Wilson, President, U.S.A., Washington, D.C.*

*Mr. President:*

*Please permit the Slovak League of America, a patriotic organization which proved during the Great War not only by its activities, but also by its sacrifices in money and blood, that it is deserving of a charter issued by one of the States of this great republic, to call to your kind attention the last ruling of the Council of Ambassadors of the Allied Supreme Council, dated at Spaa, Belgium, July 27, 1920, which is directly opposed to the fundamental conceptions of true American Democracy, the noble and supreme democratic and humanitarian principles on which rests the foundation of this great mother of republics and which you, Mr. President, as the representative of this great and liberty loving nation so forcefully expressed in your historic Message to Congress on April 2, 1917, wherein among other ideas you also emphasized the following: "We are glad, now that we see the facts with no veil of false pretense about them, to fight thus for ultimate peace of the world and for the liberation of its peoples, the German peoples included, for the rights of nations great and small, and the privilege of men everywhere to choose their way of life and obedience.*

*The Council of Ambassadors of the Allied Supreme Council decided against this principle of self determination, so beautifully and strongly expressed by you, Mr. President, by awarding to Poland, without a plebiscite and against the wish and will of the people affected by it, territory of the Counties Orava and Spiš, in Slovakia, which is a part of the Czecho-Slovak republic and which territory consists of twenty-six villages with from twenty-five to thirty thousand inhabitants. This territory formed at no time in its history a part of the Polish Kingdom, but was since time immemorial an integral part of Slovakia, and the population of its territory, according to authentic reports, voluntarily and of its own accord, expressed by a vote of preponderant majority and unanimously, that it does not desire to belong to the republic of Poland and under the sovereignty of the Polish Government of a Feudal Oligarchy which is republican in name only, that it does not desire to be torn away from its own motherland whose integral part it had been since times immemorial, and where reigns sovereignty of the citizen and civic equality.*

*The Council of Ambassadors ruled in this manner in spite of the fact that the Allied Supreme Council decided upon the motion of the United States to settle this question by a plebiscite, and regardless of the fact that, according to our information, the United States even now, and that rightfully, insists on the originally adopted motion.*

*The people of Schleswig-Holstein were granted the right to decide by a popular vote whether it wants to belong to a neutral country – to Denmark, or remain with Germany, but that part of the Slovak people who by its own contributions, goodwill, sacrifices in money and blood, in every part of the world, on all battlefields, had struggled for its own liberation and for an Allied victory, that part of the Slovak people had been denied this Supreme Natural Right. The Entente denied it this right for the sole reason of appeasing the avarice of a stronger nation for territory to which it had no claim, neither by law of precedent nor by any natural right.*

*To us, who are American citizens of Slovak descent, the principle of self- determination was, is, and will be sacred. We conceive it in the sense as taught by the Declaration of Independence of this great republic in the sense as you, Mr. President, have voiced it in the name of this great nation in several historical and memorable messages before the entrance of this country into the war; before signing of peace and thereafter.*

*For this very reason we are conscious of the fact that the ruling of the Council of Ambassadors is the grossest injustice on a defenseless people, committed by those, who during the war adopted the inspiring slogans of the United States and who are now, by their acts, dragging them in the dust. Therefore, we as American citizens, whose daily credo are the Declaration of Independence and all the inspiring ideals of this great republic, take leave to call your kind attention to this gross act of injustice and earnestly appeal to you that the United States remain firm on its original demand for the holding of a plebiscite in order to avoid becoming, even though unwillingly, a partner of the Entente in this fatal error and injustice committed on a loyal allied people. We emphasize the latter because the ruling of the Council of Ambassadors became a fact by the consent of the representative of the Czecho-Slovak republic, who submitted to this ruling by force of circumstances and under duress without having obtained the preliminary assent of the Czecho-Slovak National Assembly.*

*We emphasize it, because only eleven members of the Permanent Committee on Foreign Affairs of the National Assembly, against ten opposed, expressed their consent with this procedure; because the so called Czecho-Slovak National Council, composed of intellectuals of all political parties, voiced its discontent with the ruling of the Council of*

*Ambassadors; because the majority of the Press is opposed to it and particularly because those Slovak people who are most directly affected by this ruling have preferred rather to abandon their property and the graves of their ancestors and parents than remain under the sovereignty of Poland.*

*Finally, as loyal Americans citizens, we believe that even though this absolutely unjust ruling of the Council of Ambassadors would be ratified by the present Czecho-Slovak government, it cannot be ratified and put in to effect with the consent of the United States which, being loyal to its fundamental ideas and noble traditions, never will consent to such ruthless trammeling of human rights, the right to self determination, to a denial of the right to any people to choose their way of life and obedience.*

*Trusting that you will give this sincere appeal of American citizens your kind attention, an appeal which is dictated only by our love to this great republic and nation; that you will remain firm in your original demand for a plebiscite and will use your beneficial influential to right this wrong, we remain, Mr. President,*

*Respectfully yours,*

*Slovak League of America*

*Pittsburgh, PA*

*Sept. 18, 1920*

*John A. KocurIvan Bielek*

*SecretaryPresident*

The pleas of the Slovak League to diplomats, U.S. government officials, and Czech politicians with regard to Slovak territories being ceded to Poland fell on deaf ears. In fact, Andre Hlinka, who rushed to the peace conference to plead the case for the Slovak people being affected by this decision, was arrested by Czech officials upon his return to his homeland, imprisoned by the Czechoslovak government for daring to represent the Slovak nation personally.[6] For John Kocur and the rest of the Slovak League of America this event brought to light just how difficult the fight for true Slovak independence was to be. Not only did they have to overcome disinterest among the international community but had to once again try and wrest control of their own destiny from the very rulers that now controlled their land, life, and liberty.

The Slovaks in the United States watched the developments within their former homeland with keen interest. They had, in a sense, made the creation of the new state possible by supporting the allied war effort both monetarily and militarily. Politically, they also had the belief that when the new nation came in to existence the needs of their Slovak brothers would be addressed as promised in the Pittsburgh Agreement, signed by Thomas Massaryk, now the president of the Czechoslovak republic. When Massaryk formally became President, however, his attitude and programs completely disregarded the concept of a federation and his objectives reverted to the revival of the Czech state now enlarged by the inclusion of Slovakia.[7]

The Slovaks were not mentioned in the Constitution of the Czecho-Slovak Republic, which refers only to a Czechoslovak people. Thus, even the rights and privileges guaranteed to the minorities were not granted to the nation whose collaboration had made the existence of the new republic possible.[8] It is true that soon after the formation of the republic, cultural life in Slovakia gained a new impetus. The Slovak Cultural Society, closed by the Magyar government, was reopened and began widespread activity. Schools were re-opened and new ones built.[9] For the most part, however, these gestures on the part of the Czech-dominated government were meant only to appease the Slovak people.

John Kocur, as secretary of the Slovak League, continued to push for improvements in the new Czechoslovak republic through as many official channels as possible. The league took on the mantle of responsibility for this action due to the position of influence it held among American Slovaks, its financial resources and the close ties many of its executive members had to the highest officials in the Czechoslovak government.

Over the course of several years in the early 1920s the Slovak League of America made multiple appeals to the Prague government, issued memoranda, and even went so far as to appoint a delegation to visit "liberated" Slovakia to help implement improvements. Central to all of these formal appeals and statements was the desire to see the principles of the Pittsburgh Agreement incorporated into the constitution of the new Czechoslovak Republic. The agreement, the majority of the Slovak people believed, represented principles of Slovak freedom and self-determination and was a commitment on behalf of Czech political representatives to make an independent Slovakia a reality. For John Kocur, having come from a Slovakia where Hungarian domination had sought to virtually eliminate Slovak culture, the principles of the Pittsburgh Agreement were the only real path to independence and he was determined to make them real.

When the Czechoslovak constitution was voted on and approved by the new government, a government in which Czechs held the majority, the document not only failed to make provision for Slovakia's home rule but it did not even mention the existence of the Pittsburgh Agreement.[10] The Slovak League of America felt betrayed and outraged by this course of developments.[11] League executive members, including John Kocur, demanded that the Pittsburgh Agreement be made a part of the constitution that would govern their brothers and sisters in the Slovak homeland. This work culminated in a document authored by Kocur and Ivan Bielek that appealed directly to the National Assembly of the Czechoslovak Republic. In it the Slovak League made its strongest statement yet on what a majority of Slovaks in the U.S. and abroad believed to be the right course for achieving independence for the long-suffering Slovak people. The arguments made over the years were succinctly summed up by Kocur and Bielek in one of the document's closing passages:

> *We appeal, therefore, in the first place to the Slovak members of the National Assembly regardless of their affiliation with political parties, to adopt our request and take the initiative for the filing of a legislative bill for the supplementary incorporation of the Pittsburgh Agreement in its full contents and without whatever disparaging clauses or comments, into the constitution of the Czecho-Slovak Republic, and to the National Assembly and the government of the same to endeavor at the eleventh hour to satisfy the bilateral agreement, the obligation of honor, which was drafted by the president of the first Czecho-Slovak Revolutionary Government beyond the frontiers, Professor Thomas G. Massaryk, and which he signed when already elected first president and creator of the Czecho-Slovak Republic.*
>
> *We feel that it is our duty to emphasize that if our sincere and friendly attempt, which has at its heart the welfare, interest and future of the Republic, should fail to meet with success, the Slovak League of America would not be able to prevent American Slovaks and their factors from turning to the Court of Public Opinion of the civilized world on behalf of their natural demands, evolving on the one hand from uprightly and honestly acquired rights and on the other hand from the bilateral agreement, the Pittsburgh Agreement in order to satisfy, in case of utmost necessity the conscience and the promises made to the nation and people during the revolution, and the sacrifices evolved there from.*

Kocur and Bielek's pleas were met with silence. Prague was insensitive to the matter. Disregarding the formal petition, the authorities chose to instead spend their energies on breaking the determination of the Slovak League of America to work for attaining Slovak autonomy.[12] The Czech politicians schemed to promote anti-Slovak interests both in the Czechoslovak republic as well as in the United States; they sought to discredit the Slovak League of America and its officers; they even went so far as to intimidate concerned Slovaks with the threat of Magyar revisionism.[13] In one of the more desperate attempts by the Prague government, the very existence of the Pittsburgh Agreement was called into question; it was called a "falsification" by then President Massaryk. John Kocur and others in the Slovak League knew the agreement existed and continued to use it as a guide for their actions. With the league under attack from abroad and the very existence of the document central to its arguments called into question, the Slovak League went so far as to conceal the original Pittsburgh Agreement in the attic of Kocur's Springdale, Pennsylvania, home during some of the more tumultuous times.

The Slovak League of America weathered all this storm and fury without yielding its stand or relenting its indomitable attitude about accepted principles for establishing the republic of Czecho-Slovakia.[14] As the decade of the 1920s wore on, the Slovak League continued in its efforts on behalf of Slovaks everywhere. Not only was the battle with the Czechoslovak government ongoing but social conditions and attitudes for Slovaks in the United States were changing. After the massive waves of immigration in the early 1900s, ethnic groups were coming under increased scrutiny. Second-generation Slovak Americans had begun to come of age with no concept of their parents' life in the old country, a necessity to speak English first, and a sense of belonging to the American culture. The Slovak League began to fight what amounted to be a two-front war for the rights and freedoms of Slovaks everywhere, including those already in the United States. Executive officers of the Slovak League changed over the years as the issues of the day ebbed and flowed. One constant in the leadership of the league during this time, however, was John Kocur, still serving in the post as secretary. Kocur's principles never wavered and his focus on what was important to Slovaks everywhere never faltered. Karol Sidor in his chapter titled, "The Slovak Nation's Struggle for Autonomy" found in *Sixty Years of the Slovak League of America* summed up Kocur's role and impact to the League. Sidor wrote, "When the presidents were unable to devote full time to the Slovak League, it was the gallant secretary, Jan Kocur, who performed all the necessary tasks with devotion and ability, and kept the embers glowing in the old glorious tradition of self-government and autonomy for Slovakia."

## Endnotes

1. *Treaty of Versailles – Article 231, "War Guilt Clause"*
2. *Sidor, Karol; The Slovak Nation's Struggle for Autonomy: Sixty Years of the Slovak League, pg 52. 1967.*
3. *F.J. Dubosh and J. A. Kocur; The Slovaks and Their Right to Nationhood, pg 6. 1944*
4. *Ibid.*
5. *Ibid, pg 8.*
6. *Sidor, Karol; The Slovak Nation's Struggle for Autonomy: Sixty Years of the Slovak League, pg 61. 1967.*
7. *Mikus, Joseph A. The Slovak League of America: A Historical Survey; pg 45. 19XX*
8. *F.J. Dubosh and J. A. Kocur; The Slovaks and Their Right to Nationhood, pg 8. 1944*
9. *Ibid.*
10. *Mikus, Joseph A. The Slovak League of America: An Historical Survey; pg 45. 1963*
11. *Ibid.*
12. *Ibid, pg 46.*
13. *Ibid.*
14. *Ibid.*

## Chapter 14

# MR. SECRETARY

# Chapter 14

The 1920s was a decade of excitement, growth, and advancement in the United States. A time that started out on the heels of the largest and deadliest global conflict in history to that point changed into a time of exciting technological advancements and a step-change in the standard of living for many Americans. The roller coaster ride of the 1920s hit its high point in the middle of the decade and, in a speedy decline, reached the bottom as the decade closed and the Great Depression began.

The 1920s in the United States seemed to be a decade of contradiction. The same technological ingenuity and inventive developments that contributed to slaughter on a grand scale during World War I were deployed in a new and different way during the proceeding decade. Americans saw for the first time innovations like movies with sound, commercial radio, and mass-produced automobiles. The concept of "leisure time" began to take hold, and in concert with some of the inventions of the subsequent decade Americans began to spend more time away from work. Theaters became prominent in nearly every town and city, cars took people away from home to see the sights of their country, and forms of entertainment like jazz music multiplied and became a welcome diversion for many.

The United States also became a society of contradiction in the 1920s. The Eighteenth Amendment, a constitutional amendment banning the transport, sale, and consumption of alcohol, was ratified January 16, 1919, and went into effect one year later. The 1920s, according to the law of the land, was to be a "dry" decade. In reality, American consumption of alcohol resembled nothing of the sort. The 1920s became known as the "Roaring 20s" mostly because the decade seemed like a ten-year party fueled by bathtub gin.

An additional contradiction within American society during the 1920s continued to be many Americans' view of immigrants and minorities. Following a World War in which nearly every facet of American society contributed equally, the view that immigrants, blacks, and certain religions were somehow inferior still presided. The violent activities of the Ku Klux Klan during the decade culminated in a march in Washington, D.C. in 1928. In a move to curb a perceived source of radicalism, the U.S. government deported over six thousand foreign-born aliens accused of being radical leftists. As a response to the economic and social concerns of many "native-born" Americans, the Emergency Quota Act was passed in 1921 limiting the number of immigrants able to enter the United States and cutting back on the number of Slovaks coming to America.

America's wild ride through the 1920s ultimately came to an abrupt halt in October of 1929 with the crash of the stock market and the beginning of the Great Depression. For many Slovak Americans, however, the 1920s began as a time of promise. In the Slovak homeland, the war was over and the possibility of greater freedom and independence looked likely. In the U.S., industrial demand continued to grow and the need for a willing workforce still existed, all but guaranteeing Slovaks a place to work and money in their pockets.

As the decade of the '20s wore on, John Kocur became more engaged in leading the activities of the Slovak League of America. Kocur worked diligently on the issues facing Slovaks both abroad and at home in the United States. As a prominent voice for Slovaks, John Kocur continued to press for Slovak freedom and independence in the newly formed Czechoslovak Republic based on the principles outlined in the Pittsburgh agreement, his own Slovak pride, and the universal principles of individual freedom and self-reliance he had come to see embodied in the United States, his new adopted homeland. John Kocur had enjoyed the fruits of his labors in the United States as both a young immigrant and as a naturalized citizen; he believed in what the U.S. stood for, was willing to fight for it, and wanted to bring the same way of life to his fellow Slovaks still living in the homeland.

Many Slovak immigrants during the early part of the twentieth century followed the same path as had John Kocur; they left their families, homes, and villages to pursue a new life in America. More often than not, these immigrants improved their lot in life with hard work so that others in their families, wives, children, parents, or siblings, could follow on a trail already blazed and enjoy a better life.

While John Kocur may have been a significant contributor to bettering the lives of Slovaks in the U.S. and abroad, he shared the common story of thousands of Slovak immigrants with regard to his immigration and family. That story took on a new dynamic in late 1923 with the arrival in the United States of Kocur's wife, Margeta, from the small village of Podvysoka, Czechoslovak Republic. Margeta Zbojek Kocur arrived in New York on December 15, 1923 aboard the steam liner America. Margeta, like her husband, had sailed from the German port of Bremen two weeks earlier and had made the Atlantic crossing in frigid and torturous weather. Unlike her husband, however, the thirty-year-old Mrs. Kocur was able to forego the majority of interviews, exams, and red tape of Ellis Island. By virtue of her marriage to John Kocur in June 1913, Margeta was already an American citizen. The only questions required of her was her ultimate destination (Pittsburgh, Pennsylvania) and whether or not she had a relative to meet her (Yes, Husband).

By the time of his wife's arrival, John Kocur had been in the United States fourteen years. He spoke and wrote English well, was familiar with many areas of the United States through his military travels as well as travels as an officer in the Slovak League, and had adapted well to the customs and culture of his new country. Margeta, now called Margaret in America, knew none of these things. Margaret Kocur was not formally educated in her native country, instead working since an early age to help her family survive. She solely spoke Slovak and would learn to speak English, although never to read or write it, simply by being in American society on a daily basis. In 1923 Margaret Kocur was unfamiliar with everything from living conditions in America to daily functions like shopping, schools, and transportation. In essence, she started her life over when she finally arrived in America that winter of 1923 to live with her husband of ten years.

Throughout Margaret Kocur's life, she adapted to her new surroundings although sometimes begrudgingly. While maintaining the position that if given a choice she would never have left her home in Podvysoka, Margaret Kocur's assimilation to life in the United States was eased by fellow Slovaks in the Kocurs' new hometown of Springdale, Pennsylvania. These friends, neighbors, and acquaintances of the Kocurs eased the transition and provided much needed kinship in language and customs. As difficult as it may have been to live in the United States throughout the 1920s, '30s, and '40s it was nothing compared to the long-suffering lifestyle of a Slovak peasant that the younger Margaret surely lived. Through what must have been a difficult transition to life in the U.S., Margaret Kocur brought with her a supporting faith and religious conviction that had been a part of her since childhood. That conviction and belief was something that never left Margaret despite the trying times she would encounter in America as the wife of one of America's most prominent Slovaks, as a single mother following her husband's death, and as a widow for nearly fifty years. Religious faith and devotion would be something that Margaret Kocur would carry with her until the day she left the earth at the age of one hundred and three.

John Kocur now had his wife with him in the United States after a ten-year, "long distance" marriage. By the time Margaret had arrived in the U.S. from Czechoslovakia to begin a new phase in their marriage, John's work in the Slovak League had begun to increase. The league had become the recognized voice for Slovaks in the U.S. and abroad and John Kocur was its most consistent spokesperson. Up against this growing workload and never-ending focus came John's new responsibilities as a husband and a father. On October 29, 1924 John and Margaret Kocur welcomed a daughter, Amelia Kocur, to their family as their first born. Three short years later on May 16, 1927, a son, John Anthony, Jr. was born. Last, on December 18, 1931 John and Margaret Kocur became the parents of twins, Vera Ann and Richard Daniel Kocur.

By the early '30s the Kocurs were a six-person family. Not large by the standards of the day but in uncertain economic times and on the limited salary paid by the Slovak League, still a challenge to raise, feed, clothe, and care for. Times were tough, but the Kocurs had moved into a house in Springdale, at 918 Ross Street Rear. The house was addressed "Rear" because it sat along the black slag alley directly behind and below Ross Street. The house was not the most prominent in town by any means, however, it was larger than most Slovak families had at the time. Friends of the family or fellow Slovaks seeking to see the secretary of the Slovak League or other family members would come up the narrow sidewalk from the alley to the front door. Entering through the front door led one into an enclosed porch, which served a dual purpose as both the entryway to the first floor through a door directly inside the front door and as the waiting area for Kocur's League office, accessible via a door directly to the left after entering the porch. The Kocur house had three large rooms downstairs; one used for a dining room, one for John and Margaret's bedroom, and one for Kocur's office. It also had a small kitchen where Margaret would work to ensure her family was fed each day. The upstairs had two bedrooms for the children, a common area between the bedrooms and a small bathroom.

For John and Margaret, raising a new generation of Slovak-Americans in a country like the United States, regardless of how tight the economic conditions were, was infinitely more preferable than the life both of them had growing up in small Slovak villages. Because of where he had come from and what he now enjoyed, John Kocur was determined to make use of his position as secretary of the Slovak League to advance the cause of Slovak freedom no matter what. In many regards, this singular focus on the issues of the Slovak people and the time spent addressing these issues came at the expense of time spent with his new and growing family. Working in his office at home or in the Pittsburgh offices of the Slovak League, John Kocur's schedule was long and grueling. Kocur's duties required attention to league correspondence in the United States and abroad, legal matters, organizing league conventions, speeches, and meetings with league personnel as well as government officials. All of this left little time for the kind of direct interaction a father and child routinely enjoy. John Kocur was a rigid and disciplined father who, as a former barber, occasionally utilized his old leather barber strap for disciplining his children. Instead of sharpening razors, the strap would now be used for sharpening the children's attention to their father's directions. John Kocur's attitudes toward child rearing, however, where not much different than many parents in the 1920s and '30s who viewed "spare the rod, spoil the child" as a good rule of thumb. What made John Kocur different as a parent was most likely his family experience as a young boy and his utter dedication to the Slovak League as an adult. Orphaned before he was ten years old and raised in part by relatives in his mother's family, John Kocur did not have the opportunity to experience his own parents' behavior when it came to raising children. In addition, John Kocur's focus throughout his adult life remained on how he could advance the causes of Slovaks everywhere. On these causes Kocur spent enormous time and energy often at the expense of his family. In a newspaper article published following his death in 1948, Jozef Prusa wrote of John Kocur, "For him, his patriotic work was more important than his own health and many times in his hard work, he even harmed his family because in his deep concentration for fighting for the rights of our nation, he forgot about his personal things and duties. Lucky for us his wife did not stand between him and his devotion for our nation because she herself was one of our patriotic and devoted workers."[1] For wife Margaret and children Amelia, John, Vera, and Richard, the cause of Slovak freedom and independence would always occupy a great deal of John Kocur's time and energy. They would have accept the idea that their husband and father was working for and loving not only them but other Slovak families, wives, and children all around the world.

When Margaret Kocur arrived in the United States in December of 1923 she arrived as an American citizen due to the fact that she had married John Kocur, now a naturalized American citizen. After a long uncomfortable journey across the Atlantic, stuck in the steerage class of her ship for nearly two weeks, Margaret Kocur passed through Ellis Island as an American citizen and was on her way to Springdale. Many Slovak immigrants during the 1920s, however, were certainly not as lucky as Margaret and in fact faced an even greater challenge entering the United States due to the prevailing American attitudes towards immigrants.

Beginning shortly before America's entry in to World War I and gradually picking up momentum as the 1920s wore on was a movement among native-born Americans to limit the numbers of foreign-born immigrants entering the United States. This attitude was especially targeted toward immigrants from Central and Eastern Europe which had, over the previous ten years, made up the bulk of immigrants coming to America's shores. So while John Kocur and the Slovak League leadership were working to ensure the principles of the Pittsburgh Agreement were incorporated into the new Czecho-Slovak Republic thus ensuring freedom and autonomy for Slovaks in the homeland, they were forced to open a second battlefront at home in the United States to ensure that Slovak immigrants, like they once were, could continue to come to America and realize all its promises and potential.

Congress first instituted quotas for immigration in 1921.[2] As the decade wore on, the cries for greater immigration control increased in volume. Given the political pressure to act, Congress once again took up the immigration issue and began to debate legislative action. In his role as secretary, Kocur was a vital link for the league membership in keeping them informed on issues that directly affected their lives. The Slovak League took an active role in attempting to stop the movement toward more immigration quotas for Slovaks or at the very least minimize the impact the quotas would have.

Slovak activists on this issue, like the Slovak League, were faced not only with the problem of a direct reduction in the number of their countrymen able to come to the United States, but also the longer-term implications of such a step. Up until that point in time, first-generation Slovak-Americans represented the lifeblood of the Slovak League membership. Now with the legislative action in Congress, the league could potentially face not only a decline in new immigrants, and new members, but also a defection of the American-born, second-generation Slovak-Americans. These were younger members who were growing up in America, with command of the English language, and who didn't want to be associated with the "undesirables" tag. They were more American than Slovak.

The arguments against this legislative action were made by the Slovak community in many outlets, including both Slovak and English language publications, taking into account the evolution of their membership and the targets of their messages. The authors of such pieces in the Slovak language no doubt hoped to influence the first-generation and naturalized Slovak-Americans to take actions such as working to defeat politicians who supported immigration quotas. The English language articles were different; they targeted other readers. To be sure, these pieces constituted part of the lobbying effort directed at American politicians. However, readers of English language items consisted of the American-born second generation and probably immigrants who had come at a young age and were proficient in English.[3] Taken on the whole, the thrust of their commentary strongly suggested that the English-language articles were intended to sway a second-generation readership.[4] Activists needed to stem what they feared would be a rush by second-generation Slovaks to distance themselves from a denigrated nationality and its institutions. They were telling them not to shun their ancestral heritage because, despite contemporary disdain, they, like nationality groups before them, could ultimately gain respectability.[5]

In the end the efforts of the Slovak League and other Slovak activists failed to block the passage of the new immigration bill that was passed by Congress in the spring of 1924. The Slovak newspaper Jednota declared the law, "a defeat for Slavs and Latin peoples" and "the victory of an idea that Americans have to be Anglo-Saxon or Nordic." In essence, the newly devised plan with its aim ultimately to maintain an ethnic status quo created a permanent affront to persons of Eastern and Southern European heritage.[6]

The Slovak League, led by men like John Kocur, continued to work for its countrymen despite the setback imposed on them by the new immigration act. The 1924 legislation established an annual immigration quota based on a ratio of ethnic inhabitants to the total population in 1920. The act spells out the annual quota calculation as "a number which bears the same ratio to 150,000 as the number of inhabitants in the United States in 1920 having that national origin bears to the number of inhabitants in the United States in 1920."[7] The problem that Kocur and other members of the league encountered with this approach was that Slovak immigrants in the United States as of 1920 were often classified as something other than Slovak. From 1861 to 1918 immigration from Austria-Hungary had been recorded as "Austrian and Hungarian." Only since the census of 1910 did statistics recognize Czechs (Bohemians), Moravians, and Slovaks as national entities. The bulk of the immigration of Austria-Hungary, in excess of four million people always went to the credit side of Austria-Hungary.[8] The true numerical strength of Slovaks and Czechs in the country as of 1920 could not be attained, could not be fairly represented in the calculations, and would therefore shortchange the Slovaks in terms of the number of allowable immigrants.

John Kocur went on to draft, on behalf of the Slovak League, a resolution submitted to President Calvin Coolidge, Vice President Charles Dawes, cabinet members, the chairman of the Committee on Immigration and Naturalization of the Senate and Congress, to members of both committees, to all the members of the House and Senate and the most influential newspapers and publications of the country. The resolution was endorsed by the Slovak League as well as over a dozen Slovak organizations and newspapers in the United States.

Kocur and league president Ivan Bielek began by reminding Congress of the impact of their methods of quota calculation. They wrote:

> *By passing the Immigration Act of 1924, Congress adopted restriction of immigration as a permanent policy for the United States. There cannot be any reasonable objection by anyone against such a restrictive policy, if it is the honest belief of the majority of legislators in both houses of Congress, although there may be a division of opinion as to the correctness of the sources upon which figures, ultimately arrived at, are based. However, no argument is stronger than the premise upon which it is built, and if the fundamental idea is wrong it will be unable to support the most elaborate superstructure.*[9]

They continued:

> *In the brief which we submitted on January 3, 1924, subsequent to the hearing courteously accorded our representative by the committee on Immigration and Naturalization, while taking justified exception to evident preference given to representatives or exponents of the idea of supposed Nordic superiority, we did not deny the right of the government of the United States to determine who shall or who shall not be admissible as immigrants to the United States, but we call attention to some facts which are of vital importance in the arrival of correct and proper conclusions, and since the last available figure (2248) shows a further reduction of the immigrant quota from Czecho-Slovakia, the difference of 825 admissible going to the benefit of immigrants from Austria and Hungary, permit us not only to reiterate parts of our pleas of 1924, but also to show in brief which such arrangements would be inadequate, inequitable, and unjustified.*[10]

After outlining what they believed to be a more equitable approach to calculating Slovak "admissibles," Kocur and Bielek reiterated their arguments:

> *We claim that any figures on Czechs and Slovaks in the population of this country, based on the above methods are incorrect and work out unjustly in the determination of the final quota allowance for immigrants from Czecho-Slovakia. Who reaps the benefit of the discrepancy in figures? The immigrants from Austria-Hungary, classified as Austrians and Hungarians, the Austro-Germans and the Magyars, who are made the beneficiaries of an error in classification and who, judging from their past records are not deserving of it.*
>
> *The Czechs and Slovaks, residing in this country, are proud of their war record, both as producers in the manufacture of ammunitions, as well as of their numbers as volunteers, enlisted, and drafted members of the armed forces of the United States; as purchasers of Liberty Loan Bonds and War Savings*

*Thrift Stamps; as detectors of subversive enemy propaganda. They are proud of their records in the communities in which they live for their proclivities for law and order; for their total lack of records of criminality; for their morality manifested by a total absence of illegitimate child births; for their well regulated family lives, manifested by an absence of juvenile delinquency.*

*In view of the above we appeal to the high sense of fair play which is so typically American; which is an important part of American traditions as we have been taught to conceive them, that we base all out hope for an equitable readjustment of the final figures just on this high conception of fairness which the Government of the United States has always accorded us in all out contacts with its diverse agencies.*

*We are not seeking any favors at the expense of others; we are not claiming something which would put us in a preferred class; we are not asking for anything to which American fairness could not subscribe with a clean conscience. We are only petitioning for that which, according to all rules of equity and fair play, is our just due, and we hope that the prayer of our petition will be granted, and that the presidential proclamation, whenever issued in the future, mindful of the facts as set forth above, will allot us that figure to which we are justly and fairly entitled, without favor or prejudice.*

*Respectfully Submitted,*

*Slovak League of America*

*Ivan Bielek, President*

*Jan Kocur, Secretary*[11]

John Kocur's work on behalf of Slovak immigrants and the imposed quotas of the Immigration Act did not achieve his desired outcome. As a result of the annual quotas, just under 55,000 Slovaks immigrated to the United States during the 1920s.[12] Kocur continued, however, to aid those immigrants who did arrive and seek his advice, counsel, and help. It was known among the Slovak immigrants that this man, the secretary of the Slovak League, had time for them, lowly as they may have been in the scheme of American society.

In the wake of immigration restriction, the efforts of ethnic organizations like the Slovak League became more and more focused on installing ancestral pride among the growing numbers of second-generation Slovak-Americans. The Slovak newspaper Jednota was expressing resolve when, reacting to the national origins legislation, it proclaimed that, "if, over four generations, the Irish could maintain an affection for their own people, the Slovaks could do the same."[13]

Despite the setbacks John Kocur experienced during the 1920s with regard to his Slovak brothers and sisters in the homeland, their struggle for independence, and their ability to take part in the same life he worked for and enjoyed in the United States, he continued to work diligently on their behalf. Kocur was of the firm belief that Slovaks could and should take control of their own destiny both in the United States and in the Czecho-Slovak Republic and he was determined to do everything in his power to help achieve that goal. The coming decade of the 1930s, however, would test Kocur's resolve to a greater degree than ever before. It would provide great challenges, great joys, and great disappointments for John Kocur and for all Slovak people. It would be a decade that would test the true mettle of Kocur's beliefs under the most dire of circumstances. It would also be a decade that would bring back to the forefront the old wounds of John Kocur's service to his adopted country during the Great War. The Slovak League was in the middle of its golden age and John Kocur, its most consistent leader, was hitting his stride as a recognized voice for the causes of Slovaks everywhere.

## Endnotes

1. *Prusa, Jozef G. Catholic Sokol: Emotional Burial of Chief Secretary of the Slovak League. July 1948.*
2. *Alexander, June G.; Ethnic Pride, American Patriotism, pg 78. 2004.*
3. *Ibid.*
4. *Ibid.*
5. *Ibid.*
6. *Ibid.*
7. *Bielek and Kocur; Resolutions and Brief in Behalf of Readjustment of Quota for Immigrants from Czecho-Slovakia; pg 1. 1927.*
8. *Ibid, pg 2.*
9. *Ibid, pg 3.*
10. *Ibid, pg 4.*
11. *Ibid, 4-5.*
12. *Alexander, June G.; Ethnic Pride, American Patriotism, pg 89. 2004.*
13. *Ibid.*

## Chapter 15

# DARK CLOUDS ABOVE US

# Chapter 15

By 1931 the Great Depression was in full swing, pummeling the American economy and affecting some aspect of the lives of nearly all Americans. In the previous ten years, John Kocur had been taught hard lessons about the view many Americans had towards Slovaks and other ethnic immigrants. Kocur had also realized that Slovak-Americans, consistent with the American principle of self determination, would only have their own to rely on in times of need and the Slovak League, as representative of the majority of Slovak-Americans, would lead the way. John Kocur's love for his fellow Slovak people would fuel his desire to ensure that no matter what the economic circumstances or social attitudes, Slovaks as a community would be taken care of by their own. In Kocur's view, the charitable organizations of the day did not want to deal with "ethnics" and did not treat Slovaks with the same degree of attention and respect that others received. This fact combined with the classic Slovak traits of pride and modesty made it difficult for Slovaks in this time of need. John Kocur rallied his fellow Slovaks to the idea of self-help in the following open letter to the entire Slovak League membership:

> *My dear! Dark black clouds are above us. Dark in both meanings – national and social. The horrible Depression is like a tornado destroying our work and our businesses. Nothing seems to be sure and safe. Where are we? Well on*

*the brink of the fatal changes. The news is spreading like a plague throughout the whole country that this winter the crisis will come with its horrible and disastrous consequences.*

*Our precious magazine Catholic Sokol in its 938th issue, brought an excellent article about it. Let me quote from that article: "The winter is in front of the doors and with it is coming unavoidable poverty that our Slovak nation has never experienced in its American history". Based on the signs, the consequences of the current Depression are going to reach the peak this winter and with it also poverty and hunger will truly show with the arrival of snow and frost. We are too small to try to use our influence to get public help. Partially because we would hardly receive it and also because the Slovak pride and modesty is to the point that our people would rather suffer than to go and ask for help and support.*

*That is why any helping activities for the upcoming winter have to be initiated by us. The help for the Slovaks and their suffering families with food and clothing for their children, can only come from the Slovaks; nobody else will help us because they all have enough of their own problems...that is why we suggest here in the middle of the Slovak community to organize a Slovak self-helping agency that will take on the duties of usual charitable American agencies, on whose help needy Slovaks cannot rely. This hopeful organization will be created along with its local branches and will be responsible for the technical part of these charitable activities. And we have to start with collections! With collections that we have never seen before. We have to start with the rich organizations. They finance the building of the schools on the outside so it is their moral duty to be the first ones to sacrifice for those that spend time amongst those walls – our Slovak school children. We need to continue with the rich individuals until our last person. The situation is too serious for anyone to avoid their national and human responsibility.*

*To conclude, we express our sincerest wishes for our appeal not to be just a voice of a person lost in the desert! We hope that starting from our spiritual leaders through intelligence, dignitaries, to our last Slovak national, that everyone will accept our motto "We for our own, for our very own!" Even the Youngstown Slovak newspaper recently published an interesting article from which I would like to quote the most important parts: "...it is predicted that the upcoming winter will be the winter of poverty in America. President Hoover, himself, established a special organization that will coordinate the activities of all charitable organizations in the country as well as all job and employment centers in the country – state, municipal and private. As he said: "no good citizen should suffer from lack of food and have no roof over their head."*

*We know that to take care of needy people is the duty of the society; in spite of that we are coming with the recommendation to organize the charitable help. It is not necessary to establish a new organization as we already have the Slovak League of America with its district and local branches. These could lead the charitable help throughout the whole United States under the leadership of the main office of the League.*

*Why are we coming with this recommendation? Because in the last two years of economic hardship, we found out that without a national agency, our needy people are not getting as much help as they should be. We also found out that they who have their own charitable organization have a better chance of getting help than those who do not have it. Now is the right time to act. Let's be the human beings, let's be the Slovaks, let's be Christians, in our actions not only in our words.*

*What can I add to these important warnings and recommendations? I am adding only this: Yes, it is important to take care of your own people, it is important to help. It is not good to leave our Slovak people to rely on the help of strangers.*

*I think that even today, a lot of our people remember that "help" that they received from various city and district charitable organizations. I will mention at least one example. One of our nationals was in such a sad situation with his family that he was forced to ask for help in one of the local "charitable institutions." He needed food and clothes for his children. The directors of that institution gave him barely a crumb and turned him in to the immigration office to find out whether he could be deported. How many problems that caused to him and his family I could not describe in a few lines. It also is not needed. Those who had to deal with this one or other similar agencies can prove that a person has to go through a lot of suffering to get help and justice. This is only one little example but it clearly shows that many of our nationals were not only sorry to ask for that help but also paid for it.*

*To conclude, the Slovak League, in the past as well as today, will willingly and eagerly take on any type of difficult activity that would lead towards relieving poverty and helping the prosperity of our people. Detailed descriptions of future activities will be published in the next few days in our national newspapers and magazines. However, I am already turning to all our Slovak brothers and sisters and asking for their help and support in this noble cause. May the good Lord help us!*

*Jan A. Kocur*

*Secretary of the Slovak League of America*[1]

John Kocur's first concern during these dark days was for the younger Slovak children, the school children. Kocur knew what an important role education played in the lives of the Slovak youth and recognized its importance as an avenue to opportunity. This belief was instilled early in Kocur's youth, possibly because his father was a teacher in the state schools of Austria-Hungary and as a young boy he saw the privilege of learning taken from many Slovaks by their Hungarian rulers. Young Slovaks, Kocur believed, could also better integrate into society, get better paying jobs, and demonstrate their Slovak pride by being better educated and working harder in school. Even in those tough times of the Depression, he stood firm on the fact that young Slovaks had to graduate from high school. This extended beyond just Slovaks from Springdale and included Slovak students from the surrounding towns of Harwick, Acmetonia, and Cheswick.[2]

John Kocur's interest in the well-being of young Slovak students extended beyond their work in the class room; he also opened his home to many of them during their school lunch time as a place where they could gather, talk and eat. The Kocur household never turned a student away and if they had no lunch or could not afford lunch, Kocur and Margaret would feed the children warm soup. The secretary's house was a place where the local Slovak children could get not only soup, but attention and advice from a true giant in the Slovak community.[3]

While the public education received by the young Slovak children was important, Kocur also believed that their overall education needed to include lessons on Slovak history, language, and culture. Every Saturday throughout the entire summer and fall the Slovak youth walked to the Krivan Hall in Springdale to sit by John Kocur's chalkboard learning the Slovak language.[4] The Krivan Hall was a social hall founded and run by local Slovaks. On Slovak holidays, as well as American holidays like the Fourth of July, Kocur would organize recitals among the Slovak children of the area. Slovak families would enjoy the celebration together, children and adults alike. The youth entertained their parents at the Krivan Hall with their singing, dancing and recitals that John Kocur taught them.[5]

One of the great heroes of Slovak folklore and culture was Juraj Jánošik, the "Slovak Robin Hood" of the early sixteenth century. No doubt that John Kocur enjoyed telling the Slovak youth of Springdale and the surrounding areas the legend of Jánošik, a symbol of Slovak resistance. Any Slovak, like John Kocur, who grew up in the world of Hungarian rule would take great satisfaction in recalling the exploits of a bandit who victimized nobles, rulers, and the rich in order to help the poor and the peasant. Of even greater symbolic relevance to John Kocur was the fact that the exploits of Janosik, the bandit and robber, took place across the Slovak lands of Hungary near Kocur's home village. In fact, Juraj Janosik was reportedly born in the village of Turchova, only about forty miles from Kocur's village of Turzovka.

The legend of Janosik was handed down among the Slovak people in poems, stories, and songs. Janosik was also a favorite subject in Slovak literature, being the focus of books as early as the early 1800s. In the early twentieth century, the exploits of Janosik made a perfect fit for a feature motion picture and John Kocur did not hesitate to bring this new medium to Springdale. The Krivan Hall was the center of Slovak social activity in Springdale and it was there that Kocur set up the screening of the Janosik movie for all the local Slovaks, children and parents alike. Slovaks from all over the area packed the hall to see the movie, with many people crowded around the doorways and windows peering in to try and get a glimpse. The large gathering piqued the curiosity of many non-Slovaks in Springdale who were interested in seeing this new film that so many in the community were talking about. Tickets for this special Slovak film, however, were for Slovaks only; Kocur saw to that.[6] He knew that no matter how seemingly insignificant Janosik was to the non-Slovaks of the area, the legend was genuinely Slovak, something to be proud of, and an opportunity to educate young second-generation Slovak-Americans about their history and culture. It was also an opportunity to educate these young people, through the symbolism of Janosik, on the historical resolve and resistance the Slovak people had in the face of oppression. To John Kocur, the eighteenth-century story of Janosik had as much relevance to Slovaks in the twentieth century as it ever had and he took it upon himself to ensure that the film not only provided entertainment but a meaningful message as well.

With the Depression dragging on, communities were often brought together and had their spirits raised during special occasions and holidays. It was a time when the troubles of the day could be temporarily set aside in favor of more festive pursuits. John Kocur took an active role in two such holidays in the Springdale community. For reasons of community togetherness and as a display of patriotism for the United States, Kocur led the Slovak community's participation in both the Memorial Day and the Fourth of July celebrations. In May and July of each year the town of Springdale staged large parades to honor these uniquely American holidays; and while they were surely "American" holidays, John Kocur made sure that the Slovaks of the area played an important part. Kocur's love of his Slovak homeland was always evident in whatever he did but over the years he had also become an American citizen, served in the U.S. armed forces, and had come to deeply appreciate the values and principles that guided America. While it was important for Slovaks to recognize their own ethnic identity and be proud of their heritage, John Kocur also knew that understanding and celebrating what drove America to its special place in the world could give his fellow Slovaks a greater appreciation for their new country, give them an opportunity to outwardly demonstrate their American patriotism, and possibly stir in them a recognition of the need for freedom and self- determination, America's guiding principles, in their ancestral homeland.

The Springdale Memorial Day parades were prime examples of how John Kocur and the Slovak community chose to show their American patriotism. Kocur always made sure that the Slovak community came out to fully support this special holiday. In organizing the participation of the local Slovak community, John Kocur helped to place the Slovaks in the best position in each parade, right behind the veterans.[7] It was often that John Kocur led those veterans as a flag-bearer in the Memorial Day parades. As a veteran of World War I and leader in the community, Kocur was a slight but recognizable figure marching forward of the veteran contingent in his army uniform and carrying the flag of he United States. John Kocur not only organized the Slovak contingent that marched in the parades, he also ensured that the Slovak people of the community turned out to watch the parade, lining the sidewalks in their best Sunday clothes. They would show by their actions and appearance that they were not only celebrating America but proud to be Slovak as well; pride manifest in their numbers, actions, and even their appearance. John Kocur was no doubt proud of his service to America and honored to carry the nation's flag, but he also recognized that an overly enthusiastic display of patriotism by Slovaks could be misconstrued as disingenuous by those who did not care for "ethnics." In a typically reserved manner Kocur provided Slovaks attending the parades small versions of the American flag to wave as the parade passed by. This way, Slovaks would show that they were patriotic and supportive of their new country, but not appear too idealistic or overly patriotic.[8]

John Kocur often took center stage in what was another important social diversion during the Depression for Slovaks all across Western Pennsylvania. Every year beginning in 1922, the large community of Slovaks in Pittsburgh and the surrounding areas celebrated "Slovak Day" at Kennywood Park, an historic amusement park located just south of Pittsburgh. It was a day of fun and relaxation for Slovak families, a time to see old friends, be entertained by ethnic dance and song, eat Slovak food, and generally enjoy the large community of fellow Slovaks from across the region. As secretary of the Slovak League, the largest of all Slovak organizations in the U.S., John Kocur would often be the featured speaker of the day. Nearly everyone in the audience was familiar with the Slovak League of America and was most likely a member, so to have the national secretary and local resident as the keynote speaker was a source of pride for many in the audience. Speaking in Slovak and in English, Kocur's messages reached out to newly arrived Slovaks as well as the younger second generation. These were difficult times for every Slovak in the U.S. both financially given the hard economic times, as well as socially where the Slovak ethnic identity still faced many challenges. Kocur recognized the need for assimilation but remained convinced that the best way for Slovaks to succeed was for Slovaks to help Slovaks: "We for our own, for our very own!"[9] His speeches at Kennywood were yet another opportunity for John Kocur, a significant player in the largest national Slovak organization, to communicate at the grass roots level where he felt it could make the most difference.

In 1932, three years after the crash of the stock market, Franklin Roosevelt was elected president and his party, the Democrats, swept the congressional elections. Roosevelt's landslide victory combined with the upheaval in Congress gave the new president an unprecedented mandate to address the crisis of the U.S. Depression. Roosevelt and his congressional allies wasted no time in beginning a series of programs designed to bring the U.S. out of the grips of the Depression. Roosevelt's "New Deal" began in earnest in 1933, and continued throughout the 1930s. Reforms to the banking and monetary regulations, economic relief efforts, support for farmers, and an increased focus on reviving the industrial base of the U.S. were the building blocks of a plan that the Roosevelt administration believed could bring the United States out of its deep economic hole.

At the Depression's worst, unemployment in America reached nearly twenty-five percent and industrial output had declined by one-third. The sole focus of individuals and families became simply surviving from one month to the next and in some cases one day to the next. There was no room in the family budget of many Americans for anything other than the bare necessities. For nearly all Slovak families in the United States, American citizens or not, times were especially hard. Many Slovaks of the 1930s had not yet achieved a standard of living that would have seen them through tough economic times; and these were well beyond "tough." Slovaks had made great strides in their standing within American society since the turn of the century. The immigrants of the first ten to fifteen years of the 1900s had become firmly established, gaining citizenship and producing an American-born second-generation that was to grow up "American." Despite the economic and social advances they made, the vast majority of Slovaks in the workforce of the 1930s were still laborers working in the mills, mines, and factories of the United States. Given the blow that the Depression dealt to American industry, Slovaks were especially hard hit.

The New Deal produced a myriad of agencies designed to help Americans with everything from jobs and education to food and clothing. The bureaucratic requirements to apply for and receive the aid, however, were often enough to prevent immigrants or even ethnic American citizens, like the Slovaks, from seeking and receiving what could have rightfully been theirs. The other hurdle faced by Slovak-Americans in accessing Depression-era benefits was the characteristic Slovak pride; a simple refusal to ask for help, especially from the government or an agency not affiliated with the Slovak churches or fraternal organizations, even if one was in desperate need.

During these dark times, the Slovak League had to step up and provide leadership for the growing community of Slovaks affected by the Great Depression. John Kocur led the fight to provide help to the Slovaks hit hardest in the dire economic times of the 1930s. His view, however, was one which emphasized help from within the Slovak community rather than from the outside. In the early 1930s Kocur emphasized this need for self-help when he wrote in a Slovak newspaper editorial, "The help for the Slovaks and their suffering families with food and clothing for their children, can only come from the Slovaks; nobody else will help us because they all have enough of their own problems, that is why we suggest here in the middle of the Slovak community to organize a Slovak self-helping agency that will take on the duties of usual charitable American agencies, on whose help needy Slovaks cannot rely."[10] Kocur also recognized that a Slovak self-help agency made it easier for his fellow Slovaks to actually ask for the help they so desperately needed, noting, "We are too small to try to use our influence to get public help; partially because we would hardly receive it and also because the Slovak pride and modesty is to the point that our people would rather suffer than to go and ask for help and support. That is why any helping activities for upcoming winter have to be initiated by us."[11]

John Kocur believed deeply that the Slovak League, as the largest and most representative Slovak organization in the United States, had a duty and obligation to provide help and relief to its members. The Slovak League, however, was also feeling the effects of the Depression in a number of ways. Membership in the league began to decline during the hard economic times of the 1930s. With the Depression gripping the nation, Slovaks, like many Americans, were simply focused on surviving and the Slovak League as well as many other Slovak fraternal organizations was not where these citizens could or would spend their time and money. In addition, a new generation of Slovak-Americans was growing up not with memories of the hard times in the old country, but with the fresh perspective of growing up in America. These second-generation Slovaks did not have their parents' perspective on Slovak issues of the day and thus an organization like the Slovak League that sought to represent the interests of Slovaks in America and abroad was not as relevant to them as it was to their parents.

The combination of the economic and social challenges of the day put increased pressure on the Slovak League. Membership, and therefore dues and income, began to decline for the first time in three decades and more importantly the relevance of what the league stood for among its potential future members had the potential to become a longer term issue. Entering his second decade as secretary of the Slovak League, John Kocur was confronted with these large issues and was doing all he could to ensure that the league helped its membership in the U.S. and continued the fight for Slovak independence and autonomy abroad. When the decrease in Slovak League income threatened to slow or stop some of the league's activities, John Kocur gave of his own salary and expenses, often working without pay at all, to help continue funding the efforts of the Slovak League.[12] In fact, much of the credit for keeping the Slovak League of America alive in the late 1920s and the Depression years of the 1930s belongs largely to the determination and consistency of John Kocur.[13]

Dark days indeed. The economic situation in the United States began to look up as the 1930s wore on, only to suffer a setback when a recession struck in 1937. The Slovak League faced its own Depression both in funds and in membership and John Kocur was doing all he could to help push the organization, its membership, and its objectives forward. Kocur was still as focused as ever on helping fellow Slovaks in the United States assimilate, find jobs, housing, and the respect he knew they deserved. The secretary of the Slovak League also maintained a constant effort against the other big objective of the league, freedom and independence of his native Slovakia. Whereas in previous decades the fight for the freedom for Slovakia was aimed at the Austro-Hungarian Empire, changes in the governmental power structure post-World War I brought about not freedom for Slovakia but a new ruler with whom to deal. In the late 1920s and in to the 1930s, John Kocur and the Slovak League were dealing with the newly established Czecho-Slovak parliament but on the same old issues: Slovak autonomy and independence as laid out and described in the Pittsburgh Agreement.

The combination of challenges faced by Slovak-Americans in the United States and Slovaks abroad would have made the job of secretary in the nation's largest Slovak organization doubly difficult. John Kocur, however, never gave any indication that the mountain to climb with regard to serving Slovak-Americans or fighting for freedom and independence of his Slovak homeland was ever too high. John Kocur was like a compass on a ship in a storm, always keeping his "north," always maintaining a steady and consistent focus on his goals, and never compromising his principles.[14]

While John Kocur's emotional and intellectual strength never wavered, the decade of the 1930s brought on a new challenge over which he had little control or power. As early as 1930 the effects of the deadly poison gas that Private Kocur had been exposed to on the battlefields of France began to surface and became more pronounced as the decade wore on.

John Kocur was plagued with "disorders of the respiratory organs," as his family physicians Dr. W.T. Holland and Dr. Fisher termed it. Kocur's symptoms included shortness of breath, coughing, and wheezing, as well as pain in his upper chest. On November 7, 1930, after gathering all the necessary paperwork, military documents, and completing a mountain of government paperwork, John Kocur filed an application for service compensation as a result of his wound. The application detailed his military experience and related information including personal history, family and dependents, and a number of miscellaneous questions. All told, the application consisted of four typed pages of questions and answers, which was then signed by John Kocur and notarized by Michael Schrahm. The answer as to specifically when and where the wound was received was only vaguely answered by John Kocur with, "in service while on front." The then- Private Kocur did receive treatment while in the service but only noted, "I can't recall names of field hospital or first aid stations. All I remember it was in the vicinity of St. Mihiel and Toul, France." As standard practice, the Veterans Administration required applicants to list three references who could attest to the medical condition that prompted the veteran's application. Kocur listed as his references Ivan Bielek of Munhall, Pa., a former President of the Slovak League, Lad Keblushek of Springdale, Pa., and J.W. Johnson, also of Springdale. At the time of his application, John Kocur's wife, Margaret, as well as his children Amelia, age six, and John Jr., age three, were listed as his dependents. Kocur's responsibilities for these dependents would also be taken into consideration for the calculation of benefits to be received.

Overall, John Kocur's application for benefits as a result of his wound was very straightforward. After reviewing the application and requesting some supporting paperwork, the Veterans Administration notified John Kocur that he was to report to the U.S. Veterans Bureau in Pittsburgh on December 29, 1930 for a physical examination. The exam's purpose was to confirm, through Veterans Administration medical officers, that the patient's health status was consistent with the claim being made.

Kocur's physical exam revealed a claimant who was five feet, four inches tall and weighed 122 pounds. Nothing in his overall physical appearance was noted as unusual, although it was noted that he had a number of missing teeth. Kocur had a slightly elevated blood pressure of 144 over 86 and a resting heart rate of 108. In addition to a general physical exam, and given the difficulty he was having with regard to his lungs, John Kocur was also given a complete respiratory exam. The examination of both lungs revealed "very harsh breathing sounds accompanied by loud sibilant rales on inspiration" and, "sonorous rales on expiration which is prolonged." The summary of lung findings and diagnosis with regard to the respiratory organs after the exam was Chronic Moderate Bronchitis and Moderate Emphysema. John Kocur underwent other specific exams that day including an orthopedic exam and laboratory analysis, neither of which revealed any notable findings. It was his lungs that Kocur knew to be the problem and the exam and diagnosis by the Veterans Administration doctors helped to confirm his suffering as war related.

The wheels of government turn slowly and this was never more true than within the bureaucracy of the Veterans Administration. No fewer than four separate rating boards consisting of three physicians each had to review the examination findings and rule on the potential disability associated with each exam area (respiratory, orthopedic, dental, and general medicine). As time went by, John Kocur tried to prompt quicker action by the Veterans Administration with letters from himself as well as affidavits from others. In March of 1931 Kocur penned the following to the U.S. Veterans Bureau:

> *On December 29, 1930 I underwent a medical examination in connection with my compensation claim. At the time of the said examination I was promised prompt*

*attention, but since then three months have elapsed without any action whatsoever.*

*I do not like to annoy you with my requests, but my present financial and health situation is such that I have to urge you to be kind enough to help me in settling this long overdue matter of my justified claim.*

*Will you kindly look into this matter and find out what is holding it up this time. Thank you in advance for your kind help. I beg to remain*

*Very Truly Yours,*

*John Kocur*

To aid in having his claim reviewed and ruled upon quickly, John Kocur also had support from his local congressman, Clyde Kelly, as well as Springdale town officials. In early 1931, Kelly wrote Mr. M.J. Shortley, regional manager of the Veterans bureau in Pittsburgh in support of John Kocur's claim:

*Some of my good friends in Springdale, Pa., including the Burgess and President of the Council, have called my attention to the claim of John A. Kocur and have impressed me as to its worthiness.*

*It appears he is suffering from the effects of gas received in the service and is unable to properly carry on because of its nature. I should be glad if you will give it careful consideration with a view to granting compensation. I shall be glad to cooperate in every way possible. Thanking you, I am*

*Sincerely yours,*

*Clyde Kelly*

John Kocur's doctor, William T. Holland also wrote in support of his friend and patient:

*This is to certify that John Kocur has been treated by me on a number of different occasions suffering from an acute bronchial condition and during these attacks he is in bed for several weeks at a time.*

*He has a chronic bronchial condition as a result of being gassed while in the army and is partially disabled at all times but frequently is confined to his bed with acute attacks. This disability is permanent and he is not able to do very much work.*

*Signed,*

*W.T. Holland, M.D.*

On June 3, 1931, six months after his examination at the Aspinwall Veterans Hospital, John Kocur received word from the Veterans Administration that his claim for service-related disability compensation had been approved. The compensation was strictly related to the "chest condition" Kocur exhibited during the physical exam, that is, the chronic bronchitis directly attributable to his World War I service. The additional diagnosis of moderate emphysema was ruled not to be directly service related but aggravated by a service-related injury and so was also worthy of compensation but on a percentage basis. The amount of compensation for the moderate emphysema was related to the percentage of disability attributed to the condition. The Veterans Bureau board ruled the moderate emphysema contributed not more than twenty-five percent of the total disability and would be paid accordingly. As of the date of notification, June 3, 1931 John Kocur would be entitled to $38.40 per month as compensation for his service-related disability retroactive to the date of his physical exam, December 29,1930, and continue indefinitely.

In their letter notifying John Kocur of his disability compensation award the Veterans Bureau also noted that he was eligible for additional compensation on behalf of his wife and two children. In order to file for this entitlement, Kocur merely needed to supply supporting evidence consisting of a marriage certificate, birth certificates for the children, and a sworn statement under oath summarizing information regarding his marriage, living arrangements, and children. In addition, a statement under oath of two other people who knew and could verify the facts supporting John Kocur's family claims was also required.

Throughout the summer and fall of 1931 Kocur went about gathering the required information. The birth certificates of his children, John and Millie, were easily obtained as were the necessary sworn affidavits. The difficult piece of the additional claim requirements was the marriage certificate. John and Margaret Kocur were married on June 11, 1913 in Turzovka, Czecho-Slovakia and obtaining an acceptable record was difficult. In a letter from the Veterans Bureau dated August 14, 1931, John Kocur was informed that the copy of the certificate he submitted as proof of marriage to Margaret Zbojkova was not "properly authenticated as required by Bureau regulations." It took John Kocur an additional four months to have the marriage certificate authenticated by the U.S. Consul in Czecho-Slovakia and returned to the Veterans Bureau. Once returned, the bureau then took another four months to circulate the document first for translation and then approval. Finally on April 2, 1932, the Veterans Bureau informed John Kocur that his service-related compensation payments would increase to $48.00 per month effective from December 29, 1930 as a result of additional compensation for his wife and two children.

In the early 1930s, during the depths of the Great Depression, the compensation that John Kocur received for his service-related disability accounted for nearly all of the income on which the family had to live. While Kocur continued his work for the Slovak League and its causes with great passion, the league often did not have the funds with which to pay the salaries of their officers. Many months, in fact, Kocur either did not accept his salary and expenses or deferred them in order to ensure that the league had enough funds to survive, much to the chagrin of his wife.

As a part of the compensation award by the Veterans Bureau, John Kocur had to submit to regular examinations in order to evaluate his ongoing physical condition and keep current the status of his claim as well as associated payments. In July of 1933, Kocur received word from the Veterans Bureau that his compensation payments would be reduced to $36.00 pursuant to a change in the regulations governing the level of compensation associated with disability. The change most likely had more to do with the tightening of government funds due to the dire economic situation in the U.S. as opposed to any improvement in John Kocur's medical condition. Although a change of only $12.00, in the context of the times this reduction would have a serious impact on the Kocur family's ability to survive. In February of 1934 as an augment to the disability, John Kocur filed for relief with the Allegheny County Emergency Relief board, an organization that provided short-term relief to struggling families in the tough economic times of the Depression.

Over the next year and through 1935, John Kocur continued with his examinations at the Veterans Bureau in Aspinwall, Pennsylvania and appealed the reduction in disability compensation. Kocur was successful in bringing his level of compensation back up to $48.00 per month and with the filing of additional paperwork, including the birth certificates of his younger two children, Richard and Vera, was able to ultimately increase the disability compensation to $52.80 per month. This amount would represent the majority of what the Kocurs, now a family of six, would live on through much of the remainder of the decade.

As the 1930s were drawing to a close and the tough economic times in the United States and abroad dragged on, the work of John Kocur for the causes of Slovaks everywhere continued in typical apostolic fashion. The difficulties faced by Kocur and the Slovak League during the 1930s would have seemed to be enough to break the spirit of even the most arduous Slovak patriot. The Depression made life for Slovaks in America extremely difficult, and the league could only supply so much support to their membership. The Slovak League also suffered as a result, losing membership and revenue. Abroad, the causes for which John Kocur cared about so deeply and fought for so passionately, Slovak autonomy and independence, became hopelessly mired in the wake of a new Czecho-Slovak national government. Physically, John Kocur was beginning to suffer more and more from the wounds associated with his World War I military service, sapping his strength and energy. At home and abroad it seemed as though the relevance and influence of the Slovak League of America was losing steam. John Kocur and a handful of dedicated league officers, however, refused to give up on their vision for Slovak independence abroad and for their goal of dignity, respect, and achievement for Slovak-Americans in the U.S. As the decade of the 1930s drew to a close, rays of hope for the independence of Slovaks in Europe would begin to break through the dark skies. But these rays of sunshine would be quickly clouded by another storm gathering over the European continent; a storm that would challenge the fortitude of the world and provide the Slovak League and John Kocur its greatest test.

**Endnotes**

1. *Kocur, Jan: To the Question of Organizing and Starting Self-Help Organizations. Slovak League of America. October, 1931.*
2. *Stolarich, Imrich; Jan Kocur – Slovak's Very Own Lincoln, pg 2. 1981*
3. *Ibid.*
4. *Ibid, pg 4.*
5. *Ibid, pg 3.*
6. *Ibid, pg 4.*
7. *Ibid, pg 3.*
8. *Ibid.*
9. *Kocur, Jan: To the Question of Organizing and Starting Self-Help Organizations. Slovak League of America. October, 1931.*
10. *Ibid.*
11. *Ibid.*
12. *Pauco, Jozef; Slovak Pioneers in America – Chapter on Jan A. Kocur. 1972*
13. *Pir, Fr. Andrew V.; Jan A. Kocur: Human Rights Advocate. Jednota. 1977*
14. *Pauco, Jozef; Slovak Pioneers in America – Chapter on Jan A. Kocur. 1972*

**Chapter 16**

# THE FIRST REPUBLIC

# Chapter 16

Since the signing of the Pittsburgh Agreement in May of 1918, the Slovak League of America had led the fight to incorporate the agreement's principles into the constitution of the newly created Czecho-Slovak state. The league rightfully felt that the path to Slovak autonomy, both politically and socially, was clearly outlined in the "Pittsburghska Dohoda" (the Pittsburgh Agreement) and was legitimized by the identity of the signers but also by their current positions in the new Czecho-Slovak government. The efforts of the Slovak League and key Slovak national figures, however, had met with much resistance in the twenty years since the signing of the historic document. John Kocur, as a key figure in the Slovak League during most of the time since the signing of the Pittsburgh Agreement, helped to push forward the case for bringing the document's principles to life through various means. Alas, the efforts of Kocur and of other Slovak League officials amounted to swimming upstream for nearly twenty years; frustrated at every turn by those in control of the Czech government and by the apparent apathy of those in the U.S. government.

Over the span of the two decades since the end of World War I, there had been a number of smaller and larger delegations sent from America to Slovakia and vice versa.[1] These delegations, often coordinated by the Slovak League of America, encompassed cultural, civic, and political exchanges. One of the more important political delegations from America came to the Slovak city of Trenčín to commemorate the tenth anniversary of the Pittsburgh Agreement, joined there for the celebration by the Slovak activist Andre Hlinka. Perhaps the most important visit to America came in 1937. The delegation from Slovakia was that of the "Spolok sv. Vojtecha" (Society or Fellowship of St. Adalbert), which included Monsignor Jozef Tiso, a Catholic priest and a man destined to play a central role in Slovak autonomy.

Tiso was, by then, a growing figure in Slovak politics and a leader in the drive for Slovak autonomy and independence. Monsignor Tiso's visit included many speaking engagements with American Slovaks and meetings with Slovak fraternal groups. Tiso knew, however, that his most important ally in America was the Slovak League, and he spent his time accordingly, visiting and conferencing with each of the league's leaders, including John Kocur. When Monsignor Tiso visited the house of John Kocur, he asked, "Is this the house where the secretary of the Slovak League lives?" Kocur's work and reputation was well known by Tiso and the Slovak leader was a bit surprised at the humble way in which Kocur lived.[2] John Kocur was proud of his work in the Slovak League and was a person of great humility. For him, status was not important and stature was measured by how much one could help his fellow Slovaks, not in the type or size of his home. During Tiso's visit John Kocur took great pride in presenting his distinguished guest with a copy of the Pittsburgh Agreement and spread open the agreement in front of Monsignor Tiso with such deep feelings in his eyes and in his heart and was so honored to be the one to show the "Slovak Magna Carta" to this noble dignitary.[3] The Slovak League, at that time, was the keeper of the Pittsburgh Agreement and John Kocur was the document's protector, allegedly keeping the prized manuscript secured in his Springdale home at various times in order to ensure its safety from those who sought to discredit and even deny its very existence.

Among the reciprocal visits to Slovakia by various representatives of the Slovak League, a visit in May 1938 by a delegation headed by Dr. Peter Hletko, then Slovak League president, and Jozef Husek, an original signer of the Pittsburgh Agreement, sought to make the final push for Slovak autonomy. The delegation brought with it the original draft of the Pittsburgh Agreement to a celebration which was held on June 4, 1938 in commemoration of the twentieth anniversary of the signing of the historic document.[4] A crowd of thousands cheered as the agreement was held high by the delegates during the celebration.

The issue of Slovak autonomy simply would not go away. The Slovak people would not let it die and simply accept their fate as subjects of the Czech-dominated government and the Slovak League of America would not let it die and walk away from their fellow countrymen or a cause so many had championed for so long. Finally, on October 6, 1938 the Slovak people attained the autonomy they so longed for when the principles of the Pittsburgh Agreement were incorporated into the Constitution of the Czecho-Slovak state.[5] On page 1,161 of the "Collection of the laws and regulations of the Czecho-Slovak State" the subject of autonomy for Slovakia is addressed:

"The National Assembly, on the premise that Czecho-Slovak Republic was formed on the basis of the agreement of the sovereign will of two equal nations, that in the Pittsburgh Agreement the Slovak nation was promised complete autonomy, and motivated by the desire to bring the Slovak and Czech nations into a friendly relationship in the spirit of the Žilina agreement, approves the following laws:"

With a renewed enthusiasm, the Slovak people began to build their own new national home based on the principles outlined in the Pittsburgh Agreement. Recognizing the contributions that Slovak Americans and in particular the Slovak League of America made to the struggle, the new autonomous government was anxious to reach out to their American brothers because, as Mikulas Sprinc wrote in *Sixty Years of the Slovak League of America*, "The Slovak nation wanted to know about the life of the American Slovaks because a mutual affection and friendship develops through knowledge and understanding." Close ties between Slovak-Americans and their fellow countrymen also existed because of the close relationships between relatively new arrivals in the U.S. and family back home. With these factors in mind, the new autonomous Slovak government sent Konstantin Culen to the United States in order to establish closer cultural ties with American Slovaks and act as a lifeline between the Slovaks in their homeland and their fellow countryman overseas. Culen was also to maintain communication between the American Slovak organizations and the Slovaks at home.[6] Chief among these organizations was the Slovak League of America, to whom Culen paid a special visit in early March of 1939.

Konstantin Culen was warmly welcomed to Pittsburgh during a special meeting of the Slovak League of America's executive committee. John Kocur recorded the historic visit:

"President Husek warmly welcomed the distinguished guest, Konstantin Culen, from Slovakia. The Slovak emissary thanked him sincerely and in his brief response expressed his feelings and extended the greetings of the Slovak government and parliament to all the American Slovaks. The applause was spontaneous and enthusiastic."

Culen went on to note the gratitude of the Slovak people towards the Slovak League of America and all American Slovaks, extending an invitation for members of the league to come to Bratislava and attend sessions in the Slovak parliament when the subject of the constitution was discussed. How vitally interested the Slovak League of America was in the matter of Slovak autonomy in 1939 is evident from the same special executive meeting as a delegation to visit Slovakia was selected. The delegates chosen and unanimously approved included Ivan Bielek, John Kocur, Jozef Husek, Mrs. Gabriela Vavrek, and Dr. Peter Hletko. The executive session also passed a resolution that the above-named delegation should take the original Pittsburgh Agreement document and present it to the Slovak nation, "with due ceremony." Lastly, and most likely to Culen's great happiness, a fund raising campaign to help Slovakia was organized. This move again received unanimous approval of all present at the meeting because they realized how important it was to lend a helping hand at this particular time of the Slovak nation's history.[7]

The Slovak League and its dedicated men like John Kocur could now rejoice in the accomplishment they had worked toward for so long: the incorporation of the principles of the Pittsburgh Agreement into the Czecho-Slovak constitution and the formation of an autonomous Slovak government. For the first time since the fall of its Kingdom of Moravia at the beginning of the tenth century, the Slovaks had their own national parliament and were assured self-government.[8]

From October, 1938 to March, 1939 the Slovak parliament began the joyful work of building the governmental infrastructure necessary to support an autonomous state. National pride among Slovaks in their homeland as well as among Slovak-Americans was at its highest point in years and the future seemed bright; all were willing to work as hard as necessary to ensure that their dream of self-government would become real. The brutal reality of events unfolding in other parts of Europe in 1939, however, would shake the Slovaks from their dreams like a thunderclap in the middle of the night and force upon them the most difficult of choices, a choice requiring more than even the wisdom of Solomon.

In the late 1930s a new force was beginning to take hold in one of Europe's traditional powers, Germany. The rise of Adolf Hitler and the Nazi party can be attributed to many factors, but it is undeniable that one of the driving forces behind this rise, and Hitler's hypnotic affect on the German people, was the still relatively fresh scar of World War I. Only twenty years earlier the mighty German state was brought to its knees by the victorious allies England, France, and the United States. In 1919, with the United States far removed from the European dynamic both geographically and historically and with its president's attention focused on a higher diplomatic agenda, the terms of peace forced upon the Germans were left to England and France. Neither country, having suffered so much during the previous five years, wanted anything but the strictest military, geographic, and economic terms imposed on their defeated neighbor.

Since the end of World War I, the German people paid dearly for the mistakes of their government and military leaders. The combination of a defeated and weakened Germany, forced to swallow bitter peace terms, and the deepening world-wide Depression of the late 1920s and 1930s produced a smoldering attitude among the German people and a power vacuum in their leadership. Hitler's message of blame and victimization was something to which the German people could relate. He fully exploited the suffering of the German people and they responded to his mesmerizing delivery.

A key term of the peace to which Germany was subjected following World War I was the annexation of the Sudetenland. According to the peace terms this traditional part of German territory, nearly eleven thousand square miles, was to become part of Czecho-Slovakia. By 1938 the German government, now under Nazi control, had been able to push aside many of the post-1919 peace terms with regard to military size and economic sanctions. Territory, however, was a much more visible issue to other European neighbors and more difficult for the Germans to address. Hitler at first wanted to simply march into the Sudetenland but was persuaded by his generals that such an openly aggressive step would likely bring responses by France, Great Britain, and the Soviet Union. A confrontation between Germany and these nations, combined with the Czecho-Slovak forces defending their homeland, would likely lead to Germany being badly defeated. Hitler found himself in a difficult situation, needing the Sudetenland to consolidate German territory and validate his leadership with the German people but wanting to avoid war with an overwhelming number of European powers. In September 1938, British Prime Minister Neville Chamberlain met Hitler at his home in Berchtesgaden. In that meeting Hitler took the bold step of informing Chamberlain of his plans to invade Czechoslovakia unless Britain supported Germany's plans to retake the Sudetenland. Chamberlain, following discussion of the issue with France and Czecho-Slovakia informed Hitler that his proposals were unacceptable. The German leader knew, however, that Britain and France were unwilling to go to war for the second time in twenty years over the seemingly insignificant Sudetenland issue. Hitler also thought it unlikely that these two countries would ally themselves with the communist Soviet Union. The German leader's solution was to call another meeting among representatives of the current European powers England, France, Italy, and Germany and bargain for the Sudetenland in return for a promise of no other territorial demands. The ploy worked and on September 29, 1938 Hitler, Neville Chamberlain (England), Edouard Daladier (France), and Benito Mussolini (Italy) signed the Munich Agreement, which transferred the Sudetenland to Germany. Two days later, on October 1, 1938, German forces marched into the Sudetenland, spelling an end to the territorial integrity of Czecho-Slovakia.

Events continued to unfold with regard to the Czech territories in early 1939. Adolf Hitler, never really intending to stop at just the Sudetenland, moved further into Czecho-Slovakia and took over Bohemia and Moravia declaring these territories protectorates of the Third Reich. It appeared as through the walls were closing in on the country's now autonomous Slovak territories when, in March, 1939, Monsignor Jozef Tiso was summoned to Berlin by Hitler. There Tiso was reminded of the danger that threatened the Czecho-Slovak Republic and that a similar catastrophe would befall Slovakia if a quick decision with regard to alliance could not be reached. Slovakia, just removed from living for more than twenty years under a government where every phase of her life was centralized in Prague, without an army, without officers in the Czecho-Slovak army, without industry or separate finances, was given the choice of complete surrender as a part of the Czecho-Slovak Republic, or "independence" under the protection of the German Reich.[9] Slovakia, only so recently autonomous from the Czechs, was now between a rock and a hard place.

The momentous decision that lay before Tiso and the Slovak parliament represented the choice, as John Kocur and Francis Dubosh wrote, of national suicide or national self-preservation.[10] On one hand, refusing the option of national independence most likely meant that Slovakia would be immediately taken over by the Germans and divided among any number of interested parties. Poland, already in possession of two Slovak counties, had just recently marched into Czecho-Slovakia and shared in its partition. Hungary had never relinquished her claims to Slovakia and was now willing to barter her goodwill in exchange for all or part of the country. Rumors already circulated of the proposed division of Slovakia between the Germans and the Magyars. The Czechs themselves had repeatedly refused to recognize the right of the Slovaks to nationhood and national freedom.[11] The very future of the Slovaks, both as a nation and as a people would be in doubt should any of these scenarios come to fruition.

The Slovak struggle for independence, on the other hand, had gone on throughout the centuries. For years the people of Slovakia had struggled against kings, lords, emperors, and generals in their quest to achieve independence. The Slovaks never asked for, nor desired the support of the Germans in their national struggle. From the very beginning of their history the Germans have been the Slovaks' traditional enemies.[12] Yet in March of 1939 it was the Germans, the Slavs' enemy, who laid this difficult, near impossible choice at Tiso's feet.

After the conference in Berlin, Dr. Tiso returned to Slovakia to report on the situation. It was only after a lengthy deliberation that the democratically elected members of the autonomous Slovak Parliament decided that under the given circumstances, there was nothing else for it to do but declare independence; and that it did on March 14, 1939. Monsignor Dr. Jozef Tiso became Slovakia's first president.

Following its declaration, Slovakia was recognized as an independent state by over twenty countries including Great Britain, Russia, and the Vatican. No country, not even the United States, protested against the independence of this newest member of the European community. For Slovaks in America, Slovakia's autonomy following the Munich Agreement, Germany's subsequent invasion of Czecho-Slovakia and finally, the creation of the independent state were seismic events.[13] From the perspective of the Slovak League of America and its leadership the independence of Slovakia was the fulfillment of a lifelong dream even under the circumstances that surrounded the declaration. At the time of independence, 1939, Hitler had not yet become the scourge of Europe and the alternatives to assuming the path of independence appeared to represent certain national destruction. Tiso, as president of the Slovak state, fully recognized the great ally that the Slovak League and the many supporters in that organization represented. In his capacity as president of the Slovak state, Monsignor Tiso sent the Slovak League of America a comprehensive communication dated May 23, 1939 in which he conveyed official greetings to the Slovaks of the United States and assured them of the historic significance of the creation of the Slovak state. He saw in this momentous achievement the most effective step that could safeguard Slovak interests in the midst of the central European maelstrom.[14]

Similarly, when Tiso was duly elected president of the Slovak Republic, he sent to the 22nd Congress of the Slovak League of America, which was convened in Cleveland, Ohio on November 14-15, 1939, a cablegram expressing utmost sentiments of regard and utter devotion on behalf of the newly freed country of

Slovakia. When this message was delivered on the floor of the Congress, it was received with thunderous applause and the Slovak League of America reciprocated with a similarly hearty message forwarded by cablegram to the Slovak president.[15]

The reaction of the Slovak League was not limited, however, to simple words of encouragement. At an executive meeting in May of 1939 the officers of the league formulated their official reaction to the news in their homeland. Kocur recorded their next steps. "First, the League would establish a special committee to draw up a Memorandum to be addressed to the governments of the U.S., Britain, and France in the interest of and for the recognition of the Slovak state, a revision of the boundaries, and a provision to guarantee the cultural rights of Slovaks living inside Hungary. Second, the League would designate a reporter on its behalf and dispatch him to Slovakia to determine the situation there and investigate the exact conditions under which the Slovaks decided to terminate their alliance with the Czechs."[16]

After discussing the matter further, the members at the executive meeting agreed to authorize the Slovak League executive officers: 1) to name the necessary committees; 2) to establish an information bureau in Washington, D.C. in order to counteract false, deceitful and slanted anti-Slovak news in the American press and furnish the American press instead with information founded on facts and the truth; 3) to create memorandum and pamphlets, written in English, in the interests of the Slovak nation and its officially constituted free state, the Slovak Republic;. 4) to take the necessary steps for a hearing in the State Department in the nation's capital to obtain U.S. recognition of the Slovak Republic.[17]

As an integral part of the Slovak League of America and someone responsible for drafting much of the league's official positions and statements, John Kocur was squarely behind the new Slovak Republic. Not all American Slovaks, however, shared Kocur's views on the newly created state. Much of the disagreement, taking place before America's entry into the coming World War, was along historically religious lines. When Slovakia proclaimed independence in March of 1939, the spokespersons for various Catholic organizations (the Slovak League of America was a predominantly Catholic organization) were pleased. The

National Slovak Society, with a religiously diverse membership, had welcomed autonomy in 1938 but opposed independence and wanted Czecho-Slovakia restored to the prior federated structure. Slovak Protestants based much of their objections about independence on the apparent Catholic control of the new republic.[18]

Slovak organizations in the U.S. waged their battles in the press and there was apparently no middle ground. The independent Slovakia was either a dream come true or a nightmare. Dr. Tiso was either a hero or a traitor. Slovakia was either independent for the first time in its history or merely a puppet of the Third Reich. Events in the Slovak homeland, just as during the early days of World War I, could still engage and stir the emotions of Slovak-Americans in the U.S. For John Kocur, someone who had lived, worked, and served the causes of fellow Slovaks since his arrival in the U.S., the choice of Slovak independence in 1939 was the right decision; his principles could dictate to him no other course. Kocur's work to support the independence of his fellow countrymen, however, was about to get infinitely more difficult. In September of 1939, the German "blitzkrieg" hit Poland, viewed as a clear and outright act of aggression to everyone in the world community. In a few short years, America would be embroiled in another European war, Slovakia would be embroiled in a controversy of allegiance, and the loyalty of the Slovak League of America as well as one of its most faithful members, John Kocur, would be put to the test.

## Endnotes

1. *Sidor, Karol; The Slovak League of America and the Slovak Nation's Struggle for Autonomy – Sixty Years of the Slovak League of America, pg 67. 1967*

2. *Stolarich, Imrich; This is How Jan. A. Kocur Lived and Worked – Calendar of the Slovak League. 1981*

3. *Prusa, Jozef; Emotional Burial of Chief Secretary of the Slovak League of America. Catholic Sokol, July 21, 1948*

4. *Sidor, Karol; The Slovak League of America and the Slovak Nation's Struggle for Autonomy – Sixty Years of the Slovak League of America, pg 68. 1967*

5. *Sprinc, Mikulas; Slovak League of America and Independent Slovakia – Sixty Years of the Slovak League of America, pg 71. 1967*

6. *Ibid.*

7. *Ibid, pg 72.*

8. *Ibid, pg 73.*

9. *Kocur and Dubosh; The Slovaks and Their Right to Nationhood, pg 14. 1943*

10. *Ibid.*

11. *Ibid.*

12. *Ibid.*

13. *Alexander, June; Ethnic Pride, American Patriotism, pg 196. 2004*

14. *Mikus, Joseph; The Slovak League of America: A Historical Survey, pg 48. 1963*

15. *Ibid.*

16. *Sprinc, Mikulas; Slovak League of America and Independent Slovakia – Sixty Years of the Slovak League of America, pg 76. 1967*

17. *Ibid.*

18. *Alexander, June; Ethnic Pride, American Patriotism, pg 197. 2004*

## Chapter 17

# A QUESTION OF LOYALTY

# Chapter 17

On a cool fall day in 1940, several young Slovak school students were enjoying their lunch of noodle soup at the home of John Kocur. It was often that these local children would come to Kocur's home for the type of physical nourishment that the warm soup, made by Margaret Kocur, would provide. It was also an opportunity for these children to receive a kind of emotional and intellectual nourishment from a man who, by 1940, was arguably as important to the causes of Slovaks as anyone in the world. As important as he was, however, John Kocur had time to encourage the Slovak children to study hard in school and be proud that they were Slovak.

It was on such a day, recalled one of the students, Elena Novakova, that a large black sedan pulled up the black cinder alley below Ross Street and stopped in front of the Kocur house. Out of the car stepped five agents of the Federal Bureau of Investigation, smartly dressed in suits and ties but nonetheless carrying holstered pistols beneath their jackets. The agents approached the Kocur house and knocked on the door. Inside, several school children were having their lunch, Margaret Kocur was preparing food for later that day, and John Kocur was involved in a meeting in his home office. Kocur's daughter Amelia was also at home and answered the knock at the door. Amelia Kocur, also known as Millie, acted as her father's personal secretary often handling his correspondence on Slovak League business, arranging his appointments, and managing the affairs of his office. At age sixteen, Amelia had become her father's right hand in managing the functions of his office and had become intimately involved with and knowledgeable of the priorities and issues of the Slovak League of America.

The men from the FBI were there to see John Kocur, the secretary of the Slovak League, and Amelia let them in to wait in the enclosed front porch area of the house where a door led to her father's office. By late 1940 the joy that had spread through many parts of the Slovak community over the birth of the independent Slovak Republic had been replaced by a feeling of disappointment. With German forces on the march throughout Europe, the true and horrible nature of the Third Reich was being revealed. Slovakia, while formally independent and having gained their independence before the war under the most difficult of situations, was now being viewed by many as a nation tied closely to Germany, the ultimate expression of guilt by association. The German influence, present at the start of the first independent Slovak Republic, now hung like a dark cloud over the still-infant Slovak nation.

The U.S. government, while not yet involved in Europe's new conflict from a military sense in 1940, was supporting allies in France and Great Britain with significant material and monetary aid. Also of concern to the U.S. at that time were the activities and allegiances of certain foreign organizations and individuals. It was with that interest in mind that the agents of the FBI arrived at John Kocur's home in the fall of 1940.

As four of the FBI men waited in the front room the remaining agent went with John Kocur to his office, closing the door behind them. Kocur's wife, daughter, and the handful of school children in the house kept their distance from the agents and waited nervously in the kitchen for the secretary to conclude his meeting. At last the door opened and both men emerged from Kocur's office. The agents completed their business and left.

Such a scene had obvious affects on the children, who asked John Kocur and Amelia what had just taken place. Kocur explained that the men were from the government and had come to ask him questions about the activities of the Slovak League of America. John Kocur tried to personally reassure the children, as did his daughter Amelia, that the men meant no harm to anyone but were interested in documents and information. The secretary of the league, as holder of organizational records and correspondence, was the natural place for the men to come for such information, Kocur explained. The children proceeded back to school that afternoon but the events of the day at the Kocur house had obviously made a large impact.

Not long after the agents visited, word had spread among those in the local Slovak community that their most recognized advocate had been questioned by the FBI. The news was received with concern among local Slovaks, many of whom were still wary about the historical legacy from the old country of government agents entering homes and investigating individuals. After the FBI visit the number of callers to Kocur's home decreased as uncertainty and concern about whom else might be subject to the same type of government focus arose. Word about the situation and how John Kocur was holding up during this time was relayed to the Slovak community by Kocur's daughter Amelia and by Kocur's longtime friend and fellow barber from the early days, Juraj Gazak. Gazak continued his weekly visits to the Kocur house for Sunday dinner as he always had and was able to let friends in the community know that the secretary had not been taken away by the government men, and that he was holding up well, busy compiling the necessary information that would defend the Slovak League. John Kocur, however, was not the only member of the Slovak League of America to receive a visit from the FBI. The agents had interviewed all of the league officers on the day of their visit to John Kocur's house but had decided to concentrate their efforts on the secretary due to his position.[1]

As the investigation went on, the black sedan containing FBI agents would periodically be seen parked in front of the Kocur house. Boxes of material would be taken out of the home, screened, and sometime later returned with the marking "Cleared" stamped on them. While not known to most of John Kocur's friends and colleagues, the FBI investigation was related to fears that the Slovak League of America might be "dangerous to the national interests of the United States" and that its officers could be "subversive elements."[2] With the war in Europe going on, communications with Slovakia were unreliable at best so accurate information as to the state of affairs in the Slovak Republic and direct communication with the government was nearly impossible. This fact, combined with a very real effort among elements of the former Czech rulers to label the Slovak League and Slovakia as a loyal ally of Hitler and therefore an enemy of the United States, helped to contribute to the pressure placed on the league and its officers by the U.S. government.

Faced with what amounted to a propaganda campaign from former Czech government officials intent on gaining back Slovakia by discrediting a free Slovakia's biggest supporter, the Slovak League, and the investigations of the U. S. government the league stood fast in its defense of the truth and freedom. The Slovak League membership, its president and executive officers were men of personal integrity and loyal citizens of the United States. They met the challenge without flinching and withstood the test with courage and dignity.[3] The league and it officers like John Kocur continued to address the issue of Slovak freedom, self-government, and free statehood in all that they did.

As the year 1942 began, the United States found itself fully involved as a combatant in World War II. In two theaters of war spanning more than half the globe, America had committed her troops to help push back dual waves of aggression. In Europe specifically, the German domination and conquest of territory had nearly reached its peak. The Slovak Republic, only three years old, found itself figuratively and literally in the eye of the storm that raged throughout Europe.

During most of World War II, communication between concerned Slovaks in the United States and those in the Slovak homeland and its government was tenuous and unreliable. In particular, the Slovak League of America exhausted all available avenues and put forth incredible effort in order to maintain contact with the new Slovak Republic and support the young nation. The Slovak League of America constantly worked through U.S. diplomatic channels, Slovak national organizations, and the American press hoping to add legitimacy to the Slovak Republic and drive toward official U.S. recognition. It was, however, an uphill fight. The league was forced to battle the perception in the U.S. State Department and among many non-Slovak Americans that the Slovak Republic was an ally of Germany; a perception partially driven by the public relations machine and propaganda of former Czech government officials intent on discrediting any Slovak claims for independence with an eye toward the full restoration of Czecho-Slovakia in the post-war Europe. John Kocur and the Slovak League of America found themselves pulled in all directions once again. The league had to continue its efforts on behalf of the Slovak homeland, as well as play a part in an overall effort to support the needs of the United States in a time of war.

During World War II the efforts and contributions of all Americans were viewed as essential in helping to win the war. Beginning with America's entry into the war, the Slovak League of America undertook a widespread sponsorship of U.S. War Bonds.[4] Buying war bonds was one way in which Slovaks could visibly support the war effort. It was also a way to directly and indirectly demonstrate support for America, manifest American patriotism, and help to dispel the notion that Slovaks in America would somehow not fully support the war effort because of the controversy surrounding the perceived allegiance of their homeland.

Under the leadership of executive officers like John Kocur, the Slovak League established a national committee to manage bond drives.[5] The efforts by Slovaks and their varied fraternal and religious organizations to raise money through bond drives occurred at both the national and grass roots level. The Slovak War Bonds Committee in Western Pennsylvania was a case in point. To make Slovaks part of a local multi-ethnic drive in 1942, the committee established the "American Slovak Booth" in downtown Pittsburgh. Advertising that Slovaks would get credit for the bond purchases it launched a campaign calling on area Slovaks to buy bonds at that particular station.[6] By the end of the war the bond-buying efforts by American Slovaks had raised over 53 million dollars.[7] Local and national newspapers noted the significant efforts of Slovaks particularly, fostering a sense of ethnic pride and competition with other ethnic groups. Eleanor Roosevelt even went so far as to mention the fund raising efforts of Slovak- Americans in one of her "My Day" columns, much to the delight of Slovaks in the U.S.[8] The U.S. government, seeking to raise as much money from as many sources as possible, recognized the value of ethnic-based fund raising and encouraged it wherever possible through its ethnic mobilization campaign, a campaign specifically designed to enlist the support of America's many ethnic groups.

Slovaks were rewarded in very public ways for their activities in raising war funds. Western Pennsylvania's Slovak bonds committee, for example raised enough money through the sale of bonds to purchase a B-17 bomber. In the spring of 1943, as a tribute to the efforts of Slovak-Americans in Western Pennsylvania the B-17 bomber "The American Slovak" was dedicated. Following this dedication, John Kocur kept a large photograph of the plane on the wall of his home office. Better yet for Slovak-Americans, a picture of the plane with its name prominently visible appeared on the cover of "The Minute Man", the newsletter of the Treasury Department's War Savings staff.[9] An accompanying article inside the May 1943 "Minute Man" praised Slovaks for their efforts. Thanks to the additional fund raising efforts of John Kocur and Slovak League chapters across the country, the War Department credited the league with having paid for three war training planes, which were officially presented on an airfield in Cleveland, Ohio on May 26, 1943. The ceremony, attended by all the Slovak League officers, officially dedicated the planes each with the inscription "Spirit of the Slovak League of America."[10] Later in the war the government also named three liberty ships after prominent Slovak heroes, unknown to many Americans but household names to Slovaks. Elaborate ceremonies marked the launch of the *Stephen Furdek* (founder of the Slovak League), the *Sgt. Matej Kocak* (a WWI army hero), and the *General Milan Štefánik* (a prominent Slovak military leader). These ceremonies, also attended by Kocur and his fellow league officers, brought the Slovak League and the American Slovaks widespread publicity. Recognition of the Slovak League's efforts from the government, the American press, and the Slovak community only served to foster a greater sense of ethnic pride and grow additional support during a troubled time.

Even as the war bond efforts were getting started, the Slovak League led the charge for an increase in wartime social and charitable giving among the Slovak community. At an executive committee meeting in August, 1941, John Kocur recorded a plan to organize a Ladies Auxiliary of the Slovak League officially known as "Slovenske Vcielky" or "Slovak Bees." Slovak women from all parts of America enrolled as members in the new auxiliary, which cooperated closely with the work of organizations like the Red Cross. Details of some of the work accomplished by the Slovak Ladies Auxiliary were reported at the Slovak League Congress in February, 1943. The organization had presented the Red Cross with over sixty-six thousand surgical dressings, twenty-two hundred suits of clothes for war refugees, knitted sweaters, caps, shawls, and gloves for soldiers. In addition, blood was donated, first aid kits completed, and a total of six hundred thirty shipments were sent to American soldiers of Slovak ancestry. These American Slovak women, under the umbrella of the Slovak League, contributed invaluable service to their country and enhanced the good name of the Slovak League and the Slovaks in America generally.[11]

As World War II went on, increasing in intensity and blanketing nearly all parts of the world, John Kocur continued to help drive the war effort among Slovaks in the United States while maintaining an ever vigilant eye on developments in his homeland. The war, however, would also come to touch Kocur's family personally. On April 27, 1942 at the age of fifty-three, John Kocur did something that he had last done over twenty years before; he registered for the draft. As required at the time of all men born after April 28, 1877 and on or before February 16, 1897, John Kocur completed a draft registration card. Kocur provided on the registration card that his address was 918 Ross Street in Springdale, Pennsylvania with a telephone number of SP 371; his wife Margaret was noted on the registration as "someone who would always know your address." Also on the draft registration card, Kocur was listed as being five feet five and one-half inches tall, weighing approximately one hundred thirty-five pounds, with grey eyes, and brown hair. It was highly unlikely that any men in John Kocur's age group required to register at that time would be called upon to serve. Nonetheless, Kocur once again fulfilled his duty as a male American citizen by registering for the draft. On the same day, April 27, 1942, and possibly at the same time, Kocur's close friend George (Juraj) Gazak also completed his draft registration card. Gazak, known as GeeKee (as his initials were G. K.) was fifty-six years old at the time of his registration and listed his address as 517 Walnut Street in Springdale, approximately five blocks from John Kocur's home on Ross Street. George Gazak also listed his close friend John Kocur as the person who would "always know your address." In addition to John Kocur's registration during the early part of the war, his son John Jr. also served the United States during World War II.

In 1943 the German war machine continued to grind away in Europe and, despite America's active participation in the war up to that point, an allied victory was still not yet a certainty. At home in the United States, the Slovak League of America had stepped up its support of the American war effort and provided the U.S. government one of the best demonstrations of harnessing the power of ethnic patriotism. Slovaks from around the country contributed their time, and money, and in many cases sent loved ones to the front lines to further an allied victory. All the while the future of their homeland still hung in the balance. Part of the reason that so many Slovaks, including John Kocur, vigorously contributed to the American war effort was that an allied victory over the forces of totalitarianism would mean an infinitely better chance of true freedom and liberation for their fellow Slovaks in Europe. Kocur and other leaders of the Slovak League, having experienced both oppression in their homeland and freedom in the United States, believed that the principles of American democracy and freedom were ultimately the Slovaks' best hope.

This belief took shape and was put to paper in 1943 in one of the Slovak League's most significant documents. John Kocur and Slovak League President Monsignor Francis Dubosh co-authored an historic memorandum titled "Slovaks and their Rights to Nationhood," which reviewed the struggle of Slovaks throughout the centuries for their national freedom and their right to determine their own national destiny on the fundamental democratic principle and tradition of self-determination.[12] This memorandum was sent directly to President Franklin Roosevelt and prominently featured, on the front cover, Roosevelt's own proclamation and democratic creed that "Every nation, no matter how small, has the inherent right to its own nationhood." The position of the Slovak League within the document, however, was not one that demanded the creation of an independent Slovakia. In fact that question, Kocur and Dubosh wrote, was one that was not theirs to answer but belonged to the Slovak people. They wrote:

> *To us, the Slovak question is not one of whether or not Czecho-Slovakia should be reconstructed. It is not a question of*

> *whether Slovakia should be formed into a politically independent state. Higher and more sacred aims concern us; aims which are important not only to us because of our Slovak decent, but which are equally important to every man and woman prepared today to make the supreme sacrifice in order to assure happiness to future generations.*[13]

The historic statement by the Slovak League of America tries to ensure that the issue of Slovak freedom and independence is seen in the light of American democratic principles; ones which Slovak-Americans had come to embrace, ones which the American government promoted at home and abroad, and ones for which millions of liberty loving people around the world were fighting and dying.

The Slovak League and its leaders, many of whom had lived through oppression in their homeland and fought against those forces in the last World War, were mindful of the mistakes inherent in establishing the new order in Europe following the Treaty of Versailles. Men like John Kocur were attempting to ensure those same mistakes that so negatively affected Slovakia and other small nations post World War I were not made again following the next allied victory in Europe, rather that American principles of liberty and self-determination were the guiding forces in the building of a new order. Kocur and Dubosh wrote:

> *To the majority of Americans of Slovak descent the problem of the future of the Slovaks abroad is only one of many similar problems which will have to be solved after the war is won. We are all engaged in a gigantic struggle for survival and for the preservation of the democratic principles of life. We are determined to end once and for all, the imperialism and tyranny which have brought so much suffering and anguish to individual nations and to humanity as a whole. We are making sacrifices, willingly and cheerfully, in order that truth and justice may prevail in this world despite, and contrary to, the selfish aims of any one or more groups. We know that only in this way can peace and the happiness of mankind be assured.*[14]

In the conclusion of the historic memorandum, Kocur and Dubosh appeal to President Roosevelt and others in the U.S. government to be guided by the president's own words in their consideration of the Slovak cause for freedom once the war was concluded.

> *Every nation, no matter how small, has the inherent right to its own nationhood. This was the pronouncement of our President, Franklin D. Roosevelt. This principle, so clearly setting forth one of the aims of the present struggle, is embodied in the Atlantic Charter. It has been reiterated time and again, in the public utterances made by our leaders and statesmen. We, Americans of Slovak descent; we who sacrifice and fight today side by side with all the peoples who have dedicated their lives to the cause of freedom, appeal to our leaders in the name of this sacred cause, that, considering the fate of Slovakia, they will not permit themselves to be lead by those who would deny and who have denied the Slovaks their right to their national existence; that, the right of the Slovak people to their nationhood won by centuries of struggle against oppression and tyranny be recognized; and that, the liberty, freedom and the means to a democratic life be granted to the Slovaks in the same full measure as it shall be granted to other nations.*[15]

In the war's remaining two years, John Kocur and the Slovak League continued to press the U.S. government at its highest levels on the cause of Slovak freedom and independence in a post-war Europe. The league also continued to be a driving force among Slovaks in the United States with regard to the U.S. war effort at home. The war would draw to a victorious close for the allies and the real work of gaining a voice in the post-war European community of nations would begin.

In the final days of the war when the Organization of United Nations was being formed in San Francisco, the Slovak League commissioned two representatives to attend as delegates of the league. On April 25, 1945, these two official Slovak-American representatives distributed to all the delegates in attendance a copy of a Slovak League statement titled, "Plea on Behalf of the

Slovak People to the U.S. Congress and the World Security Organization." In this document, the Slovak League of America again sponsored the cause of Slovakia and urged the world's nations to recognize for the Slovak nation its right to a free and unrestricted opportunity to decide its own political fate and future. Most unfortunately, amid the fanfare of post-war triumphs and exhilaration, and in the whirl that found the Western powers celebrating with the Soviets over the downfall of Germany, the voice of the small Slovak nation was lost.[16]

As the dust settled following the conclusion of World War II and the allied powers began the mammoth work of restoring a destroyed Europe, both figuratively and literally, the small cadre of exiled Czech politicians attained the restoration of Czecho-Slovakia. This was due, in no small part, to the help and support of the Soviets in Moscow. Once again the Slovaks found themselves in a familiar, although unwanted, situation. The Czech majority, with backing from the Soviet Union, would once again dictate politically and socially. For the Slovak people another war had ended and peace had brought with it the prospect of a truly independent nation. Yet once again, despite all the work and preparation in anticipation of this moment's arrival, the Slovak people and their allies in the United States found themselves back at square one. For the Slovak League of America and John Kocur the war was over, but the fight would have to continue.

## Endnotes

1. *Stolarik, Imrich; Jan Kocur – Slovak's Very Own Lincoln,. 1981*
2. *Sprinc, Mikulas; Slovak League of America and Independent Slovakia – Sixty Years of the Slovak League of America, pg 79. 1967*
3. *Ibid, pg 81.*
4. *Mikus, Joseph; The Slovak League of America: A Historical Survey, pg 49. 1963*
5. *Alexander, June; Ethnic Pride, American Patriotism, pg 208. 2004*
6. *Ibid, pg 209.*
7. *Mikus, Joseph; The Slovak League of America: A Historical Survey, pg 49. 1963*
8. *Alexander, June; Ethnic Pride, American Patriotism, pg 210. 2004*
9. *Ibid.*
10. *Mikus, Joseph; The Slovak League of America: A Historical Survey, pg 49. 1963*
11. *Sprinc, Mikulas; Slovak League of America and Independent Slovakia – Sixty Years of the Slovak League of America, pg 94. 1967*
12. *Ibid, pg 81.*
13. *Kocur and Dubosh; Slovaks and their Rights to Nationhood – Slovak League of America. 1943.*
14. *Ibid.*
15. *Ibid.*
16. *Mikus, Joseph; The Slovak League of America: A Historical Survey, pg 49. 1963*

**Chapter 18**

# POST-WAR OPPORTUNITY

# Chapter 18

Following the end of World War II a sense of national exhaustion and relief seemed to come over the United States. The sense of euphoria following V.E. and V.J. days naturally ran its course and the nation seemed to collectively exhale. All the efforts of the past four years and the intensity of a war effort that touched all Americans was paid out with victory. It was as if the long distance runner, after a grueling race in which he put out his maximum effort, had crossed the finish line, celebrated his victory and was now looking for somewhere to sit down.

This attitude was not only prevalent among the post-war policy makers in the United States government but also among the people of the country itself. It was an attitude driven by sacrifice, hardship, and struggle; and it had the effect of turning the attention of the government and the American people inward rather than toward many of the issues abroad. Those issues that Washington did focus on with regard to the rest of the world were only those that were large and far reaching. Unfortunately for the Slovak League of America the issue of Slovak independence did not make the cut.

In 1945 an historic conference of allied nations was called in San Francisco in order to decide the national destinies of peoples all over the world but particularly in Europe. The Slovak League of America, the foremost voice of concern for the welfare of the Slovak nation, was denied entry and representation due to the "official" recognition of Czech delegates as spokespersons for both Czech and Slovak causes. While the Slovak League appointed Reverend John Lach as its representative to the session, he was only able to be present as an observer, not permitted to attend any meetings, and did not have a voice in any of the discussions. Despite these limitations, Father Lach attempted to lobby other national delegations on the cause of Slovak independence but to no avail. The post- war political order for the Slovak people would once again be dominated by the Czechs.[1]

Not even when the United Nations officially granted recognition to Czecho-Slovakia did the Slovak League throw in the towel. It continued its effort to fight for the Slovak nation's cause of freedom. Peter Jurcak, a writer and political leader from Pennsylvania, succeeded Monsignor Dubosh as president of the league in 1945.[2] Jurcak was the next in a long line of Slovak League presidents, including Josef Husek, Peter Hletko, and Francis Dubosh, dedicated to the fight for Slovak freedom. While the top post in the Slovak League experienced turnover in the preceding twenty years, one man, equally dedicated to the cause, was consistently present. As 1946 began, John Kocur began his twenty-fourth year serving as secretary of the Slovak League of America, his enthusiasm and dedication to the ideals he held so dear for Slovaks everywhere as strong as ever.

John Kocur continued to play a major role in crafting the positions and direction of the Slovak League of America in the post-war period. He took an active role in developing a Slovak League memorandum directed to the president of the United States, Harry Truman, U.S. congressmen, and members of the United Nations general assembly. In this appeal, published in 1946, the league once again reviewed the history of the Slovak people, called attention to their struggle for freedom, and explained the experience of trying to live with the Czechs in one state.[3]

In the early spring of 1947, John Kocur and the rest of the Slovak League leadership watched from afar as the former president of the first Slovak Republic, Monsignor Jozef Tiso, was handed over to the communist-dominated Czech government and placed on trial. Among the more than one hundred crimes of which Tiso was accused, the most serious accusations were that he contributed to the breakup of the Czecho-Slovak Republic and that during the war collaborated with the Germans. Throughout the trial, conducted and presided over by members of Czecho-Slovakia's communist party, Tiso received the support of Slovaks both in his own country and in the United States. The Slovak League of America sent more than twenty thousand letters to all possible outlets, from the smallest fraternal branch to the president of the Untied States, in an attempt to raise support for Monsignor Tiso. John Kocur and the other executive officers of the Slovak League crafted and published a distinguished brochure in the defense of Monsignor Tiso titled, "The Truth about Slovakia." Peter Jurcak, president of the Slovak League, made eight trips to Washington, D.C. to raise his voice in the cause of saving Tiso's life. In addition, the league prepared a special appeal to President Harry Truman urging him to intercede in the matter with the Prague government. This appeal evoked a huge response among American Slovaks. Indeed, it was signed by many non-Slovaks.[4]

Throughout the "trial," in which he was not permitted to select his defense counsel and three of the four judges were Czech communists, Tiso maintained his innocence of all charges. As for the charges related to his involvement in the break up of Czecho-Slovakia, Tiso had the full support of the majority of the Slovak people and he noted during the trial that, "If God allowed me to carry out my policy again under similar circumstances, I would do exactly as I have done." Also during the trial Tiso directly answered the charge of collaboration with the Nazis by characterizing Slovakia's relationship with Germany thus, "The lion finds a frog somewhere. He looks at it from all sides, plays with it, and since the small creature pleases him, he keeps it . . . This is exactly what I think about the Germans. They hold us fast, they play with us, and it has the appearance as if we liked them. And what is now our task and duty? To behave as if we like them, so that they will play longer with us, that they will let us live. For, just as the lion could devour the frog, so the Germans could devour us. It is enough for them to close their jaws and we are done for. And our most noble interest is that we should keep alive. Therefore they may continue to play with us. Our duty, from now on, is to keep them in a good mood."

As the trial drew to a close and it became apparent that a guilty verdict and therefore a death sentence for Tiso was likely, there were large-scale demonstrations and tanks were sent to Slovakia to prevent riots.[5] Considering the nature of the "trial" and the motives of those who conducted it, it was not surprising that Tiso was found guilty of ninety-seven charges. So it came that only several weeks after the trial began, Monsignor Tiso, who had been the president of his country and credited by his court-appointed defense counsel with having saved countless thousands from death during World War II, was hanged on April 18, 1947 as he said his rosary.[6] As soon as his death was announced bells tolled all over Slovakia.[7] In America, the news of Tiso's death was greeted with great sadness among the Slovak-Americans who had worked so hard in the effort to spare the priest-president's life; none more so than John Kocur and the Slovak League.

In recognizing the tragedy of Tiso's death, Slovak League president Peter Jurcak, in his report to the 29th Congress of the Slovak League of America in Cleveland, noted "We did not succeed in saving the life of the president of the Slovak state but at least we acquainted the American public, more than ever before in the history of the Slovak League, with the Slovak nation and the Slovak question. Many congressmen became our friends; the fate of the Slovak hero so touched them that they expressed their convictions about this unpleasant affair publicly in the forum of the United States Congress and thus before the whole world."[8] As a show of support for Jurcak's statement, the 29th Congress of the Slovak League of America immediately adopted the following policy statement, "The Czecho-Slovak government in Prague has committed (April 18, 1947) the gravest kind of injustice in the hanging of Monsignor Jozef Tiso, an exemplary priest, a staunch Slovak patriot, and wartime president of the Slovak Republic. This act defies the will of the entire Slovak nation and inflicts a most damaging blow to Czecho-Slovak relations. We are convinced that this is a case of the most arbitrary parody of justice and we cannot but decisively condemn Dr. Edvard Beneš and his government."[9]

Among the other business conducted at the 29th Congress of the Slovak League of America, held in Cleveland, Ohio during October of 1947, Peter Jurcak was reelected president for the second time and John Kocur was reelected secretary for the twenty-fifth time.

The war years had been a trying time for the Slovak League of America. The league's ongoing fight for the freedom and independence of the Slovak nation had been a long battle, complicated by the arrival of the World War and Slovakia's isolation by Germany. At home in the United States, Slovak citizens were faced with renewed scrutiny over the situation in their homeland but stood up well to this test of patriotism in both money and blood. Through it all John Kocur, the ever present and consistent voice for what seemed like all Slovaks, assumed much of the burden borne by his fellow countryman. Kocur worked diligently during the war to help ensure the success of the U.S. war effort at home through the support of Slovaks in the United States. In addition he continued to press the U.S. government and international organizations for the creation of an independent Slovak state in the aftermath of what all hoped would be an allied victory.

Throughout the late 1930s and early 1940s, while the issues affecting Slovaks and their homeland seemed to grow in number and significance, John Kocur continued to work with great focus. As the issues and the workload increased for the Slovak League secretary, however, his health began to steadily decline. The trajectory of workload and health were headed in opposite directions, one up and one down, and for John Kocur there was no way to change the direction of either.

John Kocur's health was negatively influenced most by the wounds he received during his service in World War I. In 1935, the Veterans Administration established the cause of Kocur's lung condition as resulting from exposure to poison gas and had awarded him disability compensation. Since that time, John Kocur was required to be regularly examined by doctors at the Veterans Administration Hospital to note any change, positive or negative, in the conditions for which he was being compensated. Typically, these exams were preceded by a letter from the V.A. asking Kocur to report to the local Veterans Hospital for the routine physical. Characteristic of the type of notice he received, a letter dated August 26, 1942 read, "Dear Sir, This is to advise you that you will be requested to report to the Veterans Administration Facility in Aspinwall, Pa. at an early date for physical examination for purpose of disability compensation." The letter went on to ask its recipient several questions about his transportation plans and once completed and returned by the patient, a travel authorization and appointment time were mailed back. Not owning a car, John Kocur usually took the Harmony Short Line bus from Springdale to the hospital in Aspinwall for his exams. Kocur also noted that he preferred to have his exams in the afternoon as in the morning he would suffer from coughing spells and was unable to travel until his lungs became clear.

The examinations at the V.A. were complete physical workups including lab analysis. In John Kocur's case a special chest examination was also part of the appointment due to the nature of his claim and disability compensation. In an examination on September 15, 1942 Kocur had indicated that he continued to suffer from frequent chest colds, extended coughing spells, shortness of breath on exertion, and occasional pains in the chest. According to the patient, the frequency and length of the chest colds had increased over time and at certain times of the year his coughing spells, most frequently occurring in the mornings, would last longer and be more severe.

The diagnosis stemming from the exam in the fall of 1942 specifically related to the chest condition was TBC Pulmonary, Inactive and Bronchitis, Chronic. In addition, a chest X-ray found "considerable fibrosis in both upper lobes, more noticeable on the right. The general appearance of the lung fields suggests a fairly well marked pneumoconiosis." The diagnosis and progression of Kocur's condition simply meant that Kocur's lung condition was not getting any better and in some aspects his symptoms were getting worse. The results of the examination were passed along to a physician review board for consideration as to whether or not John Kocur's medical condition would justify any changes in his disability compensation. As a result of the physical exam findings in the fall of 1942 John Kocur was notified on November 5, 1942 that his disability status would be changed from "temporary partial" to "permanent partial" effective December 1, 1942. In a sense the exam helped to confirm what Kocur already knew - the fact that his wounds and their symptomatic effects were not getting any better, may get worse and were in fact permanent. Unfortunately, the change in disability status did not bring with it any change in the amount of compensation received.

As one can imagine, during trying economic times and especially during wartime the government is fairly reluctant to increase compensation payments, or any form of payment for that matter, in any significant way. One of the only changes in compensation that John Kocur was notified of during the war years had to do with the amount he was receiving for his children. In the fall of 1942, Kocur received a notice from Mr. A. R. Thompson, adjudication officer of the Veterans Administration, stating that due to the fact John Kocur's daughter Amelia was to turn eighteen years of age on October 29, 1942, "the compensation you have been receiving for said child will be discontinued at that time."

The slow decline in John Kocur's health throughout the 1940s was punctuated by the onset of Type II diabetes (diabetes mellitus) around 1946 and the development of hypertensive cardiovascular disease. Kocur's lung condition as a result of poison gas exposure in World War I, diagnosed as chronic bronchitis, remained a source of near constant discomfort and resulted in his chronic cough.

In the summer of 1947, John Kocur was busy preparing for the upcoming Slovak League Congress, his twenty-fifth as secretary. As the long-serving secretary of the Slovak League, Kocur was instrumental in organizing League congresses, overseeing agenda items, and working with League officers on specific policy statements all in addition to the interaction he would have with the many local chapter representatives who would be in attendance. The post-war era had presented the Slovak League with significant challenges in regard to their continued efforts toward a free and independent Slovakia. By 1947, the influences of the Soviets and the Western allies had placed the Czech lands and Slovakia in the middle of a tug of war for territory, a small battle in a larger geo-political struggle that the Czechs and Slovaks would eventually lose. John Kocur and the members of the Slovak League, however, were not deterred in their efforts to achieve the lifelong goal of Slovak independence.

John Kocur's usual work load was made even heavier by the preparations for the upcoming 1947 League Congress. The secretary took his place among the league's officers during the July 1947 Congress and fulfilled his necessary duties. The work and attendance to the convention, however, took its toll. Following his return home, John Kocur became too weak to continue working and had to remain in bed. His condition became worse as the days went on until he became so weak that he could barely feed himself. On August 16, 1947 Kocur was taken to the Veterans Hospital in Aspinwall and was admitted.

Upon admission to the hospital, John Kocur was treated for his diabetes and heart failure with insulin, digitoxin, and oxygen. At this time Kocur's coughing spells were severe and because of this cough he was also treated with penicillin to help prevent any occurrence of pneumonia. According to hospital records, John Kocur was in the hospital for nearly eight weeks. During that time he was classified as "severely ill" and for the first few weeks following admission was unable to regain his strength. Gradually doctors gained control of Kocur's elevated blood sugar, his heart condition gradually improved, especially as a result of regular oxygen tent treatments, and his strength began to build back. Eventually he was able to slowly walk around his room and within the hospital ward without help.

Finally on October 29, 1947 John Kocur was discharged from the hospital and returned to his home in Springdale. He was sent home with a diabetic 2,000 calorie diet, directed to take insulin daily, take a maintenance dose of digitalis daily, and continue to take potassium iodide drops for his chronic bronchitis. Kocur was also told to conduct regular urinalysis and limit his physical activity. John Kocur's discharge summary read, "This man's medical prognosis is only fair. If he keeps within the limits of his endurance he should get along well for a period of time. However, another episode of cardiac decompensation will probably be fatal. This patient should do no physical work of any type. He is secretary of an organization and, with help, can continue part of the work in this position."

John Kocur was returning home physically weaker but no less dedicated to the causes he had served all his life, those of Slovak freedom and independence. Given his physical limits, Kocur's daughter Amelia now began to assume a greater role in aiding her father with the daily business of the Slovak League. Millie dedicated a great deal of her time ensuring that her father's incredible workload could be met without having to overly tax his limited physical strength. With Millie's help, John Kocur could continue to focus on the critical issues affecting his fellow Slovaks brought on by the end of World War II.

**Endnotes**

1. *Sprinc, Mikulas; Slovak League of America and Independent Slovakia – Sixty Years of the Slovak League of America, pg 98-99. 1967*

2. *Ibid, pg 99.*

3. *Ibid, pg 100.*

4. *Pauco, Joseph; Under Dynamic Leadership – Sixty Years of the Slovak League of America, pg 112. 1967*

5. *Sutherland, Anthony; Dr. Joseph Tiso and Modern Slovakia, pg 96-97. 1978*

6. *Oddo, Gilbert; Slovakia and its People, pg 315. 1960*

7. *Vnuk, Frantisek; This is Father Tiso, pg 76. 1977*

8. *Pauco, Joseph; Under Dynamic Leadership – Sixty Years of the Slovak League of America, pg 113. 1967*

9. *Ibid, pg 114.*

## Chapter 19

# REFUGEES AND EXILES

# Chapter 19

The Slovak League of America had been engaged in the fight for Slovak freedom and independence since the organization's inception near the turn of the century. Along the way many issues, large and small, and affecting Slovaks at home in the United States and abroad, had emerged and had been dealt with by the league and its officers. In the thirty-plus years of the Slovak League's existence, however, the one consistent underlying endeavor had always been the goal of freedom for the Slovak homeland based on the principles outlined in the Pittsburgh Agreement.

In the aftermath of World War II, the Slovak League strongly opposed the influences of the Communists over the government in the newly reformed Czecho-Slovakia. In a policy document approved at the league's 29th Congress in 1947 the organization expressed a decidedly anti-Communist sentiment and re-affirmed its dedication to achieving freedom in the Slovak homeland. The policy stated, "The Slovak Republic was destroyed by a self-appointed Communist political regime and by brute military force – without consultation of the will of the Slovak people," and that the new regime, "distinguishes itself with terror and the totalitarian conquest of a country by a minority which employs any means to impose its rule over Slovakia."[1] Furthermore, the declaration of the Slovak League's 29th Congress demanded free elections in Slovakia and went on to request that President Harry Truman and the Congress of the United States protest the occupation of Slovakia and the persecution of "Slovak ecclesiastical, cultural, and political leaders."[2]

For the leaders of the Slovak League, such as President Peter Jurcak and Secretary John Kocur, a serious issue resulting from the stranglehold of the Communists over the Slovak homeland was beginning to develop. These two Slovak leaders and many in the Slovak communities all across the United States turned their attention to the fate of those in the Slovak homeland who were displaced as a result of the war and the subsequent Communist takeover: the Slovak exiles. First the league faced the problem of the expatriation of nearly two hundred thousand Slovaks to the Sudetenland of Czecho-Slovakia. The move of such numbers out of the Slovak homeland proper and into traditional Czech lands was seen by many Slovaks in the United States as a means of purposefully weakening the cultural and social fabric of the Slovak people. As early as February 1947 the Slovak League's stance of the issue of expatriation was clear. President Jurcak and Secretary Kocur authored a petition on behalf of the league, which was sent to President Harry Truman. In it they called for the United States to officially protest the move and take steps to help correct this wrong or provide protection for those affected. Jurcak and Kocur wrote to Truman, "We specifically appeal with reference to the proposed expatriation of several hundred thousand Slovaks from their homeland to the Sudetenland in Czecho-Slovakia. There is reason to believe that this is another effort to dismember this small nation and defeat permanently any effort at independence by the Slovak people."[3] The league's appeal to the president, while compelling in its argument and entirely consistent with the Slovak League's position over the past twenty years, was met with little more than the courteous response of, "We're doing everything we can."

In addition to the situation faced by those affected by expatriation, the attention of the Slovak League of America and John Kocur was also being pulled by the situation faced by thousands of Slovak exiles. Many native Slovaks had fled their country at either the end of the war, fearing German reprisals, or immediately after the war, sensing the dire circumstances of the post-war occupation by the Soviets. These exiles had temporarily settled in countries like Austria, Italy, and France and now sought the help and protection of the most influential ally of the Slovak people, the Slovak League of America. The exiles, however, faced a significant hurdle in that they were not recognized by the Western powers as refugees and therefore failed to meet eligibility requirements for legal and material assistance for resettlement.[4] Without the legal protective status of "refugee," assistance in resettlement could not be secured and very often the result was deportation from the country in which they resided back to the Communist controlled Czecho-Slovak state.

The Slovak League of America took the lead in helping to secure assistance for thousands of Slovak exiles. The league worked to affect a change in the legal status of many of their exiled countryman by working with the International Refugee Organization (I.R.O.) in Geneva, Switzerland during the post-war years. The League also saw its representative to the I.R.O., Dr. Joseph Kirschbaum, received in the relief organization's European headquarters and recognized as a spokesman for exiled Slovaks across the war-torn continent. As a result of the efforts of the Slovak League and its officers the International Refugee Organization took the Slovak exile community under its protective wing.[5]

Within the Slovak League's overall efforts to help their displaced fellow countrymen, John Kocur also applied his considerable influence, time, and resources to help many faced with the dire circumstance of being a man without a country. Kocur organized drives to collect supplies, food, clothing, and other necessities; he met with friends and relatives of refugees who were eager to seek the secretary's help for their affected loved ones; and he personally made contact with those in the refugee community to ensure they knew the Slovak League of America was doing everything it could to help and support them.

One such contact that John Kocur made among the Slovak refugees during the tense and trying post-war years was with a man named Imrich Stolarik. Stolarik was a fellow countryman of John Kocur and, in fact, the two men had grown up in the same small Slovak village of Turzovka. Stolarik and Kocur maintained a friendship when both immigrated to the United States in the early part of the twentieth century and settled in Western Pennsylvania. Imrich Stolarik eventually made his way back to Europe while Kocur stayed in the U.S. and began a new life. Now, nearly thirty years after they had separated, their paths would cross again as Stolarik found himself a Slovak exile living in Austria and reaching out to his old friend John Kocur and the Slovak League for help.

Imrich Stolarik would, with help from John Kocur and the Slovak League, make it out of Austria and eventually come to North America, settling in Canada. Stolarik would go on to become a significant and recognized leader of the Canadian Slovak League, much like his fellow countryman Kocur did in the United States, and play an active role in advocating for the causes of Slovaks around the world. Immediately after World War II, however, Stolarik needed help and he found the one man he knew could provide it, John Kocur.

Later in life, Imrich Stolarik wrote of how John Kocur provided a beacon of hope for the many Slovaks living in exile across Europe. Stolarik described Kocur's actions on behalf of fellow Slovaks in exile, "He (Kocur) worked hard for the rights of Slovaks in their homeland and he did everything that was in his power to lessen the poverty and suffering of his native brothers in exile. He gave generously not only from the funds of the league but also from his own means."[6]

Imrich Stolarik was like many of his fellow Slovaks at the end of World War II, fleeing the very real potential of greater political and social oppression from the Soviets. Stolarik's journey took him to an area of upper Austria, a part of the country occupied and controlled by American military forces. A majority of Slovaks, men, women and children, living in exile gravitated towards this part of occupied Austria as it represented the best hope of freedom due to the close ties of Americans and Slovaks. In other parts of Austria, controlled by the Russians, English, or French, Slovak prospects for repatriation were not as bright. During these critical times Slovak refugees in Austria turned to the one organization they knew had the power and resources to help, the Slovak League of America, and to the one man whom they knew had the heart and strength to carry their cause forward, Secretary John Kocur.

In an article titled, "Remembering Jan Kocur," Imrich Stolarik recalled finally reaching his old friend John Kocur in hopes of finding a way to alleviate his personal suffering as well as that of his fellow Slovak refugees. "Finally, we were successful in getting connected with the Slovak League of America and its leader, Jan Kocur. There we were able to cry out about our pain and problems, whether as individuals or as a community. Besides monetary support, we were asking mainly for help with the traveling to other countries so we could find a new home and start a new life since we lost everything in Slovakia and we were very happy that we were able to save our bare lives."[7] Over the span of nearly two years, John Kocur and Imrich Stolarik exchanged over twenty letters. In them, the secretary of the Slovak League of America showed his patriotic feelings and deep Christian faith as he worked on behalf of Stolarik and other Slovak exiles through religious, government, and social agencies as well as via Slovak League representatives.

Excerpts of these letters from Kocur to Stolarik demonstrate the concern John Kocur had for the plight of his countrymen in exile and the efforts to which he and the Slovak League went in order to help. The letters began in 1946.[8]

From Jan Kocur, August 6, 1946:

> *The Slovak League of America is putting forward all of the efforts to alleviate your suffering and to get you out of these terrible predicaments and to save you as soon as possible, our dear Slovak people. The proof of this is also the following step, the acting committee of the Slovak League in its second meeting on October 2nd, 1946, single-mindedly voted for $5,000 for helping Slovak refugees in Austria. This sum of money will be given to the National Catholic Welfare Service with the instructions for the money to be used for the above-mentioned goals.*

From Jan Kocur, October 9, 1946:

> *The issue of admitting a bigger number of Slovak immigrants to the United States will be explained to you by the delegate of the Slovak League who is ready to travel to Austria right after the Congress of the Slovak League in America. At the same time, I would like to note that in September of this*

*year we sent to Mr. Augustin Zan, the Papal delegate, $1,000 to help suffering Slovaks in Austria. In addition to this monetary help, we sent to this address in Aurolzmunster in upper Austria, a large amount of helping packages. I hope that he received them. We will send more packages and money as soon as we receive a response from Mr. A. Zan.*

From Jan Kocur, October 23, 1946:

*The Congress of the Slovak League of America will meet the 29th and 30th of October, 1946. I will send you a message about its decisions regarding sending the delegation, as well as other activities in support of the Slovak immigrants as soon as possible. The letter for J. C. Hronsky (a noted Slovak author) I sent to the address of Mr. Karol Sidor. I did it because a few days ago I received a letter from J. C. Hronsky in which he writes also the following: "I am not sure whether I will be able to write to you any more or whether this is my last letter. Because this is going on: today it was already the third time for me and Hrusovsky being called to the police station and they told us bad news that we have to leave Italy within fifteen days or we will be sent back to Czechoslovakia." From this you can see that our dear countrymen in Italy are going through tough times. I am sure that you would like to know what we did for these two patriots. We turned to the Italian ambassador in Washington, D.C. to help us put off the deportation. However, it is very hard to say what the result will be.*

From Jan Kocur, November 11, 1946:

*We received the telegram from the Office of the Slovak Colony in Aurolzmunster in which our dear countrymen touchingly greeted the 28th Congress of the League and we also read it during the meeting of the Congress. Please express to them in my name my sincerest thanks for that precious greeting. Our dear countrymen living in the district Ried appealed to the Slovak League of America asking for a delegation to come to the Slovak immigrants in Europe and help them from the situation affecting the health of their immigration. That appeal was introduced not only to those members present at the Congress but also to all members of the League. And what was the result? The Congress of the League single-mindedly ordered the sending of the delegation to the Slovak immigrants in Austria, Germany, Italy, etc. It was also decided that we will do anything possible to minimize the suffering and save the suffering countrymen from their sad situation as soon as possible.*

From Jan Kocur, November 20, 1946:

*The departure of the delegation of the Slovak League in America was postponed indefinitely. The reason? The wife of Mr. P. P. Jurcak, the president of the Slovak League, became so seriously ill that he could not leave for such a trip for a while. I am very sorry that it happened, but what can we do?*

From Jan Kocur, January 6, 1947:

*Who will be in the delegation or when will they leave I cannot tell you even today. I was hoping that in January, at the latest, they will already be with you, but working on gaining the protection and support that is normally used by misplaced people postponed the departure of the delegation. Also the revision of immigration law is keeping the delegation here because we want to be sure about the number of Slovak refugees that will be allowed to enter the U.S. and Canada. As soon as these gordic knots are untied, the delegation will be able to leave. I am sorry, very sorry, that sending a delegation was postponed so much but what can be done? To leave for Europe without all of the information would not be very helpful and the hearts of suffering countrymen would not be filled with so much happiness as they will be when both of the questions will be taken care of.*

From Jan Kocur, February 7, 1947:

*During the meeting of the executive committee of the Slovak League of America that will take place sometime in March of this year, it will be determined whether and when our delegation would leave for Europe. In the beginning of March, there will be a special committee of the Slovak League of America that will meet with President Truman to find out exactly how many Slovak immigrants will be accepted into the United States this year. According to the results of that meeting, we will arrange everything else. A few days ago, I received a letter from Karol Sidor. Besides other things, he wrote to me that our dear friend, Jozef C. Hronsky, returned home from the hospital in good health. May the good Lord take care of him and protect him from everything bad for ever and everywhere.*

From Jan Kocur, February 27, 1947

*The message that the Communists took more Slovaks from Austria to their torture chambers touched me painfully as well. And my heart is mourning and crying when I see how the truth is being stepped on and how helpless we are. But let's not be desperate. Just like before, also right now, we strongly believe that there are people in the world that will listen to us and will help our suffering people. We saw it and found it out these days when we visited our state representatives and presented them a petition asking for the Slovak immigrants not to be given against their will to the hands of red Prague be-headers. What the result of this action will be I cannot tell you right now. But I am hoping for the best. Finally I would like to ask you to be strong and believe that the all-powerful God will help you go through this horrible time of spiritual darkness, the thickest materialism and slavery, because we are fighting for the truth.*

From Jan Kocur, March 24, 1947:

*A lot of time was devoted to the question of the bitter fate of Slovak immigrants during the meeting of the executive committee of the Slovak League that took place on March 14th, 1947. From the messages that we have recently received from Austria, we found out that the situation has catastrophically changed. Some of our countrymen decided to return to Czechoslovakia and other ones want to go to Brazil and some of them are willing to stay in Austria until they can; until we open the possibility of coming to Canada or the United States. Please tell what you know about it. I will be very grateful to you for explaining the things to me and sharing your opinion about the situation. You would make it much easier for me to continue in my work for securing a more humane life for our suffering countrymen.*

From Jan Kocur, April 10, 1947:

*I would like to use this occasion to let you know that Mr. P. P. Jurcak, the president of the Slovak League, left for the Dominican Republic to meet with the government regarding allowing greater number of Slovak immigrants to the Dominican Republic. I am hoping that his trip will be successful and that he will bring the ray of sunshine to the hearts of our suffering countrymen.*

From Jan Kocur, May 13, 1947:

*I cannot give you any explanation of those 25 Slovak immigrants. I have heard somewhere from somebody Dr. Zelenka is sending them to the shoemaker Bata in Brazil. Whether it is true, I could not find out. I personally like it much better to move our countrymen to the Dominican Republic. The climate there is much better for our people as well as the opportunity to make everyday bread is much easier. The truth is that the best would be to get our countrymen here to the United States. The hope is great. You can also see that from the attached publication. In my opinion, if you can, you should stay where you are. I am hoping that this year the gates will open to us or to neighboring Canada. I will also be working towards your dreams and desires to come true.*

The correspondence between Stolarik and Kocur continued, as did John Kocur's work on behalf of his fellow Slovaks, even as John Kocur's health was again suffering.

From Amelia Kocur, June 7, 1947:

*I would like to respectfully let you know that we have received your letter from May 30th of this year. The reply will come later because Mr. Secretary Jan A. Kocur became seriously ill. Please be patient in waiting for his reply.*

From Jan Kocur, July 22, 1947:

*I cannot tell you anything specific regarding Slovak immigrants moving to the Dominican Republic. Mr. Jurcak, the President of the Slovak League, after he came back from the Dominican Republic, told only that their government is willing to accept certain number of people whose occupation is farmer and who will promise in writing that they will be farming there. Other conditions are not known to me. That is why, as I already mentioned, I cannot tell you anything specific right now. I am more hoping for the bill of Congressman William G. Scranton for changing current immigration law. That would allow every year, at least 100,000 people to immigrate to the United States for fear of their life because of their religious or political beliefs. Accepting this bill will open the gate to the United States also for our Slovak immigrants. Every good and brave heart is fighting for this right now because in that we see securing better, more peaceful days for our people.*

From Amelia Kocur, August 20, 1947:

*I am respectfully announcing to you that we have received your letter dated August 6th of this year. Unfortunately, the secretary will not be able reply to your letter. The reason? He is seriously ill. On Saturday, August 16th, he was taken to the hospital where he is, even today, in a serious condition. He has been in an oxygen tent since Sunday.*

From Jan Kocur, December 2, 1947:

*I still cannot write you a longer letter. I do not have enough strength for that. I have not been this seriously and this long ill in my life. Almost three months I was fighting the horrible illness in the hospital. Today, thanks to the Lord, I am feeling much better but I am still very weak. I am hoping that the good Lord, the doctor of the doctors, will make me stronger so that I can soon continue my work for our Slovak issues and that I will be alive on the day when the freedom and the state independence for our dear nation occurs.*

From Jan Kocur, February 26, 1948:

*Please accept my sincere thanks for your letter from February 17th of this year that I have just received. I am also confirming the receiving of the petition for the Slovak League written by the representatives of the Slovak schools in Aurolzmunster (Austria). I will present it to the executive committee of the Slovak League during our next meeting. I will send you the results of the meeting as soon as possible. Whether the Stratton's bill will pass or not is hard to say but the hopes are great that it will pass. Professor Hrusovsky visited me a few days ago. He also mentioned that you wrote to him and that he will do everything that you asked him for.*

From Jan Kocur, April 9, 1948:

*Thank you very much for your nice letter dated March 16th, 1948. Yes, I agree with you that the situation in Slovakia is a clear proof that everything that was even slightly democratic has fallen apart to that extent that Czechoslovak Republic is becoming a totalitarian, military-police Bolshevik state, where there is no protection or safety for people or their property.*

From Jan Kocur, May 26, 1948.

*Regarding the permission for Slovaks to enter the United States, the situation is as follows: Our American government is giving the permission that you mentioned only to people not belonging to the real quota. It means: children for their parents, parents for their children, husband for his wife, wife for her husband, etc., can ask in Washington D.C., for such permission. Situation with the Slovak immigrants is completely different. I am hoping that the gate will open this year also for our immigrants. The fact is that there are a lot of people here that are against allowing any more immigrants from Europe. What do you think about the activities of Mr. Beniak and Dr. Izakovic? They are trying to help Slovak people to settle in France. I would like to know your opinion about that.*

The letter of May 26, 1948 from John Kocur to Imrich Stolarik was the last one exchanged between the fellow countrymen from Turzovka. Shortly after the spring of 1948, with the issues of Slovak refugees being the pressing issue of the day for the Slovak League, John Kocur's health again turned for the worse. Beginning with his initial hospitalization in August of 1947 and continuing with subsequent and increasingly lengthy hospital stays in January and April of 1948, Kocur's health had become markedly worse.

On July 6, 1948 John Kocur was visited in his Ross Street home by his personal physician, Dr. Boyd Couch. Kocur had been suffering from shortness of breath, fatigue, and a severe cough for nearly three weeks prior to the doctor's visit and Couch, upon examining his patient, immediately ordered an ambulance to transport John Kocur to the hospital with instructions for admission. The reason given by Dr. Couch for admission was "Cardiac decompensation," a condition marked by an inability of the heart to maintain adequate circulation.

Physically, John Kocur looked and acted every bit of someone who was chronically and seriously ill. The initial physical examination upon admission to the Aspinwall Veterans Hospital in the summer of 1948 found Kocur to be in moderate distress, suffering severe dyspenea (difficulty breathing), edema, and cyanosis of lips, earlobes, and nail beds; the lack of blood flow and circulation due to his weakened heart contributed to his overall symptoms. The assistant chief of the medical service at the Aspinwall Veterans Hospital, Dr. R. D. Yoder, approved the official hospital diagnosis as hypertensive cardiovascular disease due to hypertension of lesser circulation associated with emphysema, poisoning of heart by digitalis and cardiac insufficiency (heart failure). In addition he also noted conditions including chronic bronchitis, emphysema, diabetes, and arteriosclerosis. Kocur was seriously ill; so much so that the hospital registrar on July 9, 1948 sent Margaret Kocur a telegram, "to advise that the physical condition of your husband, John Kocur, is considered serious." The telegram went on to note that the patient "...may be visited at any time, disregarding regular visiting hours."

During the time immediately following his hospitalization, Kocur's condition steadily became worse. The difficulty breathing and poor circulation were relieved slightly with the administration of oxygen but immediately regressed when the oxygen treatments were discontinued. As a result, John Kocur was placed in an oxygen tent on the third day of his hospital stay. A short time later, Kocur's condition stabilized but did not improve.

Also of concern to the physicians caring for John Kocur at the Aspinwall Veterans Hospital was the status of his diabetes. A contributing cause of his previous hospital admissions, Kocur's diabetes was not well controlled leading up to the July 1948 hospitalization, this despite regular testing, a prescribed diabetic diet, and daily insulin. Perhaps like many diabetics diagnosed later in life the change in lifestyle (especially in diet, so necessary to long-term sugar control) were difficult for John Kocur to consistently maintain. Upon admission the doctors treated Kocur's blood sugar level as a case of impending diabetic coma, a condition brought on by an uncontrollable overload of sugar in the blood, and acted aggressively to reduce this risk. Despite the physicians' best efforts to bring down the blood sugar level to near normal, their patient did not respond with an improvement in his clinical symptoms.

The third area of major concern for the doctors in John Kocur's case was the worsening condition of congestive heart failure, or cardiac insufficiency. Kocur's heart was not pumping as much blood as his body needed and thus contributed to his symptoms of fatigue, shortness of breath, fluid build up, and cyanosis. After a previous hospital stay, doctors had prescribed digitalis for John Kocur, which he used to treat his cardiac symptoms. At this point, however, Kocur had taken so much digitalis that doctors suspected a "digitalis intoxication of the myocardium." John Kocur's heart muscle had absorbed so much of the drug that it became ineffective and, in fact, dangerous to use any more.

For John Kocur's condition to have stabilized after initially being admitted as "seriously ill" was viewed as a minor victory. Kocur was not getting any better, but he was not getting any worse either. Doctors continued to treat the secretary with a combination approach designed to address the three main areas of concern, the lungs, the diabetic condition, and the congestive heart failure. Kocur was given orders for bed rest, oxygen, penicillin, and aminophyllin to treat his lung condition; insulin and a restricted diet to treat his diabetes; and potassium to help reduce the fluid build up as a result of congestive heart failure. Despite having successfully stabilized John Kocur's condition over the course of three days, the doctors now saw their patient's condition begin to decline.

Still considered in serious condition, John Kocur was visited by his family, close friends like Juraj Gazak and Anton Hranec, and a small number of colleagues from the Slovak League. As a patient in serious condition, Kocur's visits from those outside his immediate family were limited as was the amount of time each visitor was allowed to spend. While everyone outside of the immediate family who saw their friend and colleague was aware of the gravity of John Kocur's condition, they also knew that he had pulled through similar hospitalizations before. Their hopes and prayers for this occasion were the same as they had been before; John Kocur, their friend and rock of hope for the shared goals and dreams of Slovaks everywhere, would steadily get better, leave the hospital, and pick up the causes of Slovaks right where he had left off. This time, however, it was not to be. Despite the treatment provided by the doctors and the thoughts and prayers of his family and friends, John Kocur's condition worsened and on Tuesday July 13, 1948 he slipped into a coma. Just after midnight, as July 13 quietly turned in to July 14, John Kocur slipped free of the bonds of earth.

**Endnotes**

1. *Pauco, Joseph; Under Dynamic Leadership – Sixty Years of the Slovak League of America, pg 114. 1967*
2. *Ibid, pg 115.*
3. *Ibid.*
4. *Ibid, pg 116.*
5. *Ibid.*
6. *Stolarik, Imrich; Remembering Jan Kocur. Slovaks in America; February 6, 1974*
7. *Ibid.*
8. *Ibid.*

## Chapter 20

# THE GOOD FIGHT

# Chapter 20

Bureaucracy. Government is famous for it and no part of the government is immune to its effects and complications. In 1948, only three years after a massive U.S. war effort with millions of American participants, the Veterans Administration was as big a bureaucracy as the U.S. government had. Administering the needs and requirements of America's most recent veterans as well as all her past veterans, including some dating as far back as the American Civil War, was a mammoth task. The United States Veterans Administration, however, seemed up to the task with a specific form for seemingly any want or need of America's veterans.

Private John Kocur, a veteran of Ambulance Company 36, 7th Sanitary Train, 7th Division, American Expeditionary Force, died on July 14, 1948 after an extended hospitalization. Kocur's death was brought on by conditions partially attributed to and aggravated by his service during World War I. Immediately following John Kocur's death the Veterans Administration paperwork machine kicked in to gear.

The Kocur family found itself wading through a sea of paperwork as a result of its patriarch's death. Minor details like those captured in Veterans Administration Form 2687, "Inventory Report of Personally Owned Effects" and Form 1171, "Notice to Person Designated by Veteran Regarding Personal Effects" were captured within the government documents and provided to the family. In addition, Form 11-2008 was completed to allow for issuance of a United States flag for use in the burial. Also associated with the burial was Form 530, an application for a burial allowance to cover the expenses of the funeral, transportation, and burial, an amount totaling $322. In addition to the stream of paperwork requiring immediate completion, the surviving members of the Kocur family also turned their attention to Veterans Administration form 8-534, an application for death compensation and pension to be paid to the surviving widow and dependent children. Although John Kocur left his family insurance money from policies with the National Slovak Society, First Catholic Slovak Union, and the Slovak Catholic Sokol, an ongoing stream of income from his veteran's pension was an absolute necessity for Margaret Kocur and her children.

Of critical importance to the approval of the veteran's pension Margaret Kocur would receive was establishing the fact that John Kocur's death was service related. Beginning shortly after Kocur's death in 1948 and continuing over the course of the next eighteen months, letters and forms were exchanged between Margaret Kocur, the Veterans Administration Hospital, and the Veterans Administration itself seeking to establish a service-related cause of death. At first, the ruling of the VA was that John Kocur's death was not service related and thus the pension award Margaret Kocur was to receive would be lower than if a service-related cause was shown to have been a contributing factor. Knowing her husband's military service and health history, and in an effort to support the remaining members of the family, an appeal was made by Margaret Kocur, using the appropriate Veterans Administration forms, to have the ruling in her husband's case reviewed. On December 10, 1948, the Veterans Administration notified Margaret Kocur that, "a review of the entire records of this (John Kocur) case indicated that no basis has been found which would warrant any change, alteration, or amendment in the present status of the case. Accordingly, the previous rating of non-service connected death has been confirmed and continued." The next level of appeal was to the Board of Veterans Appeals in Washington, D.C., a course of action accompanied, of course, by the appropriate form.

After gathering additional support and records from physicians, nurses, and hospital staff and completing the necessary VA forms, an official appeal of the non-service-related ruling was made in the fall of 1949, more than a year after John Kocur's death. Finally the case was referred to the Dependents Pension Board for review and adjudication. On October 31, 1949 the board reached a decision and notified the Kocur family. After considering the supporting evidence as well as a letter from Amelia Kocur, the board reversed the decision of the initial review panel from September 1948 and ruled in favor of the claim that John Kocur's death was indeed service related. This meant that the death benefits and pension Margaret Kocur and her family would receive would be increased, retroactive to her husband's death.

Throughout this long process of appeals, letter writing, and information gathering it is clear that Margaret Kocur, although her name and signature appears on most of the letters, did not navigate through the VA bureaucracy by herself; she had a great degree of help. Margaret Kocur had come to the United States in 1923 with very little, if any, formal schooling; she could sign her name in English but was not proficient in writing the language and spoke very little English. The nature of the information supplied to support the Kocur family's claim, the need to work through medical channels at the VA hospital, the completion of endless forms, and the eloquence of the ongoing correspondence from the Kocurs points to someone else as the primary driver in the pursuit of the claim. In some cases, correspondence between the Kocurs and the Veterans Administration was signed by Amelia Kocur, the eldest daughter of John and Margaret. It is very likely that Amelia, given her close working relationship with her father in the Slovak League, doggedly pursued his claim with the Veterans Administration and ultimately succeeded in convincing the Appeals Board to rule in her family's favor. Amelia Kocur, therefore, deserves much of the credit for ensuring her mother and siblings were able to receive the level of compensation to which they were legitimately entitled and who ultimately secured a level of ongoing income necessary to support the other members of the family.

John Kocur, the longtime secretary of the Slovak League, was buried on July 16, 1948. Kocur's funeral, held at two o'clock in the afternoon at St. Alphonsus Church in Springdale was attended by dignitaries and representatives from nearly every Slovak organization in the United States, including the Slovak

League, Jednota, and National Slovak Society. The event was covered by Slovak newspapers from around the United States and around the world. John Kocur's funeral also was attended by many local Slovaks who came to know his kindness, friendship, and help through past personal contact. The mass was conducted by no less than nine Slovak priests including several from as far away as Youngstown and Cleveland, Ohio. The service was presided over by Father Theodore Kojis, Abbott of the Cleveland Benedictines.[1]

In his homily, Monsignor Klemet Hrtanec graciously commended the achievements of the late Slovak patriot and noted how Kocur not only worked tirelessly for his Slovak homeland but also how he loved his new home, America. It was noted how John Kocur contributed to the survival of the Slovak League at a time when the league lacked the financial support to continue. Kocur was called one of the bravest workers on behalf of the Slovak nation, someone who did not care about the money or fame but cared for uplifting the Slovak nation to its full freedom.[2]

Given John Kocur's military service and his membership in the American Legion, the funeral was attended by many veterans of both World Wars. When the service was concluded, Kocur's flag-draped coffin was carried by a military honor guard to the hearse that would in turn take it to the local Slovak cemetery, St. Clements Cemetery in Tarentum, Pennsylvania. At the cemetery, Father Kojis concluded the service with a blessing of the gravesite and all those paying their respects. In a time- honored tradition, the military honor guard accompanying the casket carefully folded the American flag which had covered the casket and presented it to Margaret Kocur. The military guard then honored their fellow veteran with a firing salute.

Peter Jurcak, the president of the Slovak League, then said his official goodbye to John Kocur, his long-time friend and fellow League officer. Jurcak had been the fifth league president to work alongside John Kocur; and Jurcak, as had each of his four predecessors, learned and benefited from John Kocur's experience, work ethic, and principled focus.

Following his remarks, President Jurcak then turned to the new Slovak League secretary, Pavol Jamricka, who gave a eulogy on behalf of the entire Slovak League. As recorded by Jozef

Prusa, a writer for the newspaper of the Slovak Catholic Sokol, Secretary Pavol Jamricka honored the late John Kocur at the crowded gravesite with these heartfelt comments (as translated from Slovak to English):

"Endlessly kind, and just, and marvelously directing the fate of the world, as well as very forgiving, is God's hand. That hand is what called us here to this sacred place to say goodbye and put into the depth of the ground the body of our dearest Janko Kocur. His body was exhausted by a lifelong, uncompromising fight for the rights of the Slovak Nation, as well as a long illness, but his spirit remained great and generous. Janko, as like every good soldier, gave the biggest sacrifice for his country and the nation. It is extremely hard to talk when your heart is bleeding, when your mind is overtaken by feelings, when you cannot focus your thoughts; it is very hard to realize what our nation lost in this soulless body of Janko Kocur, especially right now in this cruel time of the world's intrigues and quarrels, when we need him the most.

We, the old colleagues of Janko Kocur, got this ungrateful task: to give farewell to a comrade, to say goodbye and put a little bouquet of forget-me-nots for his deeds for the Slovak Nation...however, I will leave that to historians who will certainly give a well-deserved spot and a reward from the nation to its faithful and deserving son because today I cannot find the appropriate words.

But one thing we all realize is that Janko Kocur left only a little earlier; and that this sacred place of peace is awaiting us as well. We also will rest in peace at the place where all of the quarrels end, all the fights and human evil end, and envy and anger end; where after the hard life there will be true peace, blessings, and sacred quietness where enemies cannot reach us and where the 100-year-old oaks will be protecting us and the leaves of the trees will be whispering the old sweet melody of God's nature.

Yes, this is the sacred place where every human being with a conscience will bow his head and his thoughts will ascend to the heavens and he will realize that it doesn't matter how hard you are trying, how much you hate your neighbor, how much you try to spoil his life, because for sure, one day, you will meet at this place; everybody-your friend, your enemy, the rich, the poor-here there is no difference, God's son is kindly warming up the graves of everyone and that gentle rain will give the moisture equally so the beautiful flowers will decorate all of the graves of the dead.

The Slovak League of America, its thousands of members, even all of America and every good Slovak soul, is today mourning the departure of Janko Kocur because in the whole-wide America, there is no Slovak that would not highly appreciate the unforgettable deeds and achievements of our dear Janko.

During the long thirty years, he gave to his nation everything good and generous. He served his nation faithfully and honorably; he sacrificed his best years so it is only fitting that his nation is endlessly thankful and his memory will live in the Slovak hearts until they stop beating.

But you, our dear Janko, can rest in peace because you carried out your duties honorably and honestly; the threat did not break you, the bribe did not sway you, and you went through both the hard days of the Slovak League as well as your Slovak nation. We will never forget you. May our dear free, American soil be light on you and may your Slovak nation remember you forever! Our sincere condolences to the dear family."[3]

No matter how hard the loss, no matter how important the person or their job, no matter how far reaching their influence, life goes on. In reality, life never really stops. The loss of a loved one, friend, colleague, or relative momentarily slows or stops the lives of those in the immediate circle of contact. But outside of life's inner ring, the events of the day in the local neighborhood, town, state, and country, continue to swirl at an ever- increasing pace, never really slowing. John Kocur's death in 1948 had an expected ripple effect, touching the lives of those closest to him the most and extending outward with lesser impact until finally fading away.

Margaret Kocur, his wife of thirty-five years, was left to persevere on her own. Having married in 1913, Margaret spent the first ten years of her marriage apart from her husband continuing to live with her family in Slovakia. Margaret came to the United States to be with her husband only after the calamity of the Great War was over and John Kocur had established himself in the United States. Throughout the remaining years of her life (she lived to be one hundred-five years old) Margaret maintained that while the United States certainly offered her a better and more comfortable life, she had never really wanted to leave her homeland. This despite the uncertain times faced in her homeland during the 1920s, the onset of war across Europe in the late 1930s and 1940s, and the dominance of Communism throughout Eastern Europe for the five decades that followed. There is no imagining how difficult life would have been during any of these circumstances, let alone the effect of each happening in rapid succession.

After her husband's death, Margaret Kocur went on with the responsibility of raising her two teenage children still at home, Richard and Vera, and seeing her other children, Amelia, twenty-four, and John, twenty-one, to adulthood. While America's economic prospects were on the upswing in 1948, Margaret Kocur was still left with the challenge of providing for herself and her children now that the breadwinner of the family was gone. John Kocur's life work, as important as it was to him and thousands of Slovaks in the United States and around the world, was not a job that brought with it a great deal of money for living expenses or for savings. Throughout his years of service to the Slovak League, John Kocur never placed financial gain above his goals and ideals for the league or for the Slovak nation. Kocur's efforts toward a higher purpose was a noble stance and one which won him much praise and admiration and very likely helped the league survive through many tough times. The practical side of the ideal, however, often left the family in tight financial situations. The salary of a Slovak League secretary, however meager it was at times, was a helpful addition to the family's income and was now something Margaret Kocur would be without. The sources of income the family would now rely upon in order to go on fell to the veteran's pension Margaret would receive on a monthly basis, approximately $112, and additional income brought in by all the Kocur children. These sources, in addition to the small life insurance policies left by John Kocur, would serve to sustain the family over the coming years.

Apart from the immediate financial situation, Margaret Kocur now also faced the prospect of living life without her husband and partner. Always supportive of his work, work that occupied the majority of his time and energy, Margaret Kocur probably believed at some point the work would decrease and

John would have more time to dedicate to her and their family. With John Kocur's death in 1948, that all changed. All the hard work and dedication left John Kocur little time for his family, time that now could never be replaced. Margaret Kocur would go on with her life, a life eventually filled with graduations, marriages, and holidays with her children, grandchildren, and great-grandchildren. Margaret remained for over thirty years after her husband's death in the Ross Street home that she and John had shared in Springdale, Pennsylvania and eventually moved to the south hills of Pittsburgh in order to be closer to her youngest children, Richard and Vera. Living independently in an apartment for nearly another fifteen years following her move, Margaret cooked weekly dinners for her family, attended family birthday and holiday celebrations, and enjoyed watching the antics that often accompanied her large, extended family. Active and mentally sharp until the end of her life, Margaret Zbojkova Kocur passed away on February 25, 1998, nearly fifty years after her husband.

The surviving Kocur children, Amelia, John, Richard, and Vera, encountered many of the same struggles faced by their mother after John Kocur's death. The demands of their father's work left him little time for interaction with his growing children and now they were left without. Amelia had worked along side her father supporting him in his duties with the Slovak League for more than five years and most likely had the greatest insight in to her father. John, twenty-one years old at the time of his father's death, also had more time and exposure to his father as a result of his age. Richard and Vera, twins of sixteen in July 1948, had less of an opportunity to truly get to know their father well. Each grew up at a time when John Kocur's work was his primary focus and as young children, Richard and Vera were far removed from his daily activities and thus from him. Despite the limited amount of time each child had to form a strong and lasting relationship with their father and learn from him as a person and family role model, all of John and Margaret Kocur's children would go on to be happily married and raise well adjusted, stable, and loving families of their own.

On July 14, 1948 the Slovak League of America lost one of its most consistent and well known voices. John Kocur had dedicated nearly half of his sixty-one years to the Slovak League, championing its causes, acting as the public face of the organization, and dutifully representing its many members. Now he was gone. Yes, other people could and would step in to fill John Kocur's shoes but none would serve so long or dedicate so much to the causes of Slovaks everywhere. At no time since its inception was the Slovak League more relevant or influential than between 1920 and 1945. These years were the golden age of the Slovak League and John Kocur was a consistent and integral part of the organization's efforts throughout that period. In 1948 and beyond the league faced influences from both inside and outside America's shores that challenged the organization like never before. In that challenging time, the steadying and consistent influence of John Kocur was no longer present to help guide the organization to which he dedicated so much.

Perhaps John Kocur's departure coincided to a time of transition for the Slovak League, the transition from a time in which he and the league accomplished so much for Slovaks both socially and politically to a time where circumstances left the hands of the league tied with regard to power or influence. The Slovak League of America would go on after its venerable secretary's death still fighting for Slovaks everywhere and celebrating its one hundredth anniversary in 2007; but without John Kocur it would never truly be the same.

John Kocur's life was one driven by principles; fair and equal treatment of his fellow Slovaks in the United States, dedication and devotion to the ideals which made America great, and freedom and self-determination for his Slovak homeland. From his first step onto American soil on September 7, 1909 to his death on July 14, 1948 John Kocur lived his principles.

On January 1, 1993, nearly forty-five years after John Kocur's death, Czechoslovakia peacefully and agreeably separated in an event known as the "Velvet Divorce" and the dream of a truly free and independent Slovak Republic became reality.

**Endnotes**

1. *Prusa, Jozef: Emotional Burial of the Chief Secretary of the Slovak League; Catholic Sokol, July 21, 1948.*

2. *Ibid.*

3. *Ibid.*